Contents

PowerPivot Alchemy

by

Rob Collie & Bill Jelen

Holy Macro! Books,
PO Box 82 Uniontown, OH 44685, USA

PowerPivot Alchemy

Author: Rob Collie & Bill Jelen

Layout: Tyler Nash

Cover Design: Jocelyn Hellyer

Indexing: Nellie J. Liwam

Published by: Holy Macro! Books, PO Box 82, Uniontown OH 44685 USA

Distributed by: Independent Publishers Group, Chicago, IL

First Printing: May 2014. Printed in USA

ISBN: 978-1-61547-021-1 (Print), 978-1-61547-214-7 (PDF), 978-1-61547-334-2 (ePub), 978-1-61547-114-0 (mobi)

Library of Congress Number: 2013907451

Dedications

Bill:

to Steve Cox. Sometimes, it IS rocket science...

Rob:

To my grandparents: Brooks, Martha, Bob, and Marie. For showing a certain little boy that silly rules were made to be broken.

A Note on Hyperlinks

You will notice that all of the hyperlinks in this book look like this:

http://ppvt.pro/<foo>

Where <foo> is something that is short and easy to type. Example:

http://ppvt.pro/1stBlog

This is a "short link" and is intended to make life much easier for readers of the print edition. That link above will take you to the first blog post I ever published, which went live in October of 2009.

Its "real" URL is this:

http://www.powerpivotpro.com/2009/10/hello-everybody/

Which would *you* rather type?

So just a few notes:

> 1. **These short links will *always* start with http://ppvt.pro/** – which is short for "PowerPivotPro," the name of my blog.

> 2. **These links are case-sensitive!** If the link in the book ends in "1stBlog" like above, typing "1stblog" or "1stBLOG" will *not* take you to the intended page!

> 3. **Not all of these links will lead to my blog** – some will take you to Microsoft sites for instance.

> 4. **The book does not rely on you following the links** – the topics covered in this book are intended to be complete in and of themselves. The links provided are strictly optional "more info" type of content.

Acknowledgements

Rob:

Kai Hankinson and Brad Miller - for encouraging me to bet on myself, and for being so generous with your valuable time.

Scott Shealy and family - for much-needed investment and support at a critical juncture.

The Great Chandoo - for inspiring me, for always being yourself, and for giving me a way to fund the repair of the Great Trampoline Incident.

James Williams and Lori Robinson - for putting me back together (see also: Great Trampoline Incident).

Bill Jelen - for continuing to be a fantastic friend and business partner.

Dany Hoter - for being a constant force of sanity, warmth, and mirth for more than a decade.

David Churchward - for being a stand up guy in a world that often seems to lack them.

Anthony Martin - for being the most "matter-of-fact" of moral compasses, and your willingness to gamble on new approaches.

Miguel Escobar and Dominik Petri - for spreading my brand of quirk to corners of the world I cannot reach.

Mike Miskell, Donovan Kelsch, Tom Phelan, Jeff Simpson, Brad Bush, Ellen Su, and Neelesh Raheja - for re-inforcing, yet again, that these methods work at the highest of levels.

Kevin Collins - for a much-needed dose of "old school."

Matt Allington - for being my kind of crazy. You are going to love your decision.

Zack Barresse, Denny Lee, Kasper de Jonge, and Miguel Escobar (again) - for an amazing set of guest lessons.

Jocelyn Collie - for climbing into a lifeboat with me and paddling hard. (No, not that kind of paddling, you sicko).

Bill:

Thanks to Rob for proposing this book. Bruce Springsteen taught us the importance of getting the product right: "The release date is only a day. The album is forever...". This book may not sell as many copies as "Born to Run", but I am using that quote to justify why the book came out when it came out. Kitty Wilson is an amazing copy editor / project manager and I appreciate her efforts in this book. Tyler Nash put up with layout changes with a smile. Thanks to the Power BI team at Microsoft. I can always count on Igor Peev to answer a quick question when I am stuck. Thanks to the crew of the Red Falcon. Parts of this book were hatched at the Cozy Corner Cafe in Merritt Island Florida. Thanks to Georgia, Krissy, Lucy, and Corrine there. Also thanks to Donnie who will rock out a blackened mahi even at breakfast time. My family always puts up with me being late for dinner, whether that is my dad, Robert F. Jelen, my son Zeke Jelen, or the lovely MrsExcel herself, Mary Ellen Jelen.

Foreword

Walk through the halls of any office today, and you'll be surrounded by people who have favorite Excel tips and tricks. This incredible software has a 30-year history and an installed base of 750 million computers; it is easy to find people all around who can offer bits and pieces of advice about Excel. Unfortunately, this is not the case with Power Pivot. Power Pivot is new, and there aren't yet a lot of people using it. If you are trying to do something with Power Pivot, it is likely that you are the only person in your office who even knows what Power Pivot is.

I first saw Power Pivot in 2009. It was amazing. I quickly learned enough to do a demo to wow people from Peoria to Peru. But a 10-minute demo requires far less skill than actually using the product every day. As I wrote *PowerPivot for the Data Analyst*, I found myself always going back to Rob Collie, who was still a PM on the Power Pivot team, to try to figure out various quirks of Power Pivot.

Subsequently, Rob left Microsoft and started www.PowerPivotPro.com. Later, he wrote the best-selling book *DAX Formulas for Power Pivot*. I often find myself turning to Rob's book to get help with particularly difficult bits of DAX formula language. That book is a techie book—but it is a must-have if you want to do data modeling with Power Pivot.

The book you're looking at right now is far less techie. Rob doesn't force you to understand how the EARLIER() function works in DAX in order to do something cool with Power Pivot. Yes, you will see the EARLIER() function in this book, but all you have to do is follow the pattern, and you will have something awesome to show for your time and attention.

-Bill Jelen, MrExcel.com

Introduction

Underestimation – the Key Ingredient of Any Book

"Every day, every day, every day, every day I write the book."

 -Elvis Costello, 1982

 -Rob Collie, 2012 and 2014

"Never again, is what you swore, the time before."

 -Depeche Mode, 1990

 -Rob Collie, 2014

Bill Jelen is a very bad man. OK actually he's a great guy, a good friend and business partner, and a walking encyclopedia of all things Excel. But despite the truth of all of that, he's also downright sneaky. Allow me to explain.

Flash back to 2011 with me: I drove down to MrExcel Headquarters to watch the Master (Bill) at work. You see, I was contemplating the idea of writing my own first book, and Bill was in the middle of a writing marathon – about 1,200 pages in six weeks. What better research, for me, than to witness his methods firsthand?

I came away from that visit with the impression that writing a book was going to be easy. At the time, I estimated that my book on DAX would be 100-125 pages at most, and Bill was cranking out 200 pages a week. Simple – I'd be done in a week or so!

The reality was completely different. Writing that book - DAX Formula for Power Pivot (aka "DFPP") - consumed every waking hour of my life for a full month, and then multiple hours per day after that for another month. I just wasn't nearly as fast as Bill. He makes it look easier than it is, because he is a machine. If you're sitting out there thinking you want to challenge his supremacy in the Excel book writing biz, I'd reconsider :)

But I am super happy that I greatly underestimated the effort required, because if I'd known the truth, I never would have written DFPP. And that would have been a shame, because in hindsight, it marks a serious inflection point in my life.

Silly Rules Were Made to Be Broken!

I was five pages into writing DFPP in a "formal" textbook style when I gave up. The formal style was *exhausting* – there was no way I was getting through it that way. So I reverted to my conversational style - like starting sentences with the word "And." Using smileys :) Telling interesting stories that were relevant from a human standpoint but not from a formulas standpoint. Sprinkling in an occasional Dr. Seuss joke or movie reference.

That turned out to be the #1 thing people love about the book – its human approach. Many people credit me with having made that as a calculated decision, but in reality I was merely hoping to *get away with it* – the style was a survival strategy, a choice I made for myself. I never once expected the style to be received *positively* – I was crossing my fingers and hoping for *neutral* :)

In hindsight that now seems like an obvious thing – of *course* people prefer "humane" books! Back in school, we were all force-fed formal textbooks for *years* – plenty of time to decide that formal textbooks *suck* :) For most people (myself included), it takes a lot of willpower to even *pick up* a book about formulas. Why *shouldn't* the experience be as pleasant as possible?

That was a powerful lesson for me – one that today extends well beyond the arena of books and into other aspects of my professional life. My grip on the "formal by tradition" world was never particularly strong, and it was loosening throughout my entire adult life, but the public reception of DFPP gave me the courage to *truly* let go. I stopped focusing on what everyone *expects* – especially on those expectations that are formed by tradition only. Instead, I increasingly ask myself, what do people truly *prefer*, if given a choice?

That lesson applies everywhere – particularly in my consulting business. I don't think our clients get what they have come to *expect* from a consulting firm, but they instead get something better: they get what they *want*. More on this later, in another forum.

How Bill Tricked Me a Second Time

Back to sneaky Bill. I've never asked him directly, but I often wonder (humorously) if Bill *intentionally* made bookwriting look easy on that fateful day in 2011. If so, I am glad that he did. (In reality, I suspect it was not remotely intentional).

But having been through the bookwriting meatgrinder once, I vowed *never* to subject myself to that again. As a book author, I was going to be "one and done."

> It's funny how many experiences I've had that are like that – incredibly valuable, but so difficult that I'd never have the will to repeat them. My first six years working at Microsoft, for instance.

Instead I had a better idea: *Bill* is a monster author, and *I* have a bunch of techniques that would be great for a book. Wouldn't it be great to unite those two resources? I'd feed a bunch of topics to Bill, and he would work his magic. Voila! Out comes a book! It was a flawless plan.

That worked, to an extent. Longtime readers of the blog may recognize many of the techniques in this book as a "greatest hits" collection of sorts – topics polished and cleaned up to be "book worthy."

But underestimation – that fateful force - reared its head again. As we looked at early drafts of this book, it was clear to us that it could be so much more, that it *should* be so much more. For instance, "that section on New Customers analysis," Bill mentioned slyly, "shouldn't it *also* explain how to count Returning customers?"

"Yes," I admitted, "that is the next question everyone *always* asks. OK, I'll write that up." And once he had opened that door, an ocean flowed in, as *I* got in on the "let's add stuff" game too. Shouldn't there be an entire chapter devoted to commonly-needed calculated columns? What about Power View, Power Query, and Power Map – wouldn't it be just *criminal* to leave those out? And yeah, some of those older techniques could now be done in better ways, or maybe just *explained* in better ways, so let's rewrite them from scratch.

That, my dear reader, is why this avowed Never Again Author found himself boarding a plane in January 2014 – once again to visit Bill Jelen for a marathon writing session. But this time to be *part* of that session rather than an observer. I then returned home and… continued writing.

Bill knew all of this in advance, I am positive. He is the Sun Tzu of bookwriting, and cunningly orchestrated me into his trap many months in advance. Either that, or I am a silly man who likes to trick himself into things. I prefer to think Bill is sneaky. You draw your own conclusions.

-Rob Collie, April 2014

Introduction Two

A Cresting Wave

"What the heck? TWO Introductions?"

 -You, right now.

Yeah that's right. If you read the first Introduction, you know tradition no longer matters around here. We're gonna do what we want. And what we *want* is... to write two introductions. So that's what we're doing.

Besides, that theme – dispensing with tradition - is *extremely* appropriate for all of us. Turning tradition on its head is *why* you are reading this book. We stand at the intersection of two worlds that are *both* being turned upside down, and for the better: the Excel world, and the BI world.

Let's focus on the Excel world, and more specifically, the worlds of its skilled practitioners. Chapter One of "DAX Formulas for Power Pivot" was titled "A Revolution Built on YOU," and explained how the world is changing dramatically in favor of the "Excel Pro." I made some pretty bold and optimistic statements in that chapter, and I get more positive feedback on it than on any other single chapter.

I won't repeat the contents of that chapter here of course, but I do want to "check in" on those bold predictions and give you an update. After all, it has been nearly two years since I wrote those words, and a lot has happened in the interim.

From a statistical standpoint, Power Pivot (and its related family of tools) has continued to grow. For instance, today PowerPivotPro.com receives about three times the visitors that it did back when I was writing DFPP in the summer of 2012. The sales of DFPP continue to trend upward – which is the reverse of what happens with most books, whether technical or otherwise – and that is also a strong indicator of growing adoption.

Those are very good trends for sure. But when we look at the *stories* - the things I have seen, heard, and lived - we get an even more powerful picture:

Excel Pros "Moving Up" – for example, a longtime Excel Pro who was making $75k as a traditional Excel analyst changed jobs and is now making $120k as a Power Pivot analyst at a different company. And now that he is gone, his former employer is ramping up on Power Pivot because they saw what it can do before he left. Another favorite: a woman who was working as an administrative assistant two years ago got re-orged into an Analyst role where she found herself living in traditional Excel (and not liking it very much). But then she discovered Power Pivot, something "clicked," and she now works for a different company as a Business Intelligence analyst, again at a similar 50% salary increase. Two years ago, she was keeping an executive's calendar, and now she's a BI professional. Let that sink in, because it is *awesome*. I get these sorts of stories frequently – and it feels *incredibly* good.

BI Firms Hiring Excel Pros – Business Intelligence consulting firms have started to specifically target people who know DAX. As in, if you know Power Pivot, you are their ideal candidate. Doesn't matter whether you were a BI professional yesterday or not – just that you know Power Pivot, which is aimed at you. And this isn't speculation - I have advertised these sorts of positions on PowerPivotPro.com, on behalf of these firms, and monitored the interview and hiring process. It's real. We call this "career re-vectoring."

Excel Celebrities Getting Involved – In July 2012 when I was writing DFPP, I had a hard time getting the rest of the Excel community's "luminaries" to talk to me – or their audiences – about Power Pivot. Some were more interested than others, but other than Bill, they weren't quite "there" yet. Today is very different. Off the top of my head, I've recently seen Ken Puls, Chandoo, Zack Barresse, Debra Dalgleish, Bob Phillips, Mike Alexander, Jon Peltier, Roger Govier, Jan Karel Pieterse, Liam Bastick, and Charley Kyd working with and/or talking about Power Pivot. There are others too that I have certainly missed. But this is a BIG change in a relatively short amount of time.

Executive Level, Strategic Adoption – I have several clients who fit a similar profile: large firms (sometimes *very* large) who all possess "real" Business Intelligence systems of the traditional flavor, but who have still been struggling to get a handle on important business problems. A highly-placed executive in those firms who happens to be an Excel Pro gets wind of Power Pivot, decides to try it out, and in a very short period of time, it has completely changed their business, from the top down, and dramatically for the better. They then, of course, start looking to expand its impact – and that means hiring and/or training more Excel Pros in the Power Pivot martial arts.

Willingness to Commit – Back in the summer of 2012, I had been working full time as a Power Pivot professional for over two years. But that job was at a single "boutique"-style company that was an early adopter. In other words, my experiences there were a tremendous *validation* of what Power Pivot can do, because we did some amazing things, but ultimately it was still just a single small firm who had "bought in" – hardly an indicator of a broader trend right? Well, I left that firm more than a year ago, in February 2013, and have been "freelance" now for 14 months. I've worked with literally dozens of clients in that time frame – empowering them to revolutionize their businesses with Power Pivot. In parallel, I created an online training course (PowerPivotPro University) which rapidly grew to over 500 enrolled students. The key observation in all of this is that companies and individuals are now willing to *spend money* on Power Pivot projects. In 2012, most companies and individuals were still in the "try out this new toy" phase. Very few had reached the point of saying "yes, we see sufficient potential here that it's worth a modest investment." But now? I can barely keep up with the demand, and the demand grows *daily*. The past 14 months have by far been the most rewarding – both financially *and* psychically – of my entire career.

In summary, the things I wrote in Summer 2012 were *predictions*. I was both confident and sincere in those predictions of course, because I had already seen a lot, and based on those experiences, it was pretty clear (to me at least) that big change was around the corner.

But now, in Spring 2014, I could rewrite all of those predictions as... *observations*. Of things that *are* happening, rather than things that are *going* to happen. And even for me, who was so confident in those predictions, seeing the changes today still is quite meaningful. Going from 95% certain to 100% certain is still a big deal :)

If you still harbor some skepticism, please consider that this isn't just "talk" for me – I have voted with my feet (and my wallet, career, etc.) I'm not pointing at an airplane on the ground and saying "I bet that airplane will take us places." I'm already flying around in it and *visiting* those places. If the plane had crashed, well, we wouldn't be having this conversation :)

One final note: we are still very, *very* early in this revolution. Awareness is still, even today, at only a small fraction of the ultimate target audience. But these things have a way of surprising us, and 2014 has so far felt... explosive. For example, in the first six weeks of 2014, traffic to PowerPivotPro.com grew by 25%. (The opportunities I've seen in my business actually grew by quite a bit *more* than that). That's the sort of growth that, if sustained over a full year, would project out to over 600%. I won't go on record and *predict* that will happen. But it *could* - Power Pivot is a classic example of viral growth – awareness is spreading only by word of mouth rather than by edict (nor by national advertising campaign, sadly).

Malcolm Gladwell's "The Tipping Point" explains how viral growth, when sustained, almost always surprises us with a sudden explosive surge. The young year of 2014 has already exhibited that on its own scale. Now is an excellent time to be getting on board. Welcome, and I hope you find this book to be helpful.

-Rob Collie, April 2014

Chapter 1: Dashboard Tricks and Visualization Techniques

Broadly speaking, Power Pivot is a numbers-producing machine: Raw data goes in, your formulas and relationships digest it, and magically useful numbers come out. Those numbers are often *metrics* on a business, and that's a beautiful thing; very often, those metrics are being "seen" for the first time in the history of the business. Quite often, before a business adopts Power Pivot, it is forced to operate without metrics that are, in hindsight, quite clearly *critical*. This is a lot like a doctor suddenly having access to patient information such as temperature, pulse rate, and blood pressure—after lacking that information for most of a career. Such a shift is transformational.

So, Power Pivot produces numbers—incredibly *important* numbers that quite often have never before existed. It's empowering stuff for sure.

There is a natural tendency among "numbers" people to view the freshly pressed numbers as the final destination. Resist that temptation! In order for numbers to have an impact, they need to be communicated to other people who may not be fascinated with these magical digits. Furthermore, those people then need to translate them into action. So the way you present numbers is often every bit as critical as the numbers themselves.

This chapter provides a collection of tricks in that vein. We have intentionally selected techniques ranging from "bread and butter" (that you might use in nearly every report/dashboard) to "envelope pushing" (that you might not apply in precisely the manner presented but that might inspire related approaches). We start with one of the former.

Adding a "Last Refreshed Date" Readout

You've built some killer models and reports. You've published them to SharePoint. You've scheduled automatic refresh to run, say, once per week. You have this Power Pivot thing All. Dialed. In. But are the report consumers satisfied? Nope, they aren't satisfied!

You can be certain that your report consumers will *never* be satisfied. And, hey, that's kinda cool. It's a good thing. You weren't given all this new power just so you could sit on your laurels, were you? Nope. True Power Pivot pros aren't even sure they can *find* their laurels, much less sit on them. You will always be improving—both your skill set and the reports you produce.

One improvement you can make is to automatically inform report consumers of how "fresh" the data is so they don't have to deal with stale reports. Adding such a readout is actually pretty simple: It requires just two steps.

Step 1: Adding a LastRefreshed Measure

Somewhere in the Power Pivot window, you probably have a column whose most recent date is always the date on which the data was last refreshed. For instance, in a retail system, you might be able to use your Sales table for this, as long as you always have at least one transaction per day. Or perhaps the Calendar table you pull from the database is always current (and does not contain future dates). Or perhaps you can get your DB admin to add a single-cell table just for this purpose.

This example uses the TransactionDate column from a Sales table:

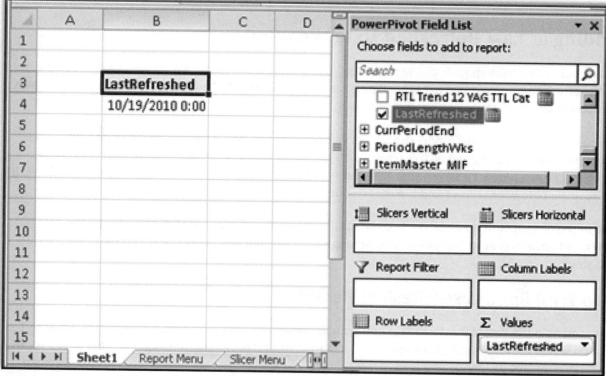

Transaction...	Sto...	S...	TransactionT
9/18/2010	151	175769	
8/5/2010	372	175769	
8/26/2010	130	175769	
10/14/2010	297	175769	
1/4/2010	165	175769	
2/7/2010	422	175769	
11/13/2009	297	175769	

[TransactionDate ▼]   9/18/2010 12:00:00 AM

Figure 1.1

Did you know that measures can return dates? They sure can, and it's killer useful. Here's how you create a measure that does this:

```
[LastRefreshed] = LASTDATE(Sales[TransactionDate])
```

LASTDATE() is kinda like MAX() but for dates. It always returns the most recent transaction date:

Figure 1.2

Neat, huh? It's a date returned as a measure, in a Pivot.

Step 2: Using the Measure in a Cube Formula

The most flexible, least intrusive way to display the `LastRefreshed` measure in a report is to create a single cube formula for it and then stuff that formula into a single cell. That way, you have complete control over its appearance.

Two things to note here:

- Given that your reports will often have columns that are oddly sized, to make everything look good, it's much better to use a single-cell formula that includes the label than to split it across two cells.

- A cube formula, when it returns a date measure, formats it as an integer rather than as a date. So you need to reformat it as a date *in the formula*. (You could just use Format Cells, but when you put the label and the date in a single cell, you can't just format the cell as a date.)

To make a long story short, here is the cube formula to use in this case:

```
="Last Refreshed: " & TEXT(CUBEVALUE("PowerPivotData",
  "[Measures].[LastRefreshed]"),"mm/dd/yyyy")
```

You can leave the result as a date serial number and then put the label in the custom format. Use `=CUBEVALUE()` to return the date serial number. Select the cell, press Ctrl+1, choose Number, Custom. In the Type box, enter "Last Refreshed "m/d/yyyy:

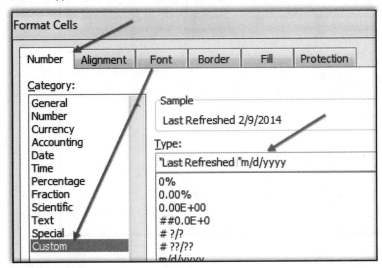

Figure 1.3

Plop this in the desired cell, and you're all set:

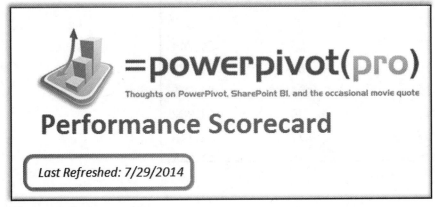

Figure 1.4

Pretty slick. The cell will refresh every time the workbook is refreshed. But it will not be reevaluated during an update, as happens with a slicer.

> **Note**
>
> For more on refreshing versus updating and the *huge* difference in performance between the two, see http://ppvt.pro/REFRESHUPDATE.

Normalizing Your Measures to First/Average/Max Values for Charts

In this chart, the line for Total Sales is quite visible, whereas the other two lines are squashed at the bottom. Even when this chart is in color, you can't tell that the line for Transaction Size is 50 times higher than the line for Active Customers.

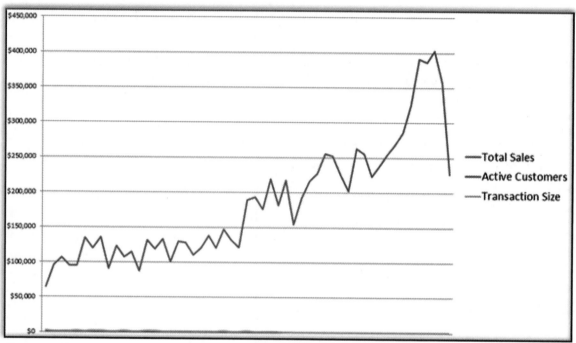

Figure 1.5

The three lines plotted on this chart are "sourced" from the following numbers:

Week Number	Total Sales	Active Customers	Transaction Size
1	$64,297	35	$1,837
2	$95,893	55	$1,744
3	$106,530	60	$1,776
4	$94,935	54	$1,758
5	$95,348	50	$1,907
6	$134,367	77	$1,745
7	$119,924	65	$1,845

Figure 1.6

These three measures are very different in their relative sizes, varying from two digits to six digits. Data like this results in crappy charts. But with a little formula magic, you can fix the chart above so it looks like this:

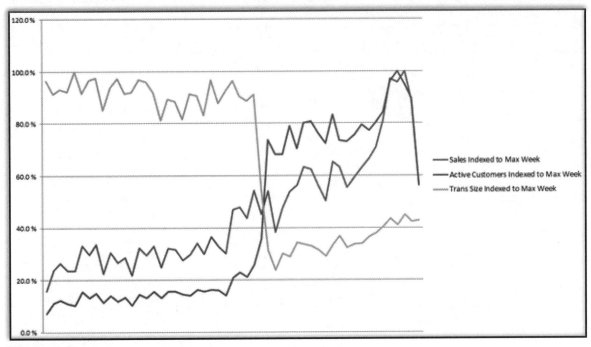

Figure 1.7

Ah, formulas make everything better. Yep, this chart uses the same data as the earlier chart, just "normalized."

A Word from the Charting Pit of Derision

Yeah, I (Rob) hear that chittering out there...the mandibles of the demonspawn chart fiends are clacking out a sound that resembles "Secondary Axis!"

Well, I need *three* axes this time. Is there a Tertiary Axis feature? I seriously don't even know. There *are* only two sides to the chart, so it would make sense, I guess, to *not* offer a tertiary axis. You'd have to start "stacking" scales side by side, and that would probably make Tufte cry.

But I'm intentionally *not* checking whether there is such a feature. Because honestly I don't even like the *Secondary* Axis feature that much.

If you are absolutely sure that none of your numbers will ever be 0 or negative, you could select Layout, Axes, Primary Vertical Axes, Show Axis with Log Scale:

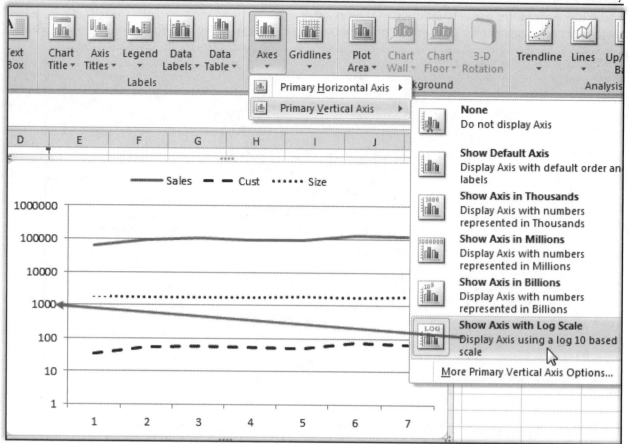

Figure 1.8

This will automatically make the smaller numbers easier to see. In a log scale, the distance from 1 to 10 is the same as the distance from 10000 to 100000. However, when, in real life, would you have a data set without a single zero point?

Numbers Are Numbers, Visuals Are Visuals, and Everyone Has a Preference

I (Rob) have a theory that you are either a numbers person or a visuals person. When you first get some new data, is your first instinct "I need to crunch this data with some formulas," or is it "I need to get this on a chart"?

Now, of course, a numbers person uses charts, and a visuals person sometimes needs to write some formulas. But which one is your *first* instinct determines which type of person you are.

I'm a numbers guy. Charts are very much a last step in the process—if that—in my world. Heck, give me some conditional formatting in a Pivot, and I am usually set. (Tellingly, though, I always *need* conditional formatting before I am happy. See, even a numbers guy can leverage visuals; it's just that I am *more* on the numbers side of things.)

So, even in a case with *two* different measures, I am tempted to correct with formulas rather than track down the Secondary Axis feature. I'm really just not that comfortable with charts. I struggle to make them do what I want. And I want to work with numbers. So this is really all just personal preference on my part.

The Formulas

Let's get back to normalizing the earlier data. Basically, you divide each measure by the maximum value of that measure and put everything on a 0 to 100% scale. Here's one of the formulas you need to do this:

```
[Sales Indexed to Max Week] =
[Total Sales Measure] /
MAXX(ALL(Calendar[WeekNumberOfYear]), [Total Sales Measure])
```

You put `Calendar[WeekNumberOfYear]` in the Rows drop zone for the Pivot (which "powers" the horizontal axis of the PivotChart). So if you change the field in the Rows drop zone, you need to change that part of the formula.

The other two measures follow exactly the same pattern, but you substitute their respective base measures for `Total Sales Measure`.

In this Pivot, all three sets of data have been normalized to be between 0 and 100%—which yields a useful chart:

WeekNumberOfYear ▼	Sales Indexed to Max Week	Active Customers Indexed to Max Week	Trans Size Indexed to Max Week
1	15.9 %	7.1 %	96.3 %
2	23.8 %	11.2 %	91.4 %
3	26.4 %	12.2 %	93.1 %
4	23.5 %	11.0 %	92.2 %
5	23.6 %	10.2 %	100.0 %
6	33.3 %	15.7 %	91.5 %
7	29.7 %	13.3 %	96.8 %
8	33.7 %	14.9 %	97.6 %
9	22.5 %	11.4 %	85.1 %
10	30.6 %	14.1 %	93.7 %
11	26.7 %	11.8 %	97.3 %

Figure 1.9

Alternative Formulas: Using the Average

Maybe 0 to 100% is too restrictive for you. Maybe you want to divide by the average instead of the max. Here's what it looks like:

```
[Sales Indexed to Average Week] =
[Total Sales Measure] /
CALCULATE([Total Sales Measure] /
        DISTINCTCOUNT(Calendar[WeekNumberOfYear]),
        ALL(Calendar[WeekNumberOfYear)
    )
```

> **Note**
>
> Again, if you have something else in the Rows drop zone, you need to replace `Calendar[WeekNumberOfYear]`.

This yields the following, slightly different (better?) chart:

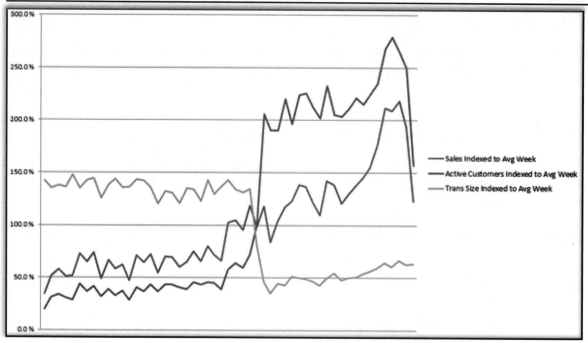

Figure 1.10

The chart is still quite readable, but the fact that Active Customers has wider variation than the other measures is no longer hidden by being squashed into 0 to 100%.

Of course, you could also just use AVERAGEX() instead of those CALCULATE() shenanigans in the denominator. In fact, that's what *does* happen for Trans Size Indexed to Average Week:

```
[Trans Size Indexed to Average Week] =
[Transaction Size] /
AVERAGEX(ALL(Calendar[WeekNumberOfYear]), [Transaction Size])
```

It doesn't make a huge difference in most cases. AVERAGEX() doesn't care whether certain weeks had higher sales volumes than others: All weeks will be averaged as equals, whereas the fancy CALCULATE() approach above computes the average as a grand total ratio, which is inherently weighted.

Building Charts That Are Dynamically Indexed to the First Value

Try using normal Excel to create a sliceable chart in which every series always begins at 100%. A chart like this is very useful for comparing the relative performance of different things over a given period of time. Setting this up is relatively labor intensive in regular Excel, and then if you want to change the selected time period, you must repeat that manual effort.

Power Pivot allows you to create such a chart with less effort than required in normal Excel, *and* the resulting chart responds dynamically to changing date range selections, with no modifications required.

In the following example of such a chart, notice how September is selected in the first image and October is selected in the second image. In both cases, all three series are indexed to 100% at the beginning of the time period:

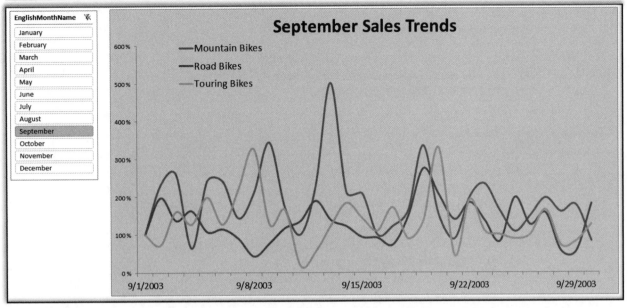

Figure 1.11

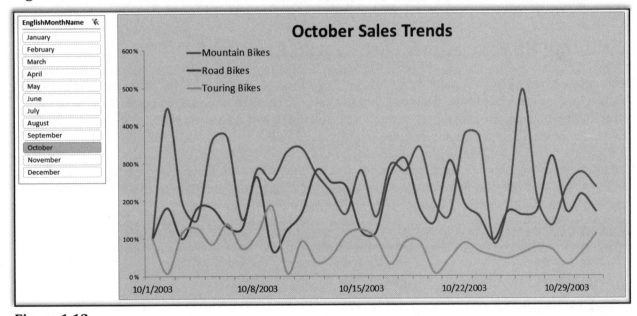

Figure 1.12

Here's the formula for the normalized measure displayed on the chart:

```
[Normalized Sales] =
DIVIDE([Total Sales], [Sales on First Date in Range])
```

This seems anticlimactic, doesn't it? But there's real magic in the Sales on First Date in Range measure:

```
[Sales on First Date in Range] =
CALCULATE([Total Sales],
        DATESBETWEEN(Calendar[Date],
                [First Date in Range],
                [First Date in Range]
                )
        )
```

Sorry, we keep teasing you. We like to write measures in intermediate steps like this. The *real* magic is in that `First Date in Range` measure:

```
[First Date in Range] =
CALCULATE(FIRSTNONBLANK(Calendar[Date], [Total Sales]),
        ALL(Calendar[Date])
     )
```

> **Note**
>
> We struggled, at first, to write this measure. We tried using `ALLSELECTED(Calendar[Date])`, but because we were slicing by the Month column (a different column than Date) and letting Month filter the date range rather than filtering by the Date column directly, `ALLSELECTED(Calendar[Date])` was returning January 1 even when we had selected December on the month slicer. `VALUES()` provided another dead end. We found ourselves desiring an `ALLVALUES()` function before realizing that `FIRSTNONBLANK()` is built for this kind of thing. All's well that ends well.

Bubbling Up Exceptions with "Sarah Problem"

Sometimes, when a Pivot has multiple fields in the Rows drop zone or the Columns drop zone, interesting "outlier" values are hidden from view until the user expands (drills down into) the correct branch of the Pivot. Rather than require consumers of your Pivots to expand and scan every node, it is sometimes valuable to "bubble up" certain details from lower levels and display them at a higher level.

For example, in the following Pivot, a flag appears at the top level (Accessories), which tells you there's a problem further down. You then expand Accessories, and then Bottles and Cages, to find that Road Bottle Cage—a product with significantly negative 1-year sales growth—is the culprit:

Product Hierarchy	Total Sales	1 Year Sales Trend	Products in Decline
⊟ Accessories	$700,760	174.3 %	⚑
⊞ Bike Racks	$39,360	128.6 %	
⊞ Bike Stands	$39,591	150.0 %	
⊟ Bottles and Cages	$56,798	50.7 %	⚑
Mountain Bottle Cage	$20,230	109.3 %	
Road Bottle Cage	$15,391	-38.3 %	⚑
Water Bottle	$21,178	100.0 %	
⊞ Cleaners	$7,219	152.9 %	
⊞ Fenders	$46,620	129.5 %	
⊞ Helmets	$225,336	131.2 %	
⊞ Hydration Packs	$40,308	78.6 %	
⊞ Tires and Tubes	$245,529	342.0 %	
⊞ Bikes	$28,318,145	-69.2 %	⚑
⊞ Clothing	$339,773	216.3 %	
Grand Total	$29,358,677	-63.4 %	⚑

Figure 1.13

At the top level, the Accessories category looked quite healthy, so you may never have known there was a problem lurking deeper down. You can use "bubbling up" techniques to prevent such lurking problems. We like to call this particular example the "Sarah Problem" technique.

Starting with a "Sarah Problem" Measure

Let's say you have a measure. It doesn't matter what it is or how it's calculated really, except that it reports on whether there's a problem. It returns 1 (or Yes or True) if there's a problem, and it returns 0 (or No or False) if there isn't. Or maybe it returns a "regular" number when it crosses a certain line that your business has decided is bad. The measure helps you determine where there's a problem, and we punnily call it Sarah Problem. (To pronounce it properly, you have to add a question mark, so, technically, it's Sarah Problem?)

> **Note**
>
> I (Rob) can't take credit for the Sarah Problem pun. Back when I lived in Seattle, my wife (girlfriend at the time, and fellow Microsoft engineer) played roller derby. She was a "Rat City Rollergirl," playing for a team called Grave Danger, and her skater name was Natalie Fatality. And she had a teammate whose skater name was "Sarah Problem." I am not making this up.

Back to the Formulas

In this example, the story of Sarah Problem starts with a measure named 1 Year Sales Trend. The formula for 1 Year Sales Trend is completely irrelevant! You just need to know that it measures "year-over-year" sales growth or decline. So it can go as low as –100% (for example, in the case of products that haven't sold at all this year) and can go as high as, well, there is no upper limit.

Say that you've decided that anything that falls below –10% is bad. So you want to flag products that have declined by 10% or more.

Here you see the 1 Year Sales Trend measure circled:

Product Hierarchy	Total Sales	1 Year Sales Trend	Products in Decline
⊟Accessories	$700,760	174.3 %	⚑
⊞Bike Racks	$39,360	128.6 %	
⊞Bike Stands	$39,591	150.0 %	
⊟Bottles and Cages	$56,798	50.7 %	⚑
Mountain Bottle Cage	$20,230	109.3 %	
Road Bottle Cage	$15,391	-38.3 %	⚑
Water Bottle	$21,178	100.0 %	

Figure 1.14

Notice that Sarah Problem is very meticulous! At the Accessories level, the trend is very positive, but it's still flagged:

Product Hierarchy	Total Sales	1 Year Sales Trend	Products in Decline
⊟Accessories	$700,760	174.3 %	⚑
⊞Bike Racks	$39,360	128.6 %	
⊞Bike Stands	$39,591	150.0 %	
⊟Bottles and Cages	$56,798	50.7 %	⚑

Figure 1.15

How do you create that Products in Decline column of the Pivot? Well it starts with another measure:

```
[Products in Decline] =
COUNTROWS(FILTER(Products, [1 Year Sales Trend]<-.1))
```

This formula counts the number of rows in the Products table (each of which is an individual product) for which 1 Year Sales Trend is below the threshold of −10%.

Here's how you do the conditional formatting:

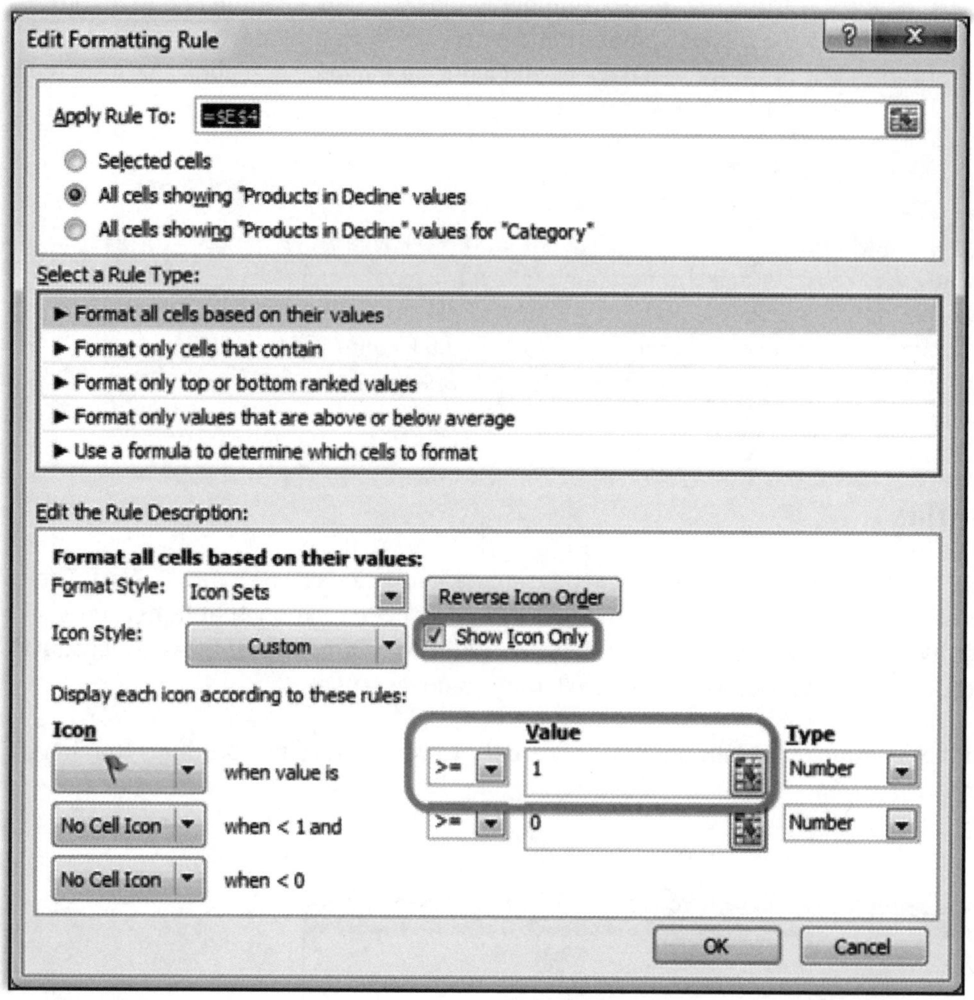

Figure 1.16

This conditional formatting rule is pretty simple: It just flags cases where there's at least one "bad" product. (Note that the Show Icon Only check box is checked.) So you get a flag whenever there's at least one "bad" product, in any level of the Pivot.

Of course, maybe you don't want to count bad products. Maybe you want to count bad stores. Or bad customers. To count anything, you just change your second measure to count rows of the proper table. Or maybe even distinct values of a column, using VALUES (*column*). Knock yourself out. But know that no one knocks people out like Sarah Problem.

Ranks and Exceptions That Bubble Up to Subtotals

Rather than bubble up the existence of problems or outliers, what if you want to display the best (or worst) value that can be found deeper down a particular branch of a Pivot?

Here's an example of bubbling up the best product rank under a branch:

Figure 1.17

Here's the measure formula:

```
[Product Sales Rank]=
IF(HASONEVALUE(Products[ProductName]),
    RANKX(ALL(Products), [Total Sales]),
    MINX(VALUES(Products[ProductName]),
        RANKX(ALL(Products), [Total Sales])
        )
    )
```

The first input to `IF()` (that is, `HASONEVALUE`) checks whether the current measure cell is in the context of a single product. If it is, the first branch performs a rank of that product against all other products:

Row Labels	Total Sales	Product Sales Rank
⊞ Accessories	$700,760	68
⊟ Bikes	$28,318,145	1
⊞ Mountain Bikes	$9,952,760	6
⊟ Road Bikes	$14,520,584	1
312	$1,205,877	1
310	$1,202,299	2
313	$1,080,638	3
314	$1,055,590	4
311	$1,005,494	5

Each of these cells corresponds to a single product, "triggering" the green branch of the formula.

Figure 1.18

So really, the first branch is just a normal `RANKX()` measure.

The second branch of the `IF()` is the nifty branch:

```
IF(HASONEVALUE(Products[ProductKey]),
    RANKX(ALL(Products), [Total Sales]),
    MINX(VALUES(Products[ProductKey]),
        RANKX(ALL(Products), [Total Sales])
        )
    )
```

So if the current measure cell is *not* a single product, the second branch "fires":

Row Labels	Total Sales	Product Sales Rank
⊞ Accessories	$700,760	68
⊟ Bikes	$28,318,145	1
⊞ Mountain Bikes	$9,952,760	6
⊟ Road Bikes	$14,520,584	1
312	$1,205,877	1
310	$1,202,299	2
313	$1,080,638	3
314	$1,055,590	4
211	$1 005 494	5

Each of these cells corresponds to *multiple* products, triggers blue branch of the formula

Figure 1.19

The boldfaced part of the formula basically does this: For each product that is "valid" in the current measure cell, it finds the product's rank among all the products. Then it returns the lowest such rank from all those products.

So It's Not Really "Bubbling Up" but Working Overtime

No measure cell *ever* impacts another measure cell. Each measure cell is calculated independently, as if it were an island.

In the case of the `Product Sales Rank` measure, the darker-shaded subtotal cells of the Pivot (the ones where there is more than one product "active" in that context) force the Power Pivot calc engine to work *much* harder than it does for the unshaded (single-product) cells:

Row Labels	Total Sales	Product Sales Rank
⊞ Accessories	$700,760	68
⊟ Bikes	$28,318,145	1
⊞ Mountain Bikes	$9,952,760	6
⊟ Road Bikes	$14,520,584	1
312	$1,205,877	1
310	$1,202,299	2
313	$1,080,638	3
314	$1,055,590	4
311	$1,005,494	5
580	$418,444	13
581	$399,733	16

Ranks all 125 bike products, but only "remembers" the lowest rank found.

Only ranks a single product – 310

Figure 1.20

So, in essence, every product in the Products table is ranked three times: once at each level of the Pivot. Don't be shocked if this sometimes results in slow Pivots. In fact, whenever you see one X function, like `RANKX()` or `MINX()`, nested inside another X function, that's generally a clue that you may see slow slicer clicks, since each X function is itself a "go do something a bunch of times" machine.

Custom ToolTips in Dashboards

It's possible to create custom "on hover" ToolTips on each cell in a dashboard. *Here's an example:*

	New Customers	Total Customers	Pct Returning Customers
2003			
July	202	511	60%
August	1,210		
September	1,112		
October	1,132		
November	1,094	1,634	33%

July was the last month in which we relied on word of mouth.

Total customer numbers were dropping off significantly.

Figure 1.21

> **Note**
>
> You could use the Input tab of the Data Validation dialog box to specify a ToolTip that appears when you select the cell. The ToolTip shown here is better, though, because it appears on hover.

The Trick: Hyperlinks to Nowhere

This trick involves a guerilla-style hack. You select a cell, choose Insert Hyperlink, and set the cell reference to the cell you just selected, like this:

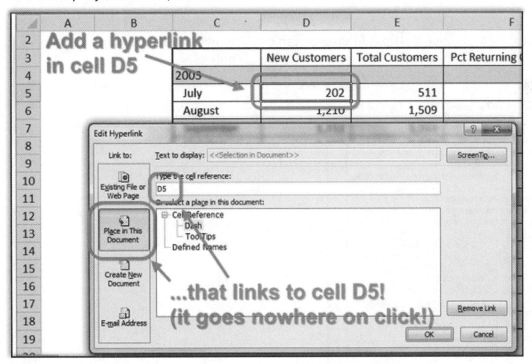

Figure 1.22

Your hyperlink in cell D5 goes to cell D5, making the hyperlink a "do nothing" link.

Now click ScreenTip and enter a ToolTip:

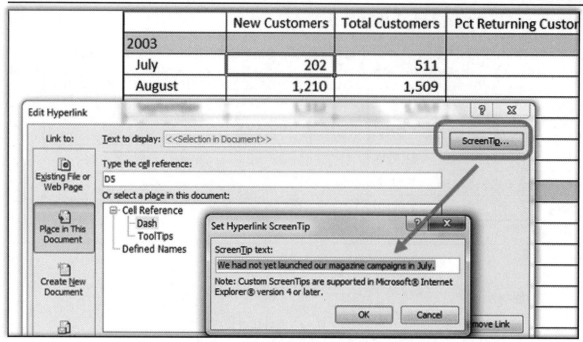

Figure 1.23

You now have an "on hover" ToolTip for cell D5!

Building a Better ToolTip Process

The problem here is that this process is incredibly tedious. Who wants to go through this process for each cell? Blech.

To make it easier to create another ToolTip in future, you can create a "mirror" sheet that has the same shape and location as the dashboard. In it, you enter other desired ToolTips:

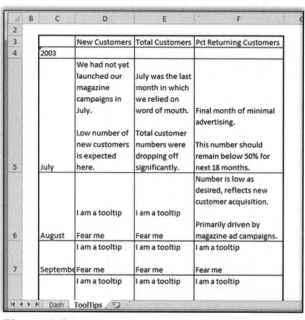

Figure 1.24

Next, you create a macro called `RunTheToolTipHack()`:

```
Sub RunTheToolTipHack()
    CubeFormulasToolTips ActiveSheet.Name, "ToolTips"
End Sub
```

Go back to your dashboard sheet, make sure your mirror sheet is named ToolTips, and run this macro. It calls these two other macros that you will also need to add to your workbook:

```
Sub CubeFormulasToolTips(sSheet As String, sToolTipsSheet As
String)
    Dim oMainSheet As Worksheet
    Dim oTipsSheet As Worksheet
    Dim oRange As Range
    Dim c As Range
    Dim sFormula As String
    Dim sAddress As String
    Dim sToolTip As String

    Set oMainSheet = Sheets(sSheet)
    Set oTipsSheet = Sheets(sToolTipsSheet)

    Set oRange = oMainSheet.UsedRange

    For Each c In oRange.Cells
        sFormula = c.FormulaR1C1
        sAddress = c.Address
        sToolTip = oTipsSheet.Range(sAddress).Value
        If Left(sFormula, 5) = "=CUBE" Then
            SetHyperlink sSheet, sAddress, "'" & sSheet & "'!" _ &
sAddress, sToolTip, True, False
        End If
    Next
End Sub

Sub SetHyperlink(sSheet As String, sCell As String, sDestAddress As
String, sToolTip As String, bFormula As Boolean, bLookLikeLink As
Boolean)
    Dim oSheet As Worksheet
    Dim sFormat As String
    Dim c As Range
    Dim iColor As Integer

    Set oSheet = ActiveWorkbook.Sheets(sSheet)
    Set c = oSheet.Range(sCell)
    sFormat = c.NumberFormat
    iColor = c.Font.ColorIndex

    If bFormula = True Then
        oSheet.Hyperlinks.Add Anchor:=c, Address:="", _
            SubAddress:=sDestAddress, ScreenTip:=sToolTip
    Else
        oSheet.Hyperlinks.Add Anchor:=c, Address:="", _
            SubAddress:=sDestAddress, _
            TextToDisplay:=c.Value, _
        ScreenTip:=sToolTip
```

```
      End If

      c.NumberFormat = sFormat

      If bLookLikeLink = False Then
          c.Font.Underline = xlUnderlineStyleNone
          c.Font.Color = iColor
      End If

   End Sub
```

The `RunTheToolTipHack()` macro "grabs" the ToolTips from your mirror sheet and assigns them all to the cells on your main sheet. It's magic.

Questions About This Trick

We're guessing you may like this hack and yet still have some questions about it:

- **Does this work with Pivots?** No, sadly, Pivots don't let you set hyperlinks on cells. In Power Pivot land, this only works with cube formula reports.

- **Can the mirror sheet be constructed using formulas?** Yes, absolutely. There's no need to manually enter ToolTips. In fact, you could use cube formulas and text measures to (cue maniacal laughter) FETCH COMMENTS FROM THE POWER PIVOT MODEL ITSELF!!!!

- **Will these ToolTips work in the web version of Excel?** Yes, they will. We have tested this hyperlink/ToolTip approach there.

- **Wait, I didn't think macros ran on the web version of Excel!** That's right, they don't. But your macros don't need to run on the server. You are merely using the macros to set the ToolTips. The macros don't even need to live in your report workbook; they can live in your Personal Macro workbook.

- **What happens when I want to change the comments?** You need to run the macros again.

- **Wait, even if I am using formulas to fetch the comments?** Yeah. You refresh your Power Pivot model, refresh the dashboards, and even refresh the mirror sheet. Everything is updated. But your ToolTips will still be the "stale" tips until you run the macro again.

- **So this won't work with Power Pivot autorefresh?** Bingo. It won't. If you have a Power Pivot server and have scheduled the reports to autorefresh, the ToolTips will still be stale. You will need to download the file and rerun the macros.

- **That's a tragedy. Can you fix this with the HYPERLINK() function?** These are good questions! It's like you were looking over our shoulders, watching us work on this. No, the `HYPERLINK` function lacks an input for ToolTips. If it had one, you *would* be able to do all this automatically.

Named Sets and "Asymmetric" Pivots: Showing Different Measures for Different Years

Here's a good challenge: How do you take the first Pivot below and turn it into the second one? This is one of those cool little (and simple!) tricks that we all need from time to time.

This Pivot has three measures (Total Sales, Sales to Parents, and Sales to Married Couples) displayed for each year from 2001 to 2004:

Row Labels	Australia	Canada	France	Germany	Northwest	Southwest
Column Labels						
2001						
Total Sales	$1,309,047	$146,830	$180,572	$237,785	$415,203	$685,346
Sales to Parents	$332,091	$38,173	$84,130	$98,354	$166,709	$249,619
Sales to Married Couples	$678,761	$91,668	$80,438	$126,238	$178,678	$314,109
2002						
Total Sales	$2,154,285	$621,602	$514,942	$521,231	$847,839	$1,278,074
Sales to Parents	$581,890	$206,473	$240,451	$278,131	$282,830	$531,319
Sales to Married Couples	$987,276	$326,177	$219,573	$280,011	$409,012	$666,246
2003						
Total Sales	$3,033,784	$535,784	$1,026,325	$1,058,406	$1,094,829	$1,733,934
Sales to Parents	$826,679	$207,887	$569,454	$533,479	$406,889	$674,797
Sales to Married Couples	$1,370,280	$305,463	$603,736	$564,248	$540,113	$942,605
2004						
Total Sales	$2,563,884	$673,628	$922,179	$1,076,891	$1,291,994	$2,020,796
Sales to Parents	$746,228	$309,998	$506,740	$550,383	$526,875	$803,774
Sales to Married Couples	$1,183,516	$354,907	$502,832	$617,875	$682,330	$1,127,661

Figure 1.25

But you *want* the next Pivot, which displays the Sales to Married Couples measure up through 2002 but "discontinues" the display of that measure in 2003, replacing it with the Sales to Parents measure:

Row Labels	Australia	Canada	France	Germany	Northwest	Southwest
Column Labels						
2001						
Total Sales	$1,309,047	$146,830	$180,572	$237,785	$415,203	$685,346
Sales to Married Couples	$678,761	$91,668	$80,438	$126,238	$178,678	$314,109
2002						
Total Sales	$2,154,285	$621,602	$514,942	$521,231	$847,839	$1,278,074
Sales to Married Couples	$987,276	$326,177	$219,573	$280,011	$409,012	$666,246
2003						
Total Sales	$3,033,784	$535,784	$1,026,325	$1,058,406	$1,094,829	$1,733,934
Sales to Parents	$826,679	$207,887	$569,454	$533,479	$406,889	$674,797
2004						
Total Sales	$2,563,884	$673,628	$922,179	$1,076,891	$1,291,994	$2,020,796
Sales to Parents	$746,228	$309,998	$506,740	$550,383	$526,875	$803,774

Figure 1.26

You cannot just filter out a measure in *some* places. A measure is either on the Pivot, or it's not. Does that mean you're stuck? Nope, you just need to use a different feature. You can create a set based on row (or column) items:

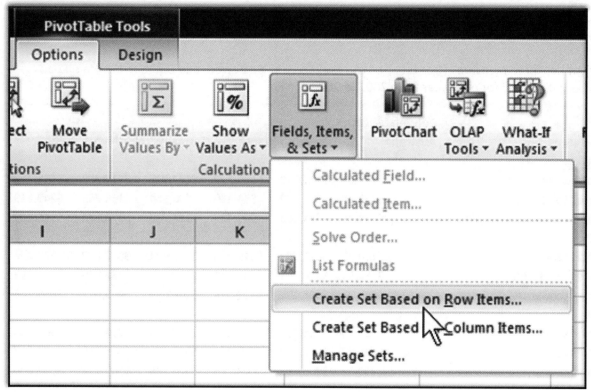

Figure 1.27

That hidden gem on the Options tab opens this dialog:

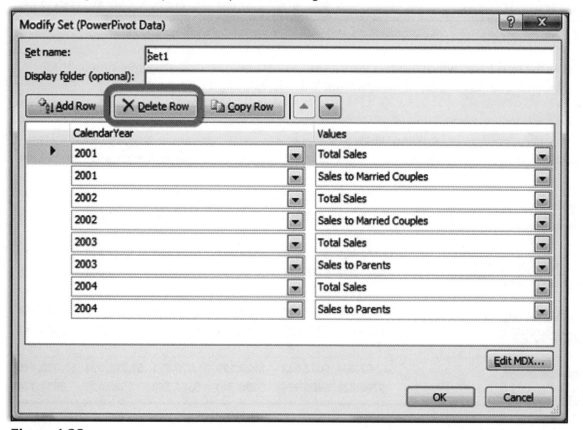

Figure 1.28

When this dialog first came up, it had more rows in it. We've already deleted some of the rows, like (2001, Parents) and (2003, Married). When you have the rows you want, click OK, and you get the Pivot you wanted in the first place:

Row Labels	Column Labels ▼ Australia	Canada	France	Germany	Northwest	Southwest
2001						
Total Sales	$1,309,047	$146,830	$180,572	$237,785	$415,203	$685,346
Sales to Married Couples	$678,761	$91,668	$80,438	$126,238	$178,678	$314,109
2002						
Total Sales	$2,154,285	$621,602	$514,942	$521,231	$847,839	$1,278,074
Sales to Married Couples	$987,276	$326,177	$219,573	$280,011	$409,012	$666,246
2003						
Total Sales	$3,033,784	$535,784	$1,026,325	$1,058,406	$1,094,829	$1,733,934
Sales to Parents	$826,679	$207,887	$569,454	$533,479	$406,889	$674,797
2004						
Total Sales	$2,563,884	$673,628	$922,179	$1,076,891	$1,291,994	$2,020,796
Sales to Parents	$746,228	$309,998	$506,740	$550,383	$526,875	$803,774

Figure 1.29

Voilà! Now you see different measures starting in 2003.

You now get a single field in the field list:

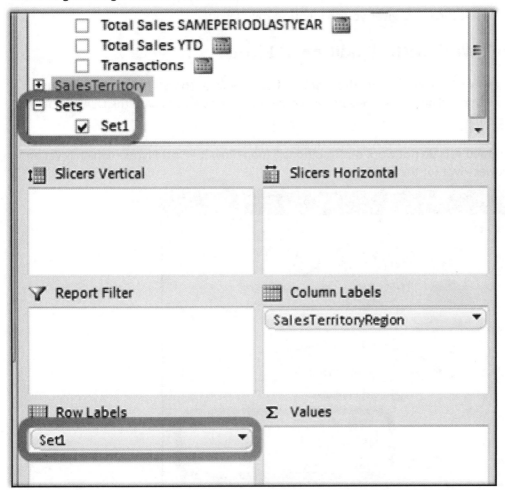

Figure 1.30

Reusable! Portable!

Just like one of Power Pivot's other great benefits, portable formulas (see http://ppvt.pro/PORTABLEFX2), sets are portable, too! To see this in action, create a new Pivot:

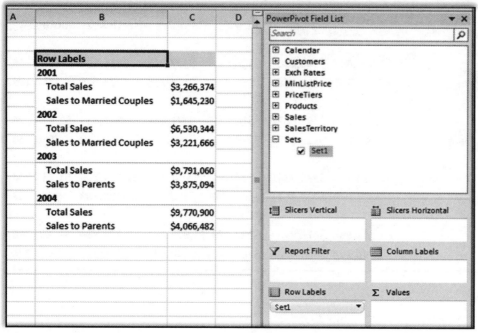

Figure 1.31

In this new Pivot, merely selecting Set1 gives you an identical-rows layout.

Named Sets Don't Work with "Traditional" Pivots

You may be wondering why you've never seen this feature of Excel before. There's a simple answer: It works only with Power Pivot and data model Pivots (as well as another flavor of Pivot, the OLAP Pivot, but that's much less common).

As you can see here, named sets do not work on "traditional" (non–Power Pivot) Pivots—which is yet another reason to use Power Pivot (or the 2013 data model):

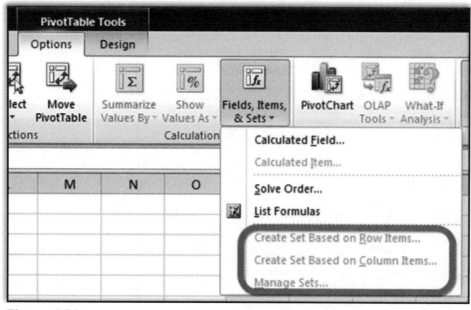

Figure 1.32

Chapter 2: Slicers: The Gateway to Interactivity

The intro to this chapter is longer than the others and offers a glimpse into the "behind the scenes at Microsoft" history of slicers, in two parts. We promise it's both relevant *and* interesting because slicers are *both* an incredibly useful feature *and* they provide a window into the "soul" of our lives as "data" people.

Part I: In 2006, I (Rob) left the Excel team to join another team at Microsoft that was working on fantasy football. (Fantasy football is a mathematical game cloaked in the trappings of American football. The siren's song of being paid to pursue my already-obsessive hobby was just too strong to resist.)

It wasn't long before I convinced my new team to spend large amounts of money on something we dubbed "Statosphere"—Excel PivotTables in the cloud (hosted on the web version of Excel), powered by an expensive OLAP database. (You don't need to know details about OLAP—just that it is a forerunner of Power Pivot.) The expensive OLAP database, in turn, was powered by even *more* expensive raw data from STATS LLC. The total price tag of this boondoggle approached half a million dollars, once Microsoft employee salaries were figured in, and it probably cost that team's general manager her job. (But let's not focus on the negatives, shall we?)

Here's an internal screenshot of one of the web pages in Statosphere, circa 2006. Yes, it's a PivotTable rendered by Excel Services (that is, the web version of Excel), "wrapped" in a custom web page:

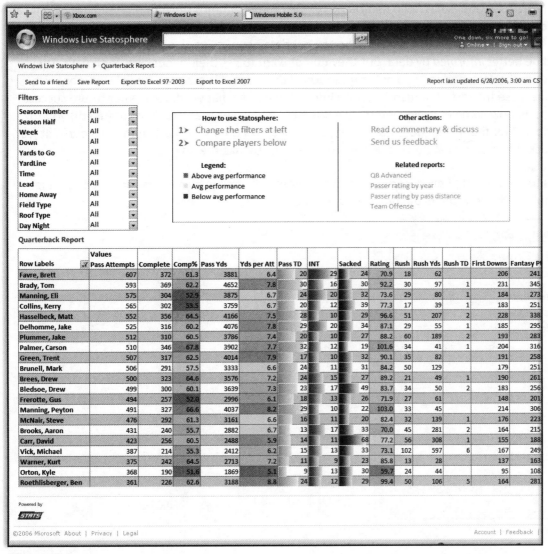

Figure 2.1

> **Note**
>
> Notice the heavy usage of report filters—Season Number, Season Half, etc.? At that point in time, report filters were available, but slicers didn't yet exist.

As part of this project, I conducted focus groups with sports fans to see what they thought of Statosphere in action. I learned two very important things from those focus groups:

- **Most human beings are not terribly interested in data.** Despite being a relatively intellectual group of people collected from the Seattle area, and despite the fact that they were all NFL fans, most participants in those groups exhibited no curiosity whatsoever when presented with the world's most expensive and amazing sports stats tool.

- **Report filters scare most people to death.** Every time we would click a report filter's little down arrow and a dialog popped up, I could see people's faces sink into frowns. They just *hated* report filters! This was shocking to me. I had spent the prior two years working on making PivotTables "friendlier," and not once during those two years had we imagined that report filters were a problem. We had always assumed that they were the easiest part of Pivots, and we hadn't bothered to test them like this.

The first of these observations has been reinforced for me dozens of times since that fateful day, and it carries tremendous relevance for *everyone* reading this book. You, my dear friends, are data people. And for every one of "us," there are about 15 people who are *not* data people. Everyone else wants to make better decisions and be better *informed* by data. But they do *not* want to get their hands dirty with data. They do not want to touch data, and they do not want to touch data tools. This is good news! Our jobs exist, in large part, because the rest of humanity has no interest in doing what we do. And your future success hinges, in part, on how completely you internalize this fact: Your colleagues largely want (need!) you to "dumb data down" for them. That does not mean your colleagues themselves are dumb, of course. It just means they lack the interest that powers us, and they need us to take the edge off.

This brings us to the second of my observations. Even something as simple as this is too much "getting dirty with data" for the consumers of our work to tolerate:

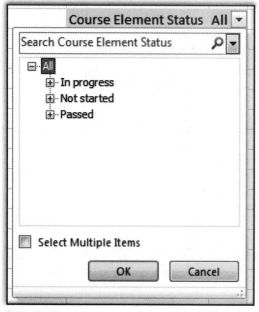

Figure 2.2

This seems pretty innocuous, doesn't it? But when you look closely, well, your colleagues' discomfort comes into focus: What starts out as a drop-down turns into a dialog, which in itself is an ugly surprise. Then there's a *treeview*, which itself starts out fully collapsed, of course, so the contents are hidden. Is it clear that you are supposed to click on In Progress and then OK if you want to open the treeview? Nope. You want to multi-select? Okay, there is a check box for that, but users may not figure that out.

This "deconstruction" of the usability of report filters may seem like overkill. All you really need to remember is that things that seem simple to you often have many nasty little sharp edges—edges that are invisible to you, as the shortcomings of report filters were to me before I conducted those focus groups. *Every* interactive report/dashboard you create runs the risk of being hard for some people to use. Always try to keep your mind open to this fact.

In parallel to the focus groups, I also demonstrated Statosphere to Francois Ajenstat, who was then in charge of Business Intelligence Marketing at Microsoft (and now holds a similar position at Tableau). He liked it but famously said he thought it needed to be more "Fisher-Price" in order to appeal broadly. (Fisher-Price is a manufacturer of toys for infants and toddlers.) I've been using that phrase—"Let's make it more Fisher-Price"—ever since.

Statosphere was a complete (and expensive!) failure. But for me, it was a turning point, and a priceless experience that informed *many* future efforts, including slicers themselves. Which brings us to the second part of this story.

Part II: After Statosphere was canceled (and, indeed, the entire fantasy football team was disbanded and folded into Bing), I started looking for a new job. Magically, as if he were reading my mind, Amir Netz (the architect behind Power Pivot) sent me an email around that time, asking if I wanted to look at a super-secret project they were working on in SQL-land—something they had code named Project Gemini.

Project Gemini was Power Pivot, of course, before it was officially named. I was hooked immediately and became one of the first handful of Microsoft engineers to work full-time on the project.

Amir and I spent the next two years in a state of "creative combat." It was emotionally charged at times, but primarily it was simply the pursuit of creating a great product. I now know that the product is better as a result of the battles I lost *and* the battles I won.

One of the key debates in the early phases of the project was whether we should rely on Excel's built-in charting and pivoting capabilities as the visualization layer of Power Pivot or whether we should build a completely new visualization layer, complete with its own charting and pivoting capabilities.

I was staunchly in favor of the "use existing" tactic, primarily because I knew how much work that would be. Teams at Microsoft that build "engines" (like the SQL team) tend to grossly underestimate the engineering cost of building user experiences. And teams that build user experiences (like Excel) return the favor and grossly underestimate the cost of building engines.

As part of our pro/con analysis of "use existing" versus "build new," Amir and I sat down one day to make a list of weaknesses of Excel's existing chart and Pivot capabilities. We both expected to emerge with a long list. We emerged, instead, with merely one item: Excel lacked *slicers*. Report filters just weren't enough.

It was Amir, not me, who pointed out the lack of slicers as a key weakness. But it resonated with me *immediately*, thanks to my experiences on the Statosphere project. We were instantly in agreement. A few days later, we were pitching the Excel team on the idea of loaning them the engineers required to implement slicers. They miraculously agreed, and the rest is history: We got slicers *and* a well-integrated experience that appeals to tens of millions of "Pivot heads" worldwide.

So what are the takeaways from this Part II?

- **Slicers are the single biggest "missing link" in Excel's "interactivity" history.** When you need interactivity in your dashboards, slicers should be one of your first and only thoughts.

- **Slicers were originally intended merely as a replacement for report filters.** This, in hindsight, *comically* understates their usefulness, as you will see in the later sections of this chapter.

For more on the topics in this introduction, see the following links:

- http://ppvt.pro/GreatFootballProject A series of blog posts, starting in 2009, in which I re-implement Statosphere using Power Pivot—my first "serious" work in Power Pivot.

- http://ppvt.pro/ReImplementGFP A two-part article on how Power Pivot radically improves the BI process, as demonstrated by re-implementing Statosphere using Power Pivot.

- http://ppvt.pro/FFLMadeMyCareer The story of how fantasy football was "the gateway drug to data" that launched my career.

- http://ppvt.pro/CultOfTheRightThing A description of that "creative combat" nerd culture from Microsoft, how essential it was, how it got diluted over time, and why I think that is one of Microsoft's biggest "downfalls." This is one of the all-time most popular posts on PowerPivotPro. com.

And now for our favorite slicers-related techniques, ranging from "just plain useful" to "mind-stretching inspiration."

"Initializing" Slicers That Contain Too Many Values to Scroll

Have you ever had a slicer like this? This customer slicer is big, displaying dozens of customers' names, and we're not even out of the "Aarons" yet:

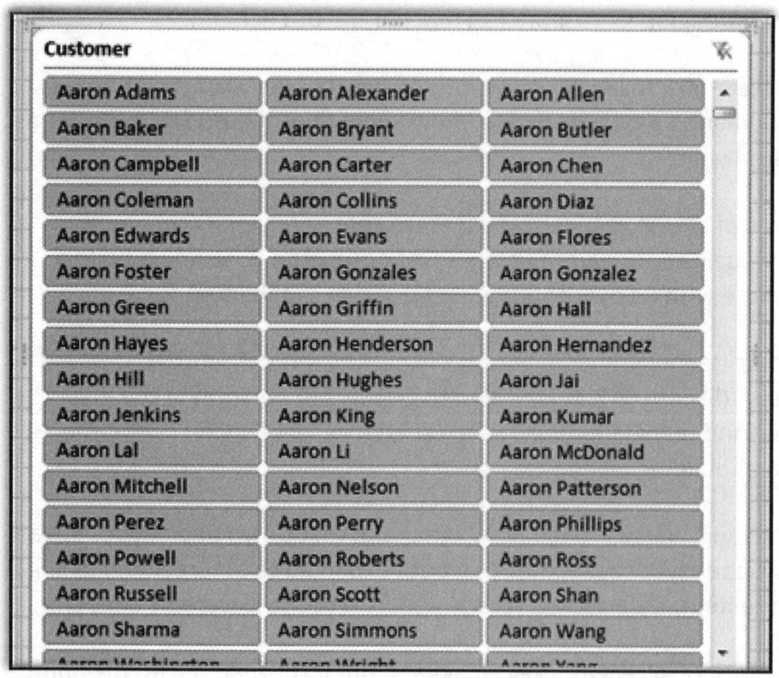

Figure 2.3

What do you do? Do you make the consumers scroll the slicer endlessly, in search of the customer they need to see? That would *not* be "Fisher-Price"! Instead, in the Customers table in the Power Pivot window, you can add a simple calculated column called Last Initial:

Figure 2.4

Then you add that field to the Pivot as a Last Initial slicer. When the consumer clicks D, the Customer slicer is instantly limited to customers with last names beginning with *D*, as shown here:

Figure 2.5

If you want, you can then go back and add a First Initial column and slicer, too:

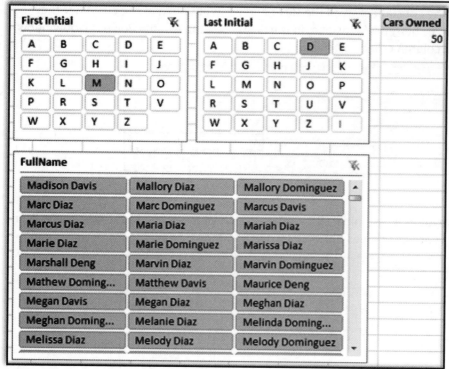

Figure 2.6

Finally, you might want to turn off cross-filtering for the First Initial and Last Initial slicers; you really only need it on for the FullName slicer, and enabling cross-filtering for the initials will slow down your report.

> **Note**
>
> http://ppvt.pro/SLICERPERF for details on cross-filtering.

Wingdings and Other Symbolic Fonts in Slicers

Someone planted an idea in my (Rob's) head one day: "Hey, can we use the Wingdings font in slicers?"

Me: "No. Wait. Maybe...50/50 likely. Hmmm...Actually, I'm gonna say 90% likely. Yeah, in fact, why WOULDN'T it work?"

If it had ended there, it wouldn't have cost me any sleep. But, of course, I was up into the wee hours, poring over every symbolic font in Windows, installing freeware character maps so I could view the "extended" characters in those fonts, writing macros. (More on macros later.)

The Symbolic Fonts Available in Slicers

Here are the symbolic fonts that we found installed on a computer running Windows Vista and Office 2010:

- Wingdings
- Wingdings2
- Wingdings3
- Symbol
- Webdings

- Bookshelf Symbol 7

- Marlett

MS Reference SpecialtyNote

MS Outlook and MT Extra are also apparently symbolic, but they contain few if any useful characters.

Wanna see all the characters you can use from each? Here are the Wingdings 1 through 3 fonts (typeable characters only):

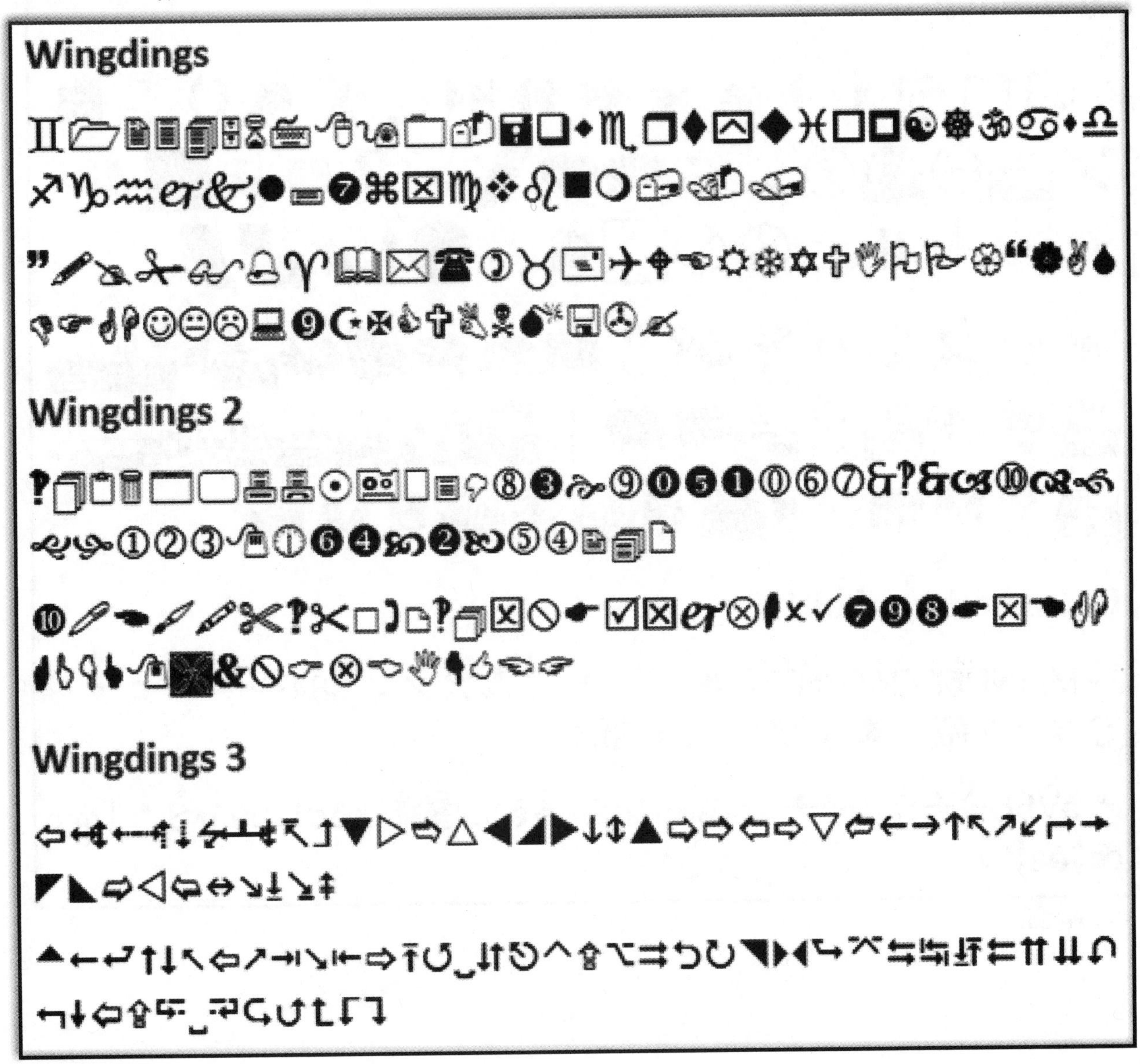

Figure 2.7

Here are the Symbol, Webdings, and Bookshelf Symbol 7 fonts (typeable characters only):

Symbol

1234567890–=θωερτψυιοπ[].∴ασδφγηφκλ;☐ζξχϖβνμ,./

~!≅#∃%⊥&*()_+ΘΩΕΡΤΨΥΙΟΠ{}|ΑΣΔΦΓΗϑΚΛ:☐ΖΞΧςΒΝ
Μ<>?

Webdings

Bookshelf Symbol 7

ᵡ⌁ḾₘṆP̣ṗṖ́Q̇q̣Q̇f́H́T⌐ ♥ ☺ ‴ ▪ ⌒ ✻✶✕↗ √ 384∽ ⋯⌒ ♮ ∘ ⅋
$ ∓ ≑ f̍ 厰 ⌣ ♠ ♩ ✻⸫ ╲ ≉ Ġ́h́ï

▪ ãV̀b́B̀C̀⌐D̊F̀F́f̀⌐G̣5æ̃ã3ɜ̃ɳæ̀ú̀ȧ⌐̓̕ ＿◉◉X̣5ầĩ̀ĩ̀ὺὺΛ̀Λ̀S̀ ▪ 1ʤá
ɶ́ȳə̀ə̓t̩t̩V́

Figure 2.8

Here are the Marlett and MS Reference Specialty typeable characters:

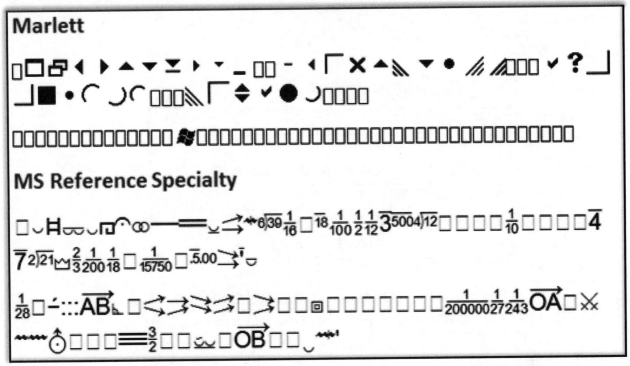

Figure 2.9

Extended Characters

Some of the available fonts contain characters that you cannot type without using the Alt key and a numeric identifier. None of those are included in the images above. In order to browse those characters, you need to use the Character Map tool in Windows. On Windows 7, find it by selecting Start, All Programs, Accessories, System Tools, Character Map:

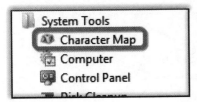

Figure 2.10

The Character Map tool gives you access to all of the other, non-typeable characters in these fonts:

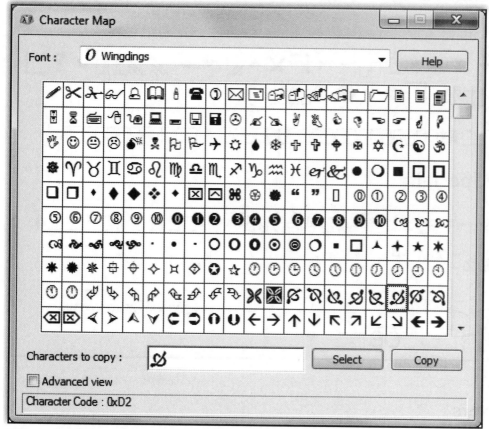

Figure 2.11

Double-click the character you want and then click Copy. Then you just paste the character into your slicer table (see below).

> **Tip**
>
> You can also create a character map in Excel. Select A1:J255. Type
> =CHAR(ROW()) and press Ctrl+Enter. Then format each column from
> B to J with a different symbolic font. Leave column A as regular letters so
> you can see what you have to type for each character.

Some of the Best Slicer Fonts

Using the Character Map tool, I pored over all eight fonts, looking for sets of characters that would be potentially useful on slicers. Here are some sets that I found interesting:

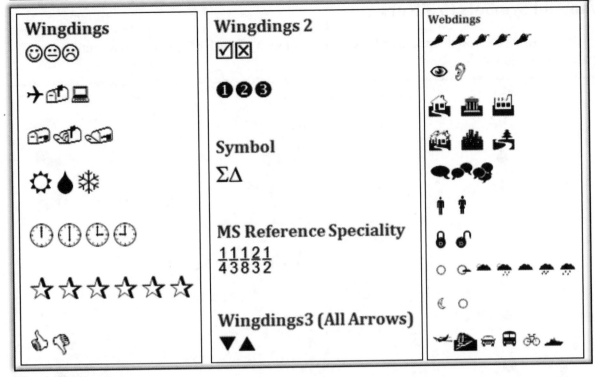

Figure 2.12

> **Note**
>
> You *cannot* mix and match characters from different fonts! If you could, that would be even more amazing. But you have to use only one font on a given slicer. You can use different slicer fonts in a single Pivot, but still only one per slicer. (More on this later.)

Some notes on the fonts for slicers shown in Figure 2.12:

- Wingdings contains clock symbols for all 12 hours.

- The two characters from Symbol would be useful in some geeky workplaces to denote total and percent change. You could use them with branching measures that switch between total and percentage change in response to slicer clicks.

- Webdings line 3 would be useful to denote sectors, like residential, government, and commercial.

- Webdings line 4 would be useful to denote suburban, urban, and rural.

- Webdings line 8 shows more weather symbols than you would ever need.

- Webdings last line gives you ways to represent planes, trains, and automobiles (and the unmade sequel *Buses, Bikes, and Boats*).

How to Add Symbols to Slicers

To add symbols to slicers, you first make an Excel worksheet with a bunch of symbols from your favorite fonts pasted into columns:

CSAT		Weather		Time		Rating			Response		Buzz
☺		☼		🕐		☆			👍		💬
☺		⬤		🕐		☆☆			👎		💬
☹		❄		🕐		☆☆☆					💬
				🕐		☆☆☆☆					
						☆☆☆☆☆					
Response		Response		Measures		Fraction					Sort
☑		❶		Σ		$\frac{1}{8}$					▼
☒		❷		Δ		$\frac{1}{4}$					▲
		❸				$\frac{1}{3}$					
						$\frac{1}{2}$					
						$\frac{2}{3}$					

Figure 2.13

Then you copy them and paste them into the Power Pivot window by selecting Home, Paste:

Figure 2.14

You repeat this until you have them all pasted over as new tables:

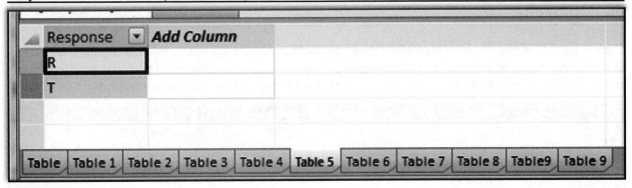

Figure 2.15

Adding the Slicers

When you add slicers on those fields, you get:

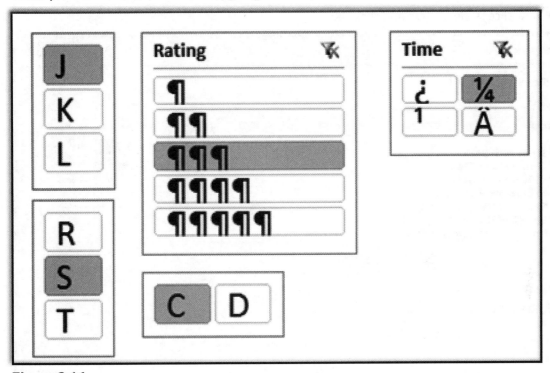

Figure 2.16

What happened to the symbols? By default, slicers don't use the font you specified, and you see the equivalent characters from Calibri, the default font in Excel. So you've got to switch those fonts next.

Changing Slicer Fonts

Changing the font in a slicer is a bit trickier than you might think, but it's not awful. You *cannot* change the default slicer styles, so you need to instead make a copy of a slicer style. The copy becomes a custom style, which you *can* modify. To do this, select a slicer, right-click in the ribbon, and select Duplicate:

Figure 2.17

Then give your new slicer style a name and click OK:

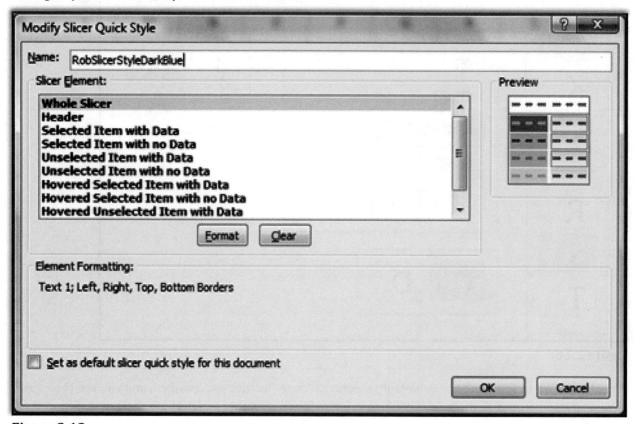

Figure 2.18

This is *very* important: Your slicer is still using the old, built-in, nonmodifiable style, so you now have to switch it to using the new style, like this:

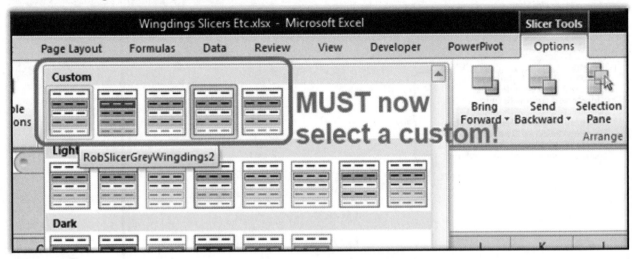

Figure 2.19

Warning
This is an important step! If you skip this step, the trick won't work.

To modify the custom slicer style, right-click your custom style and choose Modify:

Figure 2.20

Now you get the following dialog:

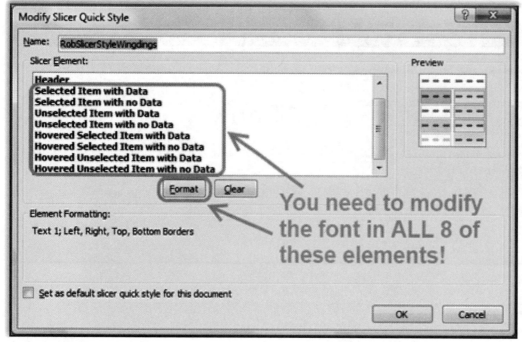

Figure 2.21

You have some clicking to do: You need to select all eight of these elements. If you don't change the font in all eight, your symbolic font won't show up all the time.

> **Note**
>
> This process is tedious, but Microsoft has the right idea here. While you would never want different fonts when you hover, you might want different colors, or maybe bold or italic.

Here's the result of all that clicking:

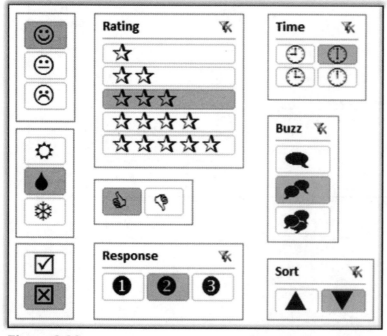

Figure 2.22

Using One Custom Style per Font

If you plan to use more than one symbolic font in a single workbook, you need to define a custom style for each of the fonts by repeating the steps above.

> **Note**
>
> Whenever you find yourself doing tedious work like modifying eight slicer item style elements, and then doing it all over again for other fonts, it may be time for a macro. For more information, see the next trick in this chapter.

Turning Off the Header

In some cases, like this, the symbols are clear enough that you may not need to use a header on the slicer:

Figure 2.23

You turn off the header by deselecting Display Header in the Slicer Settings dialog:

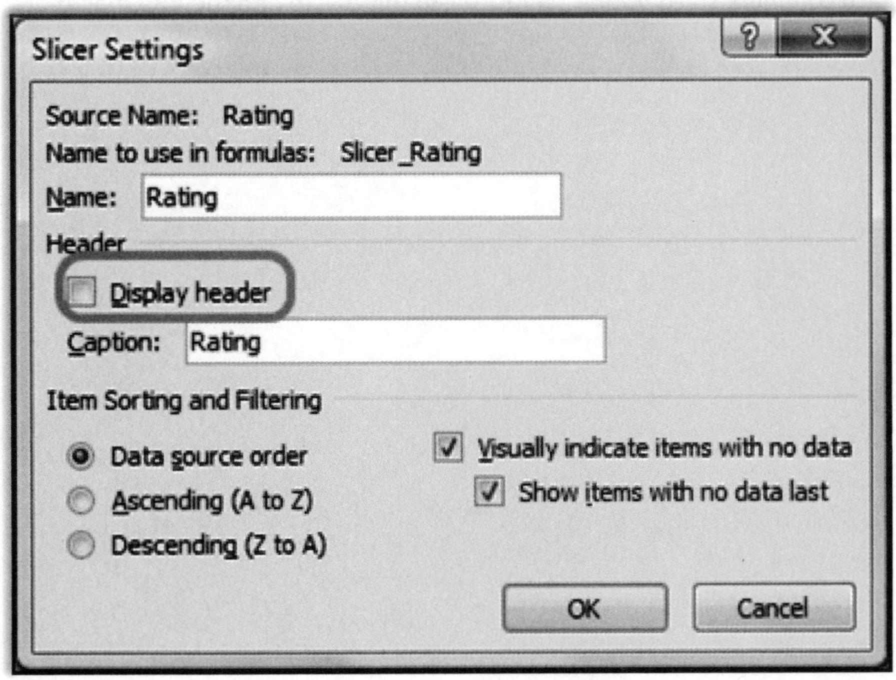

Figure 2.24

> **Note**
>
> Removing the header also removes the "clear filters" button. Trade-offs. Use this option carefully, as it may not always be clear to the report consumer what is going on.

Using Macros to Change Slicer Fonts

You just saw how to use Wingdings and other symbolic fonts on slicers for an interesting effect. But there's a lot of manual work—eight repetitive steps—involved with changing slicer style settings in order to accomplish that. This trick provides a macro that makes that process much more painless.

> **Note**
>
> Even if you're not a macro person, you should try out macro recording. There's some "how to" info at the end this post: http://ppvt.pro/PIVOTMACRO.

The ActiveSlicer Object

The one "magic ingredient" that macro recording does *not* provide is the `ActiveSlicer` object. This bad boy tells you which slicer is currently selected. Without it, you can't detect which slicer is detected, and many macros are based on knowing the name of a slicer, which is tedious to get. Macros for things like turning off cross-filtering are much easier to use when you can just select the one you want in Excel in order to run the macro.

And Now...The Macro

Here's the macro you need to use to change the slicer fonts, with the part that you edit in order to control the font boldfaced. (Note that each comment starts with a ` ' `.) Just paste this macro into the VBA macro environment:

```vba
Sub ChangeSlicerFonts()

    Dim oSlicer As Slicer

    Dim sStyle As String

    Dim sFont As String

    Dim iFontSize As Integer
        ' Set your desired font and font size here
        ' Spelling errors will not cause error,
        ' but also won't take. Lost 30 min once
        ' to that problem, so don't be like me!
        sFont = "Wingdings"
        iFontSize = 24
        ' This slicer MUST have a custom style
        ' The built-in styles are read-only and
        ' CANNOT be modified*****.
        Set oSlicer = ActiveWorkbook.ActiveSlicer
        sStyle = oSlicer.Style
        ' The 8 elements to change are conveniently
        ' numbered 28 to 35. Using this instead of
        ' xlSlicerHoveredUnselectedItemWithData etc.
        For i = 28 To 35
        ' Set the font
        With ActiveWorkbook.TableStyles(sStyle). _
            TableStyleElements(i).Font
            .Name = sFont
            .ThemeFont = xlThemeFontNone
            .Size = iFontSize
        End With
        Next i
    End Sub
```

> **Note**
>
> This macro changes all slicer fonts *except* the header font. This is pretty specifically useful in the Wingdings case and not what you'd use to modify the font of the entire slicer.

If You Are Changing the Header Font, Too...

Remember that in this example, you wanted to change just the font of the slicer items, the tiles, and leave the header alone. You didn't want Wingdings as the caption font; you still wanted it to read as the Region slicer, for instance. And that's why you had to take eight manual steps. If you instead want to change the header font, too, you can just select Whole Slicer and avoid the eight-step process:

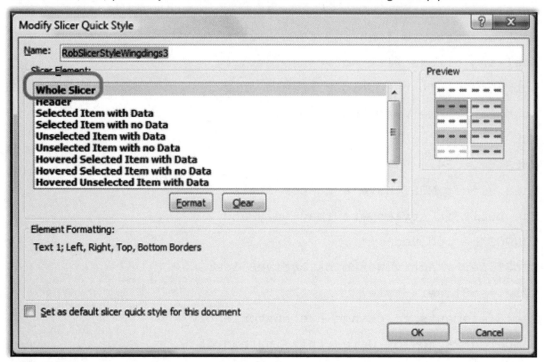

Figure 2.25

A Simple Trick for Combatting "Stale" Slicers

What do you do when your dashboard is refreshed, but its slicers are stuck in "yesteryear"? For example, two weeks of refreshes later, this report still thinks November 15 is what everyone wants to see first:

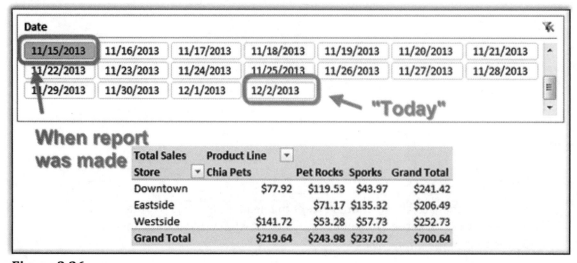

Figure 2.26

This trick is an oldie but a goodie. And enough folks are now using Power Pivot for SharePoint (PP Server) that this trick's time has come. And really, it's relevant on the desktop, too.

On the day when you first made this report, you selected the most recent date (or week, etc.) in the slicer. And you saved the report. All was right with the world! But then, when tomorrow comes, all of your slicers still have that "old" date selected, even after you refresh everything. Ick. Who wants to update all those slicers to point to the latest date? So you might just let the slicers sit on an old date (or week, month, etc.). This forces the consumers of that report to *always* click the latest date, sometimes after scrolling the slicer to the bottom—every time they open the report. They. Don't. Like. That. And neither would you.

Adding a "Shadow" Column for the Slicer Caption

You need to add a column for the slicer caption. The new column is just a duplicate of the original date column...*except* it's in the most recent row:

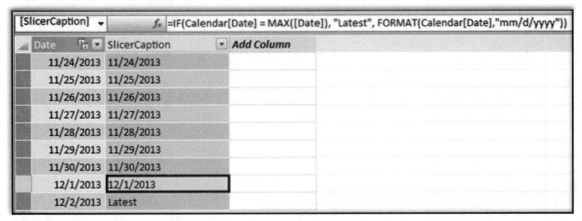

Figure 2.27

This is the formula for that column:

```
=IF(Calendar[Date] = MAX([Date]),
                "Latest",
                FORMAT(Calendar[Date],"mm/d/yyyy")
    )
```

This formula checks to see if this row is the "latest" row in the table. If it is, it returns `"Latest"`. If it isn't, it returns the original `Date` value for this row.

Why do you need the `FORMAT()` function? Why not just use `[Date]` for the "false" part of the `IF()`? Because you get this error if you do that:

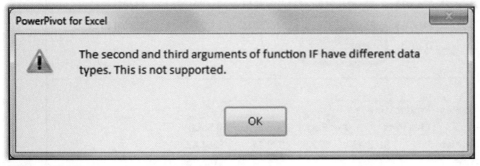

Figure 2.28

Because `"Latest"` is text, you need `Date` to also be text. So you use `FORMAT()` to return a text version of the date.

> **Note**
>
> You could also use `[Date]` & `""` to "coerce" the date to be text.

Now you need to set the column sorting so the slicer sorts appropriately:

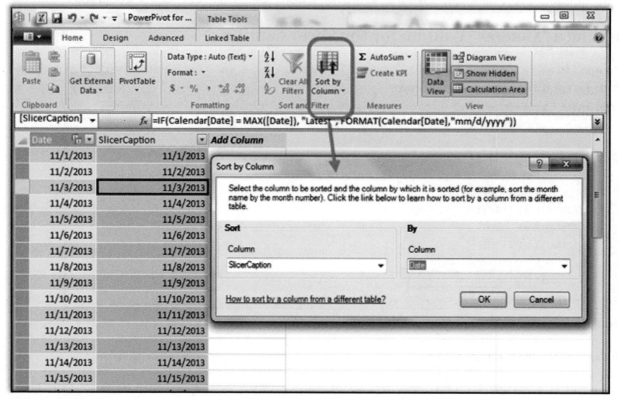

Figure 2.29

The new caption column should use the original column for its sort order.

Next, you replace the date field on the slicer with the `SlicerCaption` field. `"Latest"` is the same as 12/2/2013—for now:

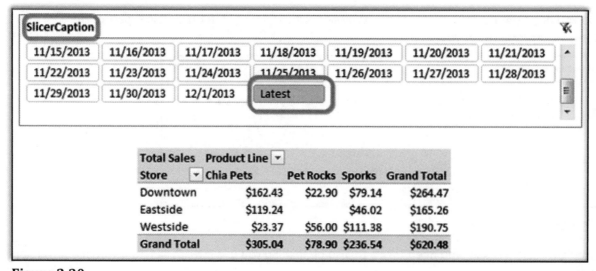

Figure 2.30

So far, so good. But then you refresh the data, and now 12/3/2013 appears in your Calendar table:

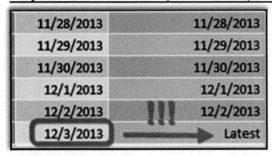

Figure 2.31

You've picked up a new date with the Power Pivot refresh, and `"Latest"` has now marched forward.

Now you refresh the Pivot:

Figure 2.32

When you simply refresh the Pivot, "Latest" is still selected, but now it means 12/3/2013.

> **Note**
>
> If you're using SharePoint, generally speaking a scheduled refresh combined with this trick will take care of this problem for you. Ditto if you're refreshing manually on your desktop, for that matter.

What if Your Calendar Is Not "Trimmed"?

The example above assumes that your Calendar table is being refreshed and that it contains only dates up until the most recent date—that is, that yours is a "trimmed" calendar.

But you may not have a trimmed calendar. Instead, you may have Calendar tables that go all the way into next year. Some calendars even go to the year 2100. What do you do in such a case? No biggie. Just change your Caption column's formula to reference the Date column in your data table (maybe the Sales table) instead of the Calendar table:

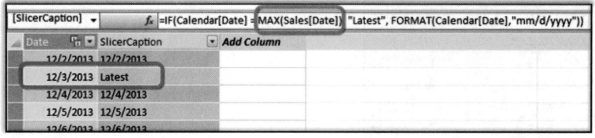

Figure 2.33

User-Friendly Report Sorting with Slicers

As discussed in the intro to this chapter, making things "Fisher-Price" for consumers is incredibly import-ant. If you aren't sensitive to this need, sometimes even the greatest analytical work goes unnoticed.

You should always be asking yourself, "How can I make the report easier to understand and use?" As your work becomes more important and makes its way further up the leadership hierarchy of your organization, it becomes more and more critical to get into this habit.

One common consumer need is sorting. Let's say you have published the following mission-critical Pivot report on UFO sightings in the United States:

State	Total Sightings per Year	Avg Sighting Len (Mins)	Sightings per 100K Residents
California	37.6	166	1.1
Arizona	17.8	142	3.5
Washington	17.1	145	2.9
Texas	11.6	204	0.6
Florida	9.8	240	0.6
New York	9.3	217	0.5
Oregon	8.8	127	2.6
Illinois	7.5	209	0.6
Ohio	6.8	188	0.6
Michigan	5.8	206	0.6
Pennsylvania	5.5	269	0.4
Missouri	4.6	196	0.8
New Jersey	4.5	166	0.5
Wisconsin	4.2	208	0.8
Colorado	3.9	216	0.9
Massachusetts	3.6	180	0.6

Figure 2.34

One of the report consumers says to you, "Great, but how do I sort by average sighting length instead?"

Well, because you're an Excel pro, you know about this little drop-down, don't you?

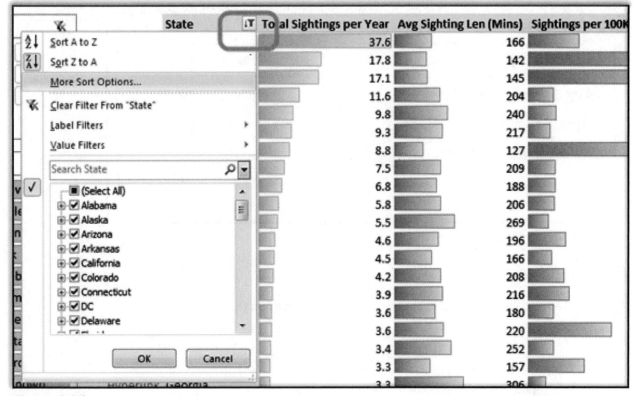

Figure 2.35

This drop-down scares most average users. Really, it does. The only people who don't find it scary are Excel nerds like us. And we, the Excel nerds, also know that we can right-click in the Avg Sighting Len column and choose a sort option. But remember: *Normal people don't know this.* Also keep in mind that doing this doesn't work on SharePoint. And really, report consumer are used to simply clicking on column headers to sort—in just about every single application they have ever used, except for Excel. Even the new Power View add-in for Excel 2013 (see Chapter 6) lets you sort by clicking the header—once for ascending and a second time for descending.

So in cases where sorting is important, can you give consumers something a little friendlier? Yes, you can.

Creating Dummy Tables for Slicers

The first table below lists all the measures you'd like the user to be able to sort by. The second table is just for ascending/descending sort orders, with the names changed to Largest to Smallest and Smallest to Largest because ascending and descending often confuse people:

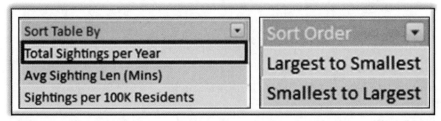

Figure 2.36

Now you add these tables as slicers on the report, even though they don't do anything yet:

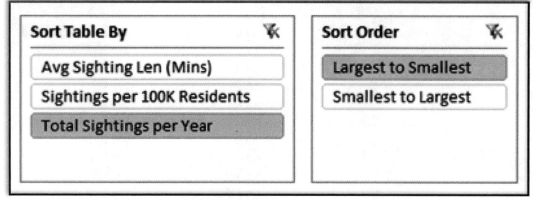

Figure 2.37

Creating Measures

The next step is to create measures that detect user selections on those slicers:

```
[SelectedSortMeasure]=
IF(HASONEVALUE(SortBy[Sort Table By]),
    VALUES(SortBy[Sort Table By]),
    "Total Sightings per Year"
)

[Selected Sort Order]=
IF(HASONEVALUE(SortBy[Sort Table By]),
    VALUES(SortOrder[Sort Order]),
    "Largest to Smallest"
)
```

Both of these measures merely return the caption of whatever is selected. And if more than one thing is selected on a slicer, Excel returns the default value `"Total Sightings per Year"` for the first measure.

Next, you create a `1, -1` measure, based on sort order:

```
[SortOrderMultiplier]=
IF([SelectedSortOrder]="Smallest to Largest",-1,1)
```

If the `SortOrder` measure defined here returns `"Smallest to Largest"`, then this measure returns −1. Otherwise, it returns 1.

Now you create a branching measure based of the Sort Table By slicer:

```
[HiddenSortMeasure]=
IF([SelectedSortMeasure]="Avg Sighting Len (Mins)",
    [Avg Sighting Length in Mins],
    IF([SelectedSortMeasure]="Sightings per 100K Residents",
        [Sightings per 100K],
        [Sightings per Year]
    )
) * [SortOrderMultiplier]
```

This measure returns an entirely different value, based on whatever the user selects on Sort Table By. Sometimes it "mimics" one measure and other times another.

> **Note**
>
> The last line above multiplies [SortOrderMultiplier], which is 1 or −1, by the whole thing.

Adding HiddenSortMeasure to the Pivot and Sorting

The next step is to add HiddenSortMeasure to the Pivot and sort by it:

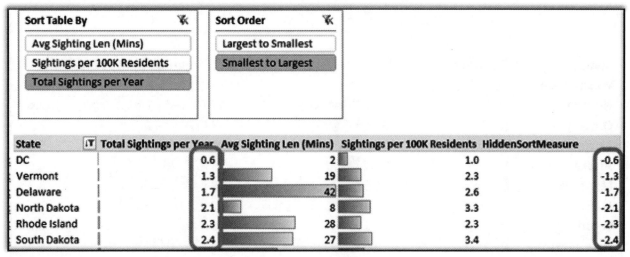

Figure 2.38

When you sort the Pivot by this measure, notice that it is the negative version of the Total Sightings per Year measure. This is expected, based on the slicer selections.

Hiding the HiddenSortMeasure Column of the Spreadsheet

Now you need to hide the HiddenSortMeasure column of the spreadsheet. You can either select the column and use Alt+O+C+H or right-click the column header and select Hide, as shown here:

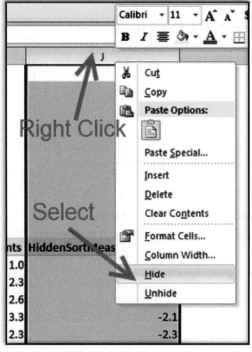

Figure 2.39

Here's the result:

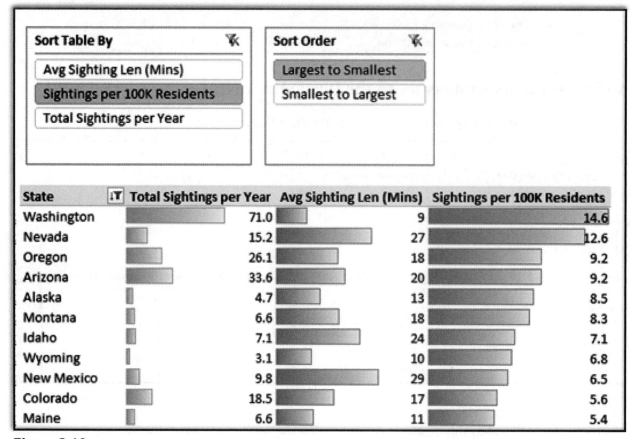

Figure 2.40

This whole process is actually really easy; it takes longer to read these instructions than to add the sorting to the report.

But what about sorting by state name? We're glad you asked, because that is the very next trick.

Adding State Alpha Sorting to the Sort-by-Slicer Trick

There are two ways to change the previous trick so that it sorts by state name: using text measures and adding a column to the States table.

Method 1: Text Measures

The first method for sorting by state name involves sorting by HiddenSortMeasure, and you some-how have to get the state name reflected in that measure. So you need a measure that represents StateName.

It's not widely known, but measures *can* return text. This measure simply returns the name of the state:

```
[StateNameMeasure]=
IF(HASONEVALUE(States[FullStateName]),
   VALUES(States[FullStateName]),
   BLANK()
)
```

> **Note**
>
> To find out how this formula works, check out
> http://ppvt.pro/IFVALUES.

If you add this measure to the Pivot and sort by it, you get this:

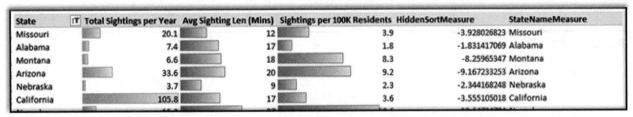

State	⊤ Total Sightings per Year	Avg Sighting Len (Mins)	Sightings per 100K Residents	HiddenSortMeasure	StateNameMeasure
Missouri	20.1	12	3.9	-3.928026823	Missouri
Alabama	7.4	17	1.8	-1.831417069	Alabama
Montana	6.6	18	8.3	-8.25965347	Montana
Arizona	33.6	20	9.2	-9.167233253	Arizona
Nebraska	3.7	9	2.3	-2.344168248	Nebraska
California	105.8	17	3.6	-3.555105018	California

Figure 2.41

Well, the measure works. But the sort order is awful. Why is Missouri ahead of Alabama? The next method clears up this problem.

Method 2: Adding a Column to the States Table

Another way to have your slicer sort by state name is to add a column to the States table, like this:

FullStateN...	State	Region	Pop Density Range	AlphaOrder
Alabama	AL	Southeast	2 - Low	1
Alaska	AK	Pacific NW	1 - Sparse	2
Arizona	AZ	SW	1 - Sparse	3
Arkansas	AR	Central South	2 - Low	4
California	CA	California	3- Medium	5
Colorado	CO	Rockies	1 - Sparse	6
Connecticut	CT	Northeast	4 - High	7
DC	DC	Mid Atlantic	4 - High	8
Delaware	DE	Northeast	4 - High	9
Florida	FL	Southeast	3- Medium	10
Georgia	GA	Southeast	3- Medium	11
Hawaii	HI	Hawaii	3- Medium	12
Idaho	ID	Rockies	1 - Sparse	

Figure 2.42

> **Tip**
>
> Getting this column into Power Pivot can be a bit tricky, especially with a copy/pasted table. If this were a serious production application, you would want to use SQL as the source for this table and ask your database colleagues to add the column for you.

Because you're working here with UFO data, you paste a second, two-column (StateName and AlphaOrder) States table into Power Pivot and relate it to your original States table. (Be sure to treat the new table as a lookup table!) Then you use =RELATED() to add it to your original States table.

Okay, now it's time for the AlphaSort measure:

```
[AlphaSort]=
MAX(States[AlphaOrder])
```

This *does* sort properly:

State		Total Sightings per Year	Avg Sighting Len (Mins)	Sightings per 100K Residents	HiddenSortMeasure	AlphaSort
Alabama		7.4	17	1.8	1.831417069	1
Alaska		4.7	13	8.5	8.544786499	2
Arizona		33.6	20	9.2	9.167233253	3
Arkansas		7.5	8	3.2	3.190505057	4
California		105.8	17	3.6	3.555105018	5
Colorado		18.5	17	5.6	5.61560032	6
Connecticut		7.0	7	2.1	2.129526308	7
DC		0.6	2	1.0	0.988630746	8

Figure 2.43

> **Note**
>
> You could use MIN(), SUM(), or even AVERAGE() instead of MAX().
> You just need something that returns the number.

Now you just add the "State Name" value to your Sort Table By slicer table and add another clause to the IF() in the original HiddenSortMeasure, and you get this:

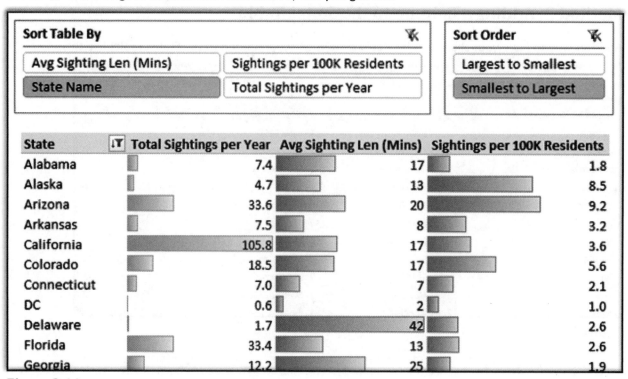

Figure 2.44

This is a bit trickier than sorting by the other columns, but it's doable.

Dynamic Top *N* Reports Using Power Pivot

Check out *this* bad boy:

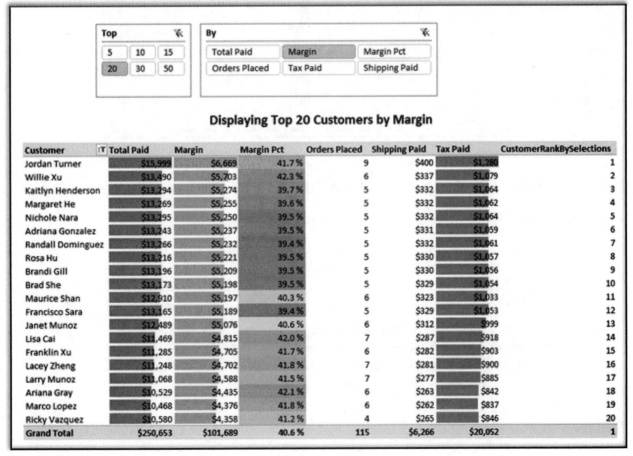

Figure 2.45

Folks, this combination of slicers and DAX is just amazing. Do you *see* that picture above? Say that a consumer of this report wants to change it completely and instead see the top 10 customers by total paid (sales). It takes two quick slicer clicks:

Figure 2.46

> **Note**
>
> This solution requires the RANKX() and SWITCH() functions, which
> were not present in the very first release of Power Pivot, but versions
> 11.x and higher all have them.

At heart, this is really just a variant of the sort-by-slicers trick described earlier in this chapter.

Creating Two Disconnected Slicers

A great technique is to create slicer tables that are only intended to populate slicers, never to be related to other tables, like this:

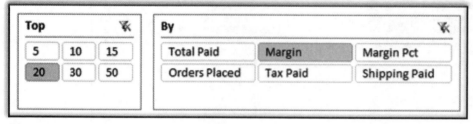

Figure 2.47

To create these slicers, you create the Measure for TopN and TopN tables manually in Excel and then copy and paste them into Power Pivot:

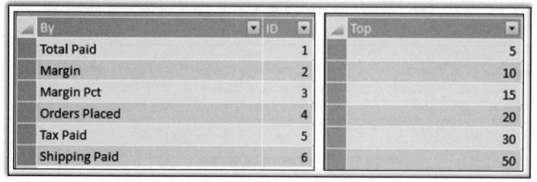

Figure 2.48

Behind-the-Scenes Measures: Harvesting Selections from Slicers

The next step is to write measures that "harvest" the user's selections from those slicers:

```
[Selected TopN Measure] = MIN(MeasureForTopN[ID])
[SelectedTopNNumber] = MIN(TopN[Top])
```

> **Note**
>
> Here you use MIN() to break ties in case the user is silly and selects
> more than one value on a slicer. You could just as easily use MAX(), or
> do an IF(HASONEVALUE()) test, catch the case where more than
> one is selected, and specify a default value.

Then you write a branching measure—a measure that becomes different measures, based on conditional tests. Refer to the ""Adding State Alpha Sorting to the Sort-by-Slicer Trick" on page 50. That section uses a nested IF, but you can also use SWITCH(), which is much better:

```
[Selected TopN Value] =
SWITCH([Selected TopN Measure],
        1, [Total Paid],
        2, [Margin],
        3, [Margin Pct],
        4, [Orders Placed],
        5, [Tax Paid],
        6, [Shipping Paid]
)
```

This measure returns the `[Total Paid]` amount if the user selects Total Paid on the slicer. Cool, huh?

> **Note**
>
> If you have a hard time writing nested `IF`s, rejoice. The Power Pivot team has provided `SWITCH()`, which makes your life much easier!

Using RANKX()

Next, you use `RANKX()` with the measure that ranks each customer according to the selected measure:

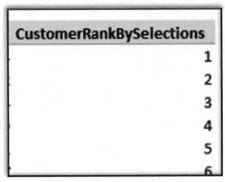

Figure 2.49

Here's the formula:

```
[CustomerRankBySelections] =
RANKX(ALL(Customer[FullName]), [Selected TopN Value], ,0)
```

Here are a few observations on `RANKX()`:

- **It's amazing…even better than SWITCH().** Although `RANKX()` is a little weird, you can't live without it.

- **Why do we have to specify ALL() in the first param?** We struggled here at first. The function text for `RANKX()` just says "Table" for that first param. So we were throwing `VALUES(Customer[FullName])` in there, and every customer was coming back ranked as 1. This is the right function design if flexibility is your overwhelming design goal. But for the 99% case, this is incredibly counterintuitive. For the Excel crowd, it would be much better to have a simpler function where all you need to do is specify a column—no `ALL()` and no `VALUES()`, just a "raw" column.

- **That third parameter is deeply mysterious and very rarely used.** You can leave it blank, and it doesn't cause any harm. So, um, leave it blank. (A use for that parameter is covered in *DAX Formulas for Power Pivot*, in the chapter on the X functions.)

• **Set the fourth parameter to 0 when you want the largest number to be ranked 1.** If you omit this parameter, it defaults to the other direction, which seems backward for a function named RANK(). (Think of the best team in the NFL each year...is the team's rank 1 or 32?)

• **There is a fifth argument in RANKX() for dealing with ties.** The choices for the fifth argument are Skip and Dense. With Skip, if you have two items tied for #1, they both get a rank of 1, and the next item is ranked #3. This is similar to the decades-old RANK() function, which was renamed RANK.EQ() in Excel 2010. With Dense, if you have a three-way tie for the second position, all three items will be ranked #2, and the next item will be ranked #3.

Caution from Bill

Dense, described above, is equivalent to the method mysteriously introduced in Excel 2010 PivotTables when you chose Options, Show Values As, Rank Largest to Smallest. It's fair to say that this Dense option is the fourth method of handling ties to be introduced to Excel.

Statisticians will be disappointed that Power Pivot lacks an equivalent to the RANK.AVG() function introduced in Excel 2010. With this method, if you have two items tied for #1, they are both ranked 1.5.

Excel pros will continue to be disappointed that no one on the Excel team can fathom the need to have every rank represented exactly once, as shown in column G of this figure:

G4			f_x	=RANK(B4,B3:B$12)+COUNTIF(B$2:B3,B4)			
	A	B	C	D	E	F	G	Q
1			DAX CHOICES		EXCEL CHOICES			PT CHOICE
2	Row Labels	TotalSales	RankXSkipTies	RankXDense	=RANK.EQ	=RANK.AVG	What the Excel Pro Wants	PT Show As Rank
3	Fig	49	1	1	1	1.5	1	1
4	Eggplant	49	1	1	1	1.5	2	1
5	Dill	47	3	2	3	4	3	2
6	Apple	47	3	2	3	4	4	2
7	Banana	47	3	2	3	4	5	2
8	Guava	45	6	3	6	6	6	3
9	Cherry	35	7	4	7	7	7	4
10	Ice	31	8	5	8	8	8	5
11	Herbs	24	9	6	9	9	9	6
12	Jicama	21	10	7	10	10	10	7
13	Grand Total	395	1	1				
14								
15								
16			A	D	A	B	C	D
17								

Figure 2.50

> **Reaction from Rob**
>
> What??? Why would I ever want what's being displayed in column G?
> (Hrm, I guess I am showing my Microsoft roots here.)
>
> **Reaction from Bill to Rob's Reaction**
>
> I thought it was obvious! To sort with a formula, you
> need a column that returns every rank exactly once to
> act as the second argument in the `MATCH()` function:
> `=INDEX(A$3:A$12,MATCH(ROW(1:1),G$3:G$12,0))`. What
> do the Excel PMs do all day if they aren't struggling to sort with a
> formula?

The Should Customer Be Included Measure

At this point, if you were always just doing top 10, and not a slicer-controlled top *N*, you'd be done. You'd just set a filter on the Pivot to always show the top 10 customers by `CustomerRankBySelections`, and everything would be great. (In fact, you could have skipped `CustomerRankBySelections` altogether and just done a top 10 filter by `Selected TopN Value`, the branching measure itself.) But you need one more simple measure:

```
[Should Customer Be Included] =
IF([CustomerRankBySelections]<=[SelectedTopNNumber],1,0)
```

Then you filter the Pivot such that only the top *N* are included, via the `IF()` measure. To do this, you filter the Pivot to only show rows where that measure is greater than 0 or equal to 1:

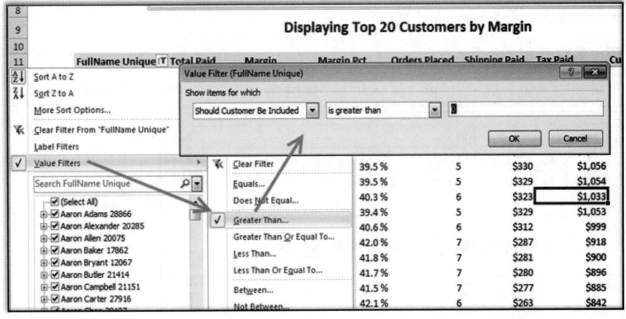

Figure 2.51

Ensuring That Customer Names Are Unique

Some data sets contain a name field that might have different people with the same name. Your data might have more than one customer named Willie Xu, for instance. The approach described in this trick combines those customers into one "super customer" who unfairly sneaks into the top 10. There are a couple ways to avoid this problem. The first is to create a unique customer name and use that on your Pivot:

Figure 2.52

Or, in theory, you can change your RANKX() measure to use the behind-the-scenes unique ID instead. But when you use ALL(), as in the original measure, it is so slow that the Pivot never finishes calculating, and you'll end up canceling it:

```
[CustomerRankBySelections] =
RANKX(ALL(Customer[CustomerKey]), [Selected TopN Value], ,0)
```

When you use VALUES() instead, every customer comes back ranked as 1:

```
[CustomerRankBySelections] =
RANKX(VALUES(Customer[CustomerKey]), [Selected TopN Value], ,0)
```

So let's call this a work in progress.

The Readout

To add some class and usability, you might want to create a readout that responds to slicer selections:

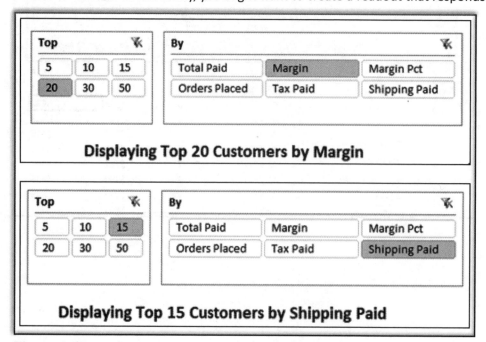

Figure 2.53

This readout is just a formula that uses Center Across Selection:

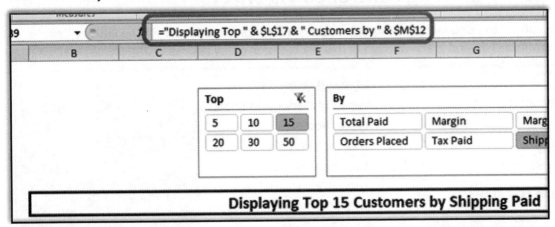

Figure 2.54

The two cells referenced in this formula are interesting. One is a cube formula:

Figure 2.55

Here's the formula in text:

```
=CUBEVALUE("PowerPivot Data", "[Measures].
        [SelectedTopNNumber]",Slicer_Top)
```

Do you see how the formula is parameterized by the name of a slicer? This allows the formula to be sliced by the slicer, just like a Pivot.

The other cell is the top cell in the Rows drop zone in a Pivot:

Figure 2.56

This Pivot has a slicer connection established to the same measure-selector slicer, and it also has the same field on rows as the slicer field itself. It has nothing in the Columns or Report Filter or Values drop zones.

Note that there are two alternate ways of accomplishing this without using a "dummy" Pivot. One is to write a measure that returns text and fetch that with a CUBEVALUE() formula. The other is to use CUBESET() and CUBERANKEDMEMBER() to directly fetch user selections from the slicer, which is covered later in this chapter.

> **Note**
>
> For more on text measures, see
> http://ppvt.pro/TXTMEASURES.

Conditional Formatting Controlled via Slicers

It's possible to control conditional formatting via slicers. For example, in this case, at the 65th percentile, model name profits are shaded green (though in this printed book, they appear as a shade of gray):

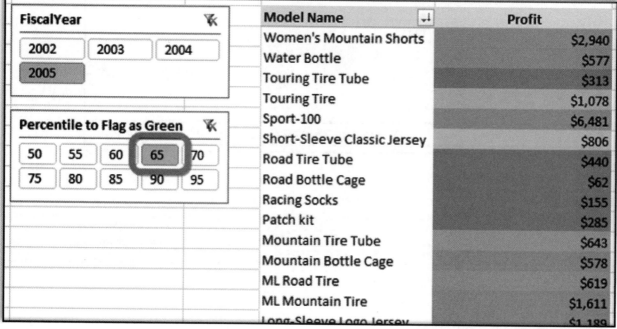

Figure 2.57

In this case, xxx:

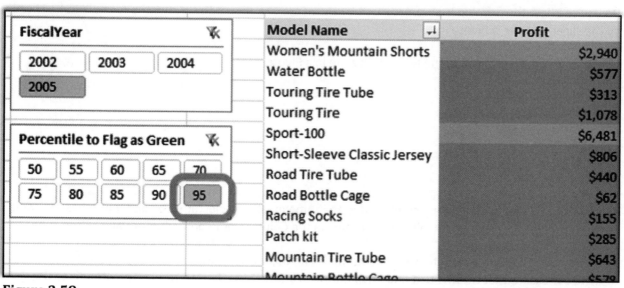

Figure 2.58

Another Disconnected Table Technique

This disconnected table technique is, of course, a recurring favorite. First, you create a single column in Excel, fill it with the numbers that you want to appear on your slicer, and copy that whole column:

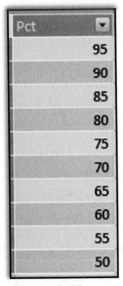

Figure 2.59

Then you paste the column as a new table in Power Pivot:

Figure 2.60

Here is the resulting CFMinBar table:

Pct
95
90
85
80
75
70
65
60
55
50

Figure 2.61

Then you write a measure on your new table:

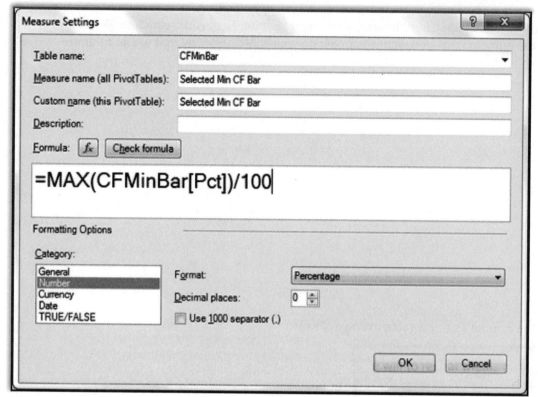

Figure 2.62

This measure harvests the selection from the slicer.

> **Note**
>
> In this case, you could just as easily have used MIN() rather than MAX().

It looks like this in a Pivot:

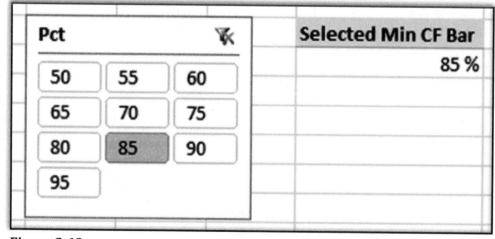

Figure 2.63

Using the New Slicer and Measure to Control Conditional Formatting

Now you need to make a real Pivot—one with a useful measure on it:

Pct		
50	55	60
65	70	75
80	85	90
95		

Row Labels	Profit
Women's Mountain Shorts	$49,111
Water Bottle	$14,583
Touring-3000	$166,858
Touring-2000	$188,109
Touring-1000	$1,245,393
Touring Tire Tube	$5,113
Touring Tire	$18,665
Sport-100	$155,166
Short-Sleeve Classic Jersey	$21,801
Road-750	$311,651
Road-650	$274,733
Road-550-W	$617,974

Figure 2.64

Rather than display `Selected Min CF Bar` on the pivot, you can use a cube formula, off to the side, to capture that measure:

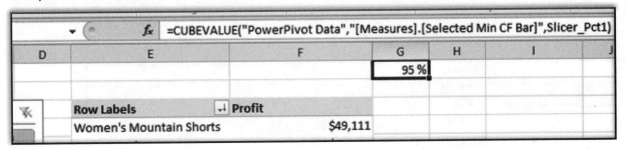

fx =CUBEVALUE("PowerPivot Data","[Measures].[Selected Min CF Bar]",Slicer_Pct1)

D	E	F	G	H	I	J
			95 %			
	Row Labels	Profit				
	Women's Mountain Shorts	$49,111				

Figure 2.65

Note how this formula references the slicer, too. If it didn't, it would always return 95%.

Adding a Color Scale Rule

Now you add a three-color scale rule to the Pivot:

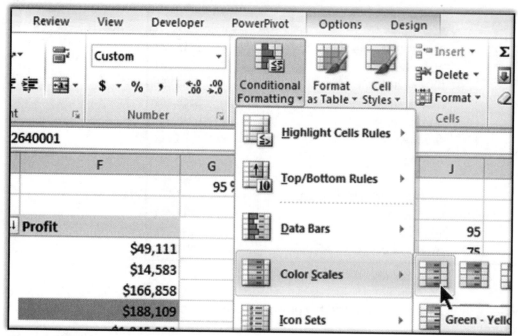

Figure 2.66

Then you set it to affect the entire measure:

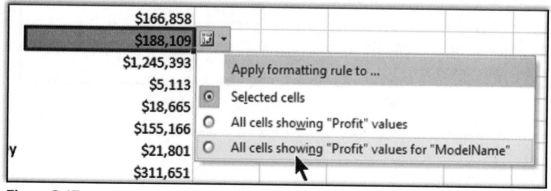

Figure 2.67

You get this result from the simple three-color scale conditional formatting rule:

Row Labels	Profit
Women's Mountain Shorts	$49,111
Water Bottle	$14,583
Touring-3000	$166,858
Touring-2000	$188,109
Touring-1000	$1,245,393
Touring Tire Tube	$5,113
Touring Tire	$18,665
Sport-100	$155,166
Short-Sleeve Classic Jersey	$21,801
Road-750	$311,651

Figure 2.68

Now for the Trick

Here's the sneaky part. Go to Manage Rules:

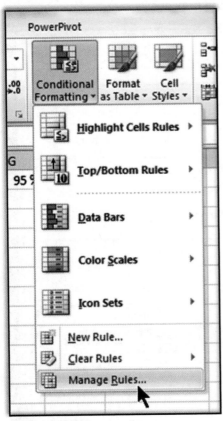

Figure 2.69

Edit the one rule you have on the Pivot, and you get this dialog:

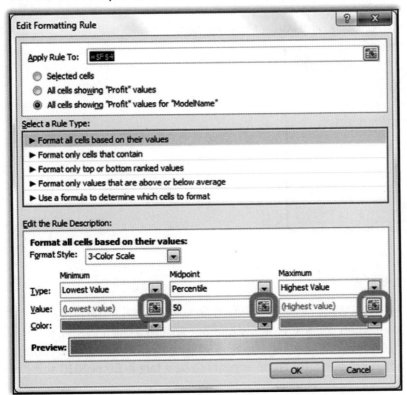

Figure 2.70

Note the circled buttons. These are RefEdit controls. The thresholds in the conditional formatting rule can be cell references.

You now set the controls to reference the cube formula cells you created previously:

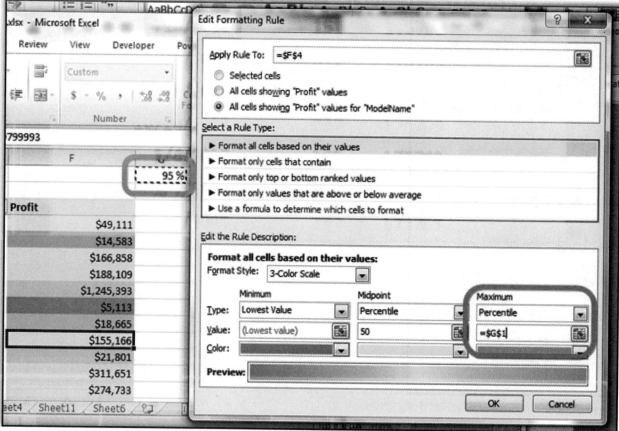

Figure 2.71

And then you hit what appears to be a bug. Click OK, and you get this message:

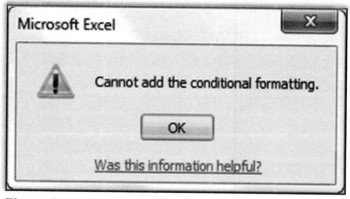

Figure 2.72

Don't you love the "Was this information helpful?" link?

Excel is expecting an integer like 90 rather than a percentage value like 0.90, which is what the measure returns. But you get this error message even when you just type the number 90 into a cell and then reference that cell. However, you don't get the error message when you type 90 directly into the RefEdit control rather than use a cell reference. Something is broken here: There appears to be a bug in Excel 2010 and Excel 2013 conditional formatting.

Correcting the Bug

It seems that only the Percentile option doesn't like cell references because the Number option works:

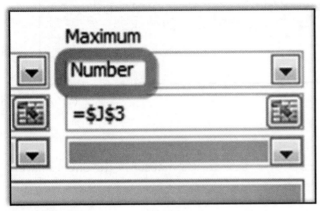

Figure 2.73

Also, the Percent option works. If your data is evenly distributed, you can get away with using Percent instead of Percentile. However, if the data is heavily skewed with a few large records, you will want the exactness of using Number.

In order to use the Number option to let the user control percentile-based conditional formatting with a measure like Profit, however, you need to get a bit more sophisticated with your measures. If you can get the actual Profit value for, say, the 80th percentile model name into a cell, you can reference that. And that's precisely what those three cells in this image contain:

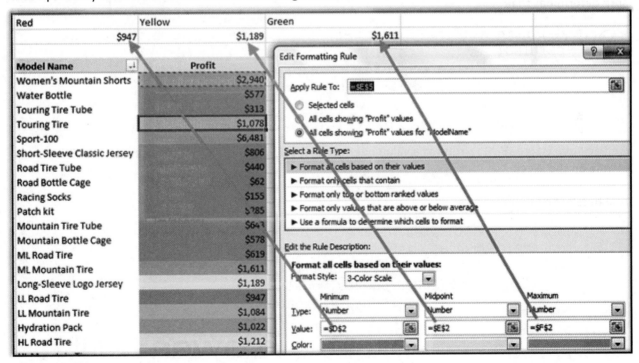

Figure 2.74

In this figure, each number RefEdit in the Edit Formatting Rule dialog points to a different cell on the sheet.

Here you can see that cell F2 contains a cube formula that returns the measure Profit Required for Green CF:

=CUBEVALUE("PowerPivot Data","[Measures].[Profit Required for Green CF]",Slicer_FiscalYear, Slicer_Pct)			
E	F	G	H
w	Green		
$1,189	$1,611		

Figure 2.75

Setting the Green Threshold

Here's the formula for calculating the Profit Required for Green CF measure—the one displayed in cell F2 above:

```
[Profit Required for Green CF]=
    MINX(TOPN([Model Name Rank for Green CF],
              ALL(Products[ModelName]),
              [Profit]
          ),
        [Profit]
    )
```

The TOPN() function returns a set of rows from ALL(Products[ModelName]), ranked by the Profit measure. But how many rows does it return? The Model Name Rank for Green CF measure determines that:

```
[Model Name Rank for Green CF] =
    CEILING(
            (1-[Selected Min CF Bar])*
            [Number of Model Names with Profit],
            1
        )
```

Selected Min CF Bar returns a value between 0 and 1, such as 0.90 if the user selects 90th percentile on the slicer.

And here's the other measure:

```
[Number of Model Names with Profit] =
CALCULATE(COUNTROWS(VALUES(Products[ModelName])),
        ALL(Products[ModelName]),
        FILTER(ALL(Products[ModelName]),
            NOT(ISBLANK([Profit]))
          )
    )
```

The purpose of this measure is essentially to tell how many products have actually sold. It weeds out products that are in the catalog but have not sold yet or have not sold recently enough, and so on—depending on slicer selections.

So if you have 100 products that have actually sold, and the user has selected 90th percentile on the slicer, Model Name Rank for Green CF becomes:

```
CEILING(
        (1-0.9)* 100,
        1
        )
```

which is 10.

And then `Profit Required for Green CF` becomes:

```
MINX(TOPN([10, ALL(Products[ModelName]),[Profit]),
        [Profit]
    )
```

This grabs the `Profit` value of the lowest-ranked product in the top 10. And this is the value that is returned into cell F2, which is what the conditional formatting rule references! Any product with a `Profit` value greater than or equal to the `Profit` value of the 10th-most-profitable product will be colored green.

Setting the Yellow and Red Thresholds

There are multiple ways to handle the yellow and red thresholds. You could give the users three separate slicers and let them control each one independently. That seems like overkill in this case, and you can instead hard-wire those to be 20% and 40% lower than the green threshold, respectively:

```
[Model Name Rank for Yellow CF]=CEILING((1-
        [Selected Min CF Bar]+.2)*
        [Number of Model Names with Profit],1)
```

```
[Model Name Rank for Red CF]=CEILING((1-
        [Selected Min CF Bar]+.4)*
        [Number of Model Names with Profit],1)
```

Then the rest of the measures are the same for both red and yellow as they were for green.

Catching Slicer Selections in a Formula

A lot of people want to catch slicer selections in formulas. It's actually very simple to catch users' slicer selections in Excel formulas, if you are using Power Pivot (aka the 2013 data model feature):

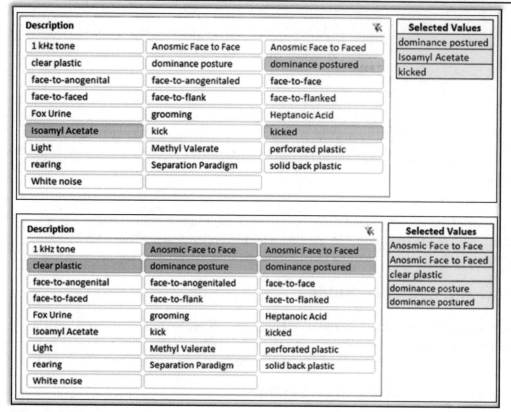

Figure 2.76

Sometimes you want to catch a user's slicer selections and use them in a measure. Other times you want to catch them and use them in "normal" Excel formulas in a worksheet. Here we examine the latter option.

Using a CUBESET() Formula

The first step is to write a single CUBESET () formula, as shown here:

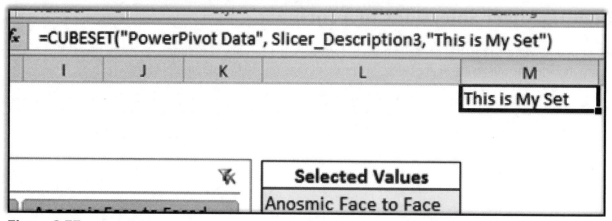

Figure 2.77

In Power Pivot v1 and v2, the first argument is always PowerPivot Data. In Excel 2013, it's ThisWorkbookDataModel.

The second argument is the "formula-approved name" for the slicer. To see it, click the slicer and check its Slicer Settings dialog:

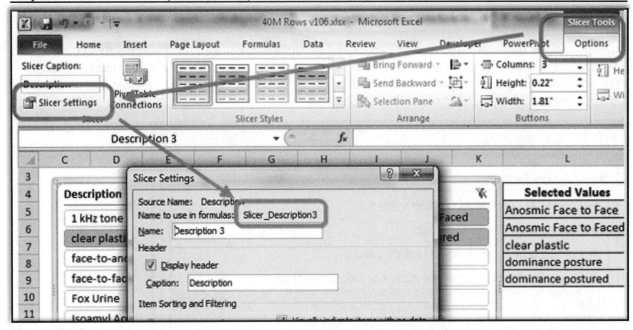

Figure 2.78

The third argument can be left blank, but then you get a blank cell in your sheet. If you set it to `"This is My Set"`, as shown here, you can see where the set lives.

Using a CUBERANKEDMEMBER() Formula

Next, you write a CUBERANKEDMEMBER() formula, wrapped in an IFERROR():

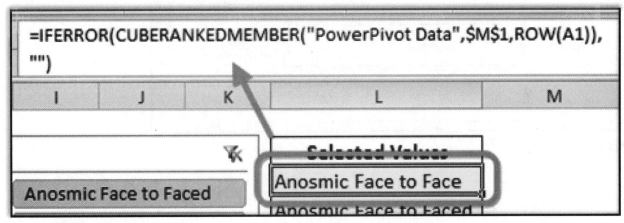

Figure 2.79

You then fill this formula down enough cells to handle every slicer tile (about 26 cells down in this case).

Note the following:

- You use `IFERROR()` to handle the case where the user has not selected enough slicer tiles. `CUBERANKEDMEMBER()` returns an error when you "fall off the edge" of the user's selections. `IFERROR()` returns a nice blank cell instead.

- `ROW(A1)` returns 1, and when you fill the formula down, you get `ROW(A2)`, `ROW(A3)`, etc., so that each cell grabs the first, second, third, and so on values from the set of user selections.

- `$M$1` is the cell where you create the `CUBESET()` formula, and you do not want that reference to autoadjust.

Applying More Formatting Rules

Now you can use other formulas to concatenate all selections into a single, comma-separated string. Or you can apply conditional formatting to the cells so that they "light up" when there's a selection. In this case, you can leverage the "unique values" flavor of conditional formatting, since all slicer tiles always have unique names:

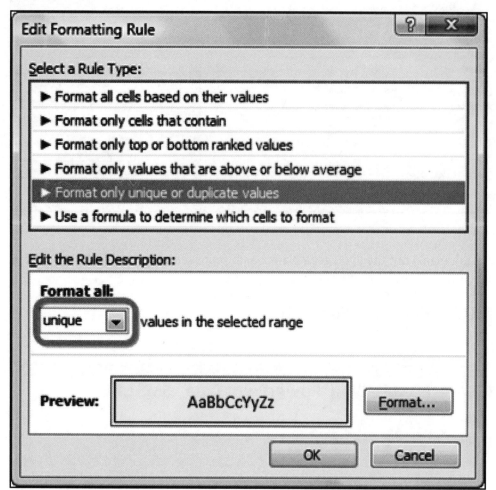

Figure 2.80

> **Note**
>
> You need to make sure you always have at least two blank cells in your conditional formatting rule. If you don't, when the user selects all slicer tiles except one, the single blank CUBERANKEDMEMBER() formula *will* be formatted.

Dealing with No Selection

If the user makes no selection, you get this:

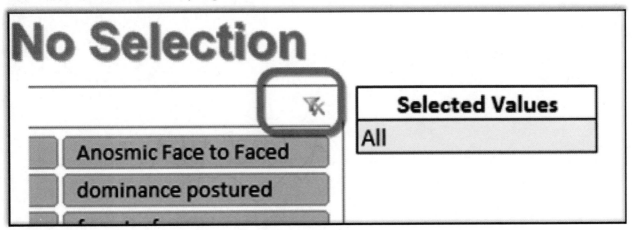

Figure 2.81

This is probably okay in most cases.

If it's not okay, and you want to show all individual values "lit up" instead, you can use an alternative trick to fetch each individual value. We won't go into that here in great depth, but these steps will get you started:

1. Establish a second CUBESET() formula and rather than use the name of the slicer as the second argument, use something like "[*TableName*].[*ColumnName*].[All].children" (including the double quotes and substituting the name of the table and column that the slicer is based on).

2. Establish a second series of CUBERANKEDMEMBER() formulas that reference the second CUBESET() cell.

3. Now wrap your original CUBERANKEDMEMBER() formulas with an IF() to detect the case where the first CUBESET() returns "All" for its first member, which happens only when the slicer is cleared of any selections.

4. When you get "All" from that first CUBESET(), switch over to using a cell from that second series of CUBERANKEDMEMBER() formulas (the ones established in step 2).

Here's an example of a formula for step 3:

```
IF(CUBERANKEDMEMBER(<original CUBESET cell>,1)="All",
    <relative ref to cell in the 2nd series
     of CUBERANKEDMEMBER cells>,
    <original CUBERANKEDMEMBER formula>
     )
```

Chapter 3: Conquering Common Calculated Column Conundrums

For years, we've been saying that calculated columns aren't a "strength" of Power Pivot as compared to normal Excel. Sure, the ability to write a calculated column in a table of more than 1 million rows is certainly a distinction, and we've even written calculated columns on tables with more than *100 million* rows. Hey, that's pretty hot.

But if you set that one new capability aside, calc columns in Power Pivot do not enable you to *create* anything that you could not create in normal Excel. In the end, a calc column in Power Pivot produces a column full of values—just like a calc column in Excel.

By contrast, measures (called calculated fields in Excel 2013) absolutely *do* empower you to create dramatically more flexible, insightful, and useful results than are possible in regular Excel. When it comes to Power Pivot formulas, measures are the main attraction, and calc columns are the warm-up band.

In that light, Power Pivot calc columns often require more of an adjustment for long-time Excel users than do measures. The lack of "A1"-style references in the DAX formula language is much more noticeable in calc columns than in measures, and that sometimes leaves newcomers exasperated ("This was so easy in Excel, but I can't figure it out in Power Pivot").

> **Note**
>
> This confusion strikes at the moment when you first need to reference a value (or values) that *isn't* in the current row. Up until that point, Power Pivot calc columns are in fact easier to write than normal Excel calc columns, thanks to the named reference syntax. So "current row" calc columns are a dream, but what we call "cross-row" calc columns require some adjustment.

Hey, I (Rob) have been to "cross-row confusion land." But I've grown to love Power Pivot calc columns over time, even for cross-row cases, and the intent of this chapter is to help speed you to that same happy place.

An Excel Pro's Primer on Calculated Columns

If you're an Excel pro trying to learn to use calculated columns in Power Pivot, you may face a few hurdles that could trip you up. There are 400 different functions in Excel, and only one-fifth of them work in Power Pivot—but it is definitely the best one-fifth of the functions. If you want to use `MID()`, `LEFT()`, `RIGHT()`, `IF()`, and other popular functions, go right ahead...they will work as you expect.

The TEXT()/FORMAT() Oddity

Whereas some functions work the same in Power Pivot as in Excel, there are some oddities. The `TEXT()` function in Excel is useful for converting dates to month names or weekday names, and you might eventually want to use this function. But for some reason, the Power Pivot team chose to use the VBA function `FORMAT()` instead of the Excel function `TEXT()`. We like to joke that is it simply a typo—they misspelled T-E-X-T as F-O-R-M-A-T—but there are some important differences between these two functions.

If you usually use =TEXT(A2, "MMMM") in Excel, this correctly translates to =FORMAT([Date], "MMMM") in Power Pivot. Both of these functions take a date field and return a full month name, like January.

The FORMAT() function accepts a few format codes that TEXT() does not accept. For example, Q returns a quarter number (from 1 to 4), and W returns a week number (from 1 to 51). Such differences make FORMAT() superior to TEXT(), but the uninitiated may not understand this.

Where is VLOOKUP()?

The number-one function for many Excel pros is VLOOKUP(). This function is not available in Power Pivot, and for good reason: in most cases, you no longer need it! Relationships allow us to use fields from table A on the same pivot as fields from table B, without having to "merge" the two tables. But in cases when you truly do need to reference another table in a calc column, Power Pivot offers you several great methods like the RELATED() function (covered in DFPP) and LOOKUPVALUE() (covered in this chapter).

You Can't Point to a Column by Using the Arrow Keys

There is no workaround for this. Excel pros should be thankful that Rob Collie was on the Power Pivot team. But Rob is too young. Younger Excel pros might build their formulas by clicking on columns with the mouse. Others might actually type to enter formulas. But older Excel pros will often point to a column using the arrow keys. This technique dates back to Lotus 1-2-3. For example, if you start in E2 and want to build the formula =B2*C2/D2, you can use the arrow keys technique as follows: =, left arrow, left arrow, left arrow, *, left arrow, left arrow, /, left arrow, Enter. It sounds horrible to read, but it is fast to do, once you get used to the technique. In our seminars, 70% of the room uses the mouse, 10% type the formulas, and 20% use the arrow keys to build their formulas. The Power Pivot grid allows you to use the mouse or to type a formula, but it does not support the arrow keys method.

No One Ever Named Their Kid "CalculatedColumn1"

There is no workaround for this. I've tried every possible syntax to specify a name and the formula at the same time (ie Month:=RELATED...), and there simply is no way to prevent CalculatedColumn1. In regular Excel, you might type a heading in row 1 and then a formula in row 2. In the Power Pivot grid, you cannot enter a column heading until you've added the formula. Once you add the formula, Power Pivot uses the default names CalculatedColumn1, CalculatedColumn2, CalculatedColumn3, and so on. We don't really care for these names, but they're easy to change: After you enter the first formula, you can right-click the heading of CalculatedColumn1, choose Rename, then type the field name you want.

Subtotaling Calc Columns and the EARLIER() Function

Say that you have a very simple table like this:

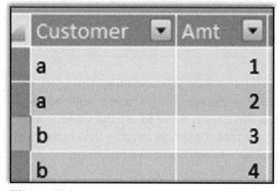

Figure 3.1

And you want to add a third column that is the total for each customer:

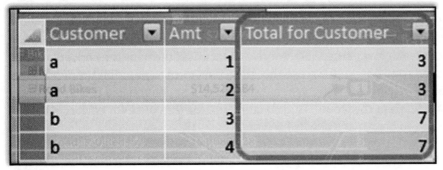

Figure 3.2

This is the calculated column formula for that third column:

```
=CALCULATE(SUM(Table[Amt]),
        FILTER(Table,
            Table[Customer]=EARLIER(Table[Customer])
            )
      )
```

If you don't really understand row context (described in just a bit), you can simply follow the pattern laid out here to add that third column. We suggest, for starters, that you just use the formula above as a pattern, substituting your own table and column names. Then you can move on without worrying about understanding what you've done. It's fine. You have our permission and encouragement to do so, especially in the early days.

Seriously, you can just move on to the next trick in this chapter. You only need to read the rest of this section if and when you are ready for the next level of enlightenment.

Oh, you're still here? Okay then, here is an explanation of what's going on in that subtotal calc column: Since there are four rows in the table, the calc column formula needs to "run" four times—once to calculate each row's resulting value (in this case, 3, 3, 7, and 7, as pictured above). Within each one of those four steps, a reference to a column will evaluate to the value of the specified column from that "current" row. So, for instance, in the second row of the table, a reference to `Table[Amt]` will return 2. Just like you want it to.

On the off chance that this seems complex already, we want to illustrate that there is nothing complex here *yet* because this is precisely the way you *already* understand things. Now say that you write another calc column, this time with the following formula:

```
=CONCATENATE('Table'[Customer], 'Table'[Amt])
```

You get, of course, precisely what you expect:

Customer	Amt	TotalForCustomer	CalculatedColumn2
a	1		a1
a	2		a2
b	3		b3
b	4	7	b4

Figure 3.3

This is because, at each one of the four "steps" in the calc column (one step per row), a reference to a column is essentially limited to the current row. It would be quite bizarre if, in the first row, a reference to the [Amt] column evaluated to 2! Of *course* you want it to evaluate to 1.

As a calc column evaluates, once for each row in the table, there's a fancy DAX term for the concept of "current row at each step." It's called *row context*. If we use this fancy new term to describe the simple concepts conveyed earlier, it goes something like this: "When evaluating a calc column in a four-row table, the DAX engine steps through four different row contexts, evaluating the formula once for each row context." So far so good, right? Take a deep breath and slowly let it out...

The problem is that the formula for the TotalForCustomer column contains a FILTER() function, and FILTER() is quite sneaky. Just as the calc column formula itself is evaluated once per each row context, FILTER('Table',...) also steps through each row in Table, one at a time, much like the calc column formula itself!

One of the key characteristics of FILTER() is that it ignores the row context of the calc column and operates on the *entire* table. This makes it simultaneously confusing (at first) and awesome (once you grasp it).

Since Table has four rows, every time FILTER('Table',...) is evaluated, FILTER() has its own four steps to process. At each step, it looks at a row and says, "Hey, should I keep this row or filter it out?"

All in all, then, there are 16 steps involved in evaluating the calc column:

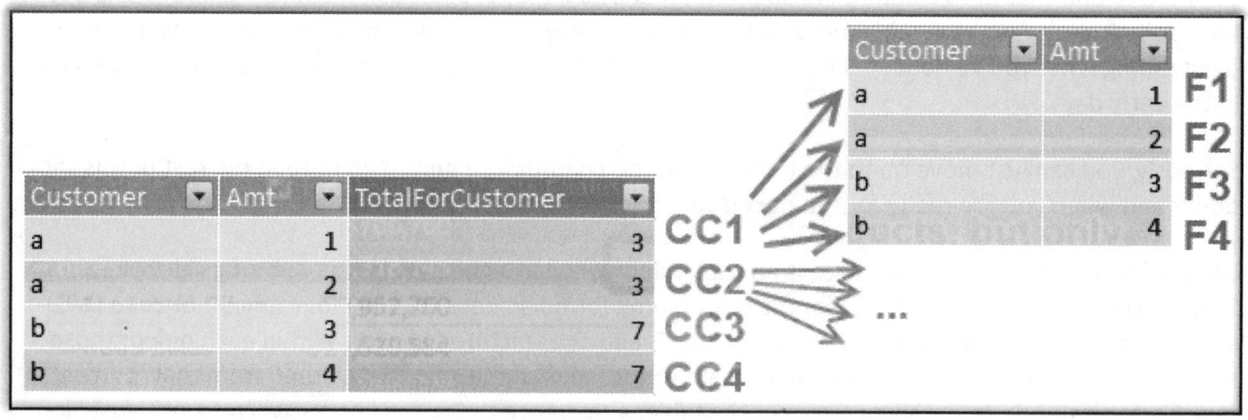

Figure 3.4

In this illustration, CC1 denotes "the first row context evaluated by the calculated column," and F1 means "the first row context evaluated by FILTER()."

You might want to imagine the "names" of each of the 16 row contexts examined by this calc column formula. They would be something like CC1/F1, CC1/F2, etc., all the way up through CC4/F3 and CC4/F4. (These names are completely unofficial. There are no names for individual row contexts in DAX. We are just using this as an explanatory trick.)

So there are four "calc column row contexts," and tucked inside *each* of those four, there are *also* four "FILTER() row contexts"—an *outer* loop of four row contexts and an *inner* loop of four row contexts.

Now, within a FILTER() function, a "naked" reference to a column will evaluate according to the row context of the FILTER() function itself, not the calc column row context. Get it? Inside FILTER(), the reference to 'Table'[Customer] will be evaluated according to that "inner" row context of F1, F2, etc.—completely ignoring the "outer" row context of CC1, etc.! (Remember that FILTER() has to look at every row in the table to see if it should be kept or discarded.) So even when the formula is evaluating in the CC2 "outer" row context (where [Customer]="a"), the "naked" reference to

'Table'[Customer] inside FILTER() will sometimes evaluate to "b"—in contexts CC2/F3 and CC2/F4.

Within FILTER(), how do you "get back" to the outer loop and see what the value of [Customer] is in CC2? You use the EARLIER() function! EARLIER() basically says "pop out of the current row context and look at the outer (earlier) row context instead, when evaluating the value of the specified column." You will therefore often hear us refer to EARLIER() as the CURRENTROW() function. This allows you, within FILTER(), to examine every row in the table and compare it to the current row of the calc column. That is, you can to focus on a given row of a table and then go look at *all* the rows in the table, saying to each row "Hey, are you similar to me? If so, I want to count you."

And yes, it is possible (but *very* rare) to end up in situations where you have *more* than two nested loops of row contexts. That's why EARLIER() has the optional second argument Number—because you can specify how many loops "outward" you want to step. When you omit that argument, it defaults to 1. This is also why there is an EARLIEST() function: Its purpose is to get back to the *absolute* outermost row context, no matter how deeply nested you might find yourself.

> **Note**
>
> For perspective: At this writing, your dear authors have never en-countered a need for more than one outward step and, accordingly, have never used either the Number argument to EARLIER() *or* the EARLIEST() function. For now, we merely aspire to *encountering* such a need.
>
> A long time ago, when I (Bill) was working on *Power Pivot for the Data Analyst*, I desperately tried to get a working example of EARLIER() or EARLIEST(). Now, several years later, we are using EARLIER() to essentially do a SUMIF(), and it looks so simple and powerful.

Referencing the Previous Row and Similar Calcs

This is a very common question in the world of calc columns: "How do I reference the row immediately 'above' this one?"

For example, how do you create a calc column like the one pictured here?

Date	Value	Yesterday Value
1/1/2014	74	
1/2/2014	40	74
1/3/2014	22	40
1/4/2014	40	22
1/5/2014	22	40
1/6/2014	75	22
1/7/2014	34	75
1/8/2014	45	34
1/9/2014	39	45

Figure 3.5

As it happens, the answer is *very* similar to the subtotal example we just looked at:

```
=CALCULATE(SUM(LookingBack[Value]),
           FILTER(LookingBack,
           LookingBack[Date]=
                   EARLIER(LookingBack[Date])-1
                   )
           )
```

In fact, the only difference is the −1 at the end of the third line!

Note the following here:

- Sort order of the table has *no* impact on this formula. This formula finds the row(s) whose date column is one less than the current row's date and sums them up.

- If you want to grab the following row(s) rather than the previous row(s), change the −1 to +1.

- Similarly, if you want to go back a week, change the −1 to −7.

- This technique works with columns other than Date. If you have a column like MonthNumber, subtracting one from that will work, too.

- Many times when you are writing a calc column like this, you'd be better off writing a measure instead, but a full discussion of that is beyond the scope of this book. (You will see examples of such measures later in this chapter and in Chapter 4, however.)

- There *are* definitely cases where such a calc column is required, hence this technique's inclusion here.

Referencing Rows "Within Range" of the Current Row

As you read the last trick, you might have wondered why you used a SUM() when you just wanted to grab the previous row. Well, Power Pivot does not trust you that it's only going to find a single row when you send FILTER() off to do its work. It always assumes it's going to find more than one, which is why it always requires an aggregate function like SUM(). Of course, if it *does* find only a single row, the aggregation function you choose is often unimportant; SUM(), AVERAGE(), MAX(), etc. are all going to return the same result.

Let's look at a few examples. In this starting table, note that there are *multiple* rows for each date:

Date	Value
1/1/2014	78
1/1/2014	32
1/1/2014	46
1/2/2014	40
1/2/2014	52
1/2/2014	55
1/3/2014	60
1/3/2014	79

Figure 3.6

Here you see a sum of yesterday's values:

Date	Value	Sum of Yesterday
1/1/2014	78	
1/1/2014	32	
1/1/2014	46	
1/2/2014	40	156
1/2/2014	52	156
1/2/2014	55	156
1/3/2014	60	147
1/3/2014	79	147
1/3/2014	25	147

Figure 3.7

The formula for this table is *precisely* the same as in the previous trick, just updated to the new table name:

```
=CALCULATE(SUM(MultiValue[Value]),
         FILTER(MultiValue,
                MultiValue[Date]=
                     EARLIER(MultiValue[Date])-1
                )
         )
```

And here is an example of a running total that includes the current row's date:

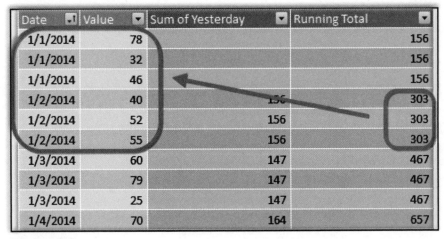

Date	Value	Sum of Yesterday	Running Total
1/1/2014	78		156
1/1/2014	32		156
1/1/2014	46		156
1/2/2014	40	156	303
1/2/2014	52	156	303
1/2/2014	55	156	303
1/3/2014	60	147	467
1/3/2014	79	147	467
1/3/2014	25	147	467
1/4/2014	70	164	657

Figure 3.8

Here's its formula:

```
=CALCULATE(SUM(MultiValue[Value]),
         FILTER(MultiValue,
                MultiValue[Date]<=
                     EARLIER(MultiValue[Date])
                )
         )
```

> **Note**
>
> To exclude the current row's date, just change <= to <.

Continuing in this vein, here's a three-day moving sum of the current date, the previous date, and the following date:

Date	Value	Sum of Yesterday	Running Total	3 Day Moving Sum
1/1/2014	78		156	303
1/1/2014	32		156	303
1/1/2014	46		156	303
1/2/2014	40	156	303	467
1/2/2014	52	156	303	467
1/2/2014	55	156	303	467
1/3/2014	60	147	467	501
1/3/2014	79	147	467	501
1/3/2014	25	147	467	501
1/4/2014	70	164	657	472
1/4/2014	84	164	657	472
1/4/2014	36	164	657	472
1/5/2014	34	190	775	445

Figure 3.9

And here's its formula:

```
=CALCULATE(SUM(MultiValue[Value]),
        FILTER(MultiValue,
            MultiValue[Date]>=
                EARLIER(MultiValue[Date])-1 &&
            MultiValue[Date]<=
                EARLIER(MultiValue[Date])+1
            )
        )
```

> **Note**
>
> Of course, you can change SUM() to MAX(), for instance, and find the amount of the single "best" day in this three-day window. And again, *many* times when you are writing a calc column like this, you'd be better off writing a measure instead—but not *always*.

Cross-Table Lookups: LOOKUPVALUE() and Other Techniques

All the examples so far in this chapter involve looking across rows in the same table. But what if you want to grab values from other tables? Let's look at an example of such a problem. First, you have a Sales table:

Date	Product	Quantity
1/1/2014	A	33
1/1/2014	B	39
1/1/2014	A	40
1/1/2014	B	36
1/2/2014	A	49
1/2/2014	B	30
1/2/2014	A	27
1/2/2014	B	38
1/3/2014	A	27
1/3/2014	B	41
1/3/2014	A	44
1/3/2014	B	28

Figure 3.10

> **Note**
>
> In the Sales table, for each pair of Date and Product, you have multiple rows.

You also have a Prices table:

Date	Product	Unit Price
1/1/2014	A	$1.50
1/1/2014	B	$3.10
1/2/2014	A	$1.60
1/2/2014	B	$3.25
1/3/2014	A	$2.00
1/3/2014	B	$2.75

Figure 3.11

> **Note**
>
> In the Prices table, for each pair of Date and Product, you have a *single* row.

Now, using a calc column in the Sales table, you want to grab the appropriate Unit Price amount from the Prices table.

The "simplest" answer would be to use the RELATED() function. And if you had a relationship established between these two tables, that would work quite well. But alas, you do not have a relationship here. Furthermore, you don't have a column on which you could establish a relationship. In order to create a relationship, you'd have to create a new column in each table (Sales and Prices) and concatenate the Date and Product columns. *Then* you could relate the two tables via those "Frankencolumns." That's a lot of busy work. Plus, calc columns can add a lot of weight to a file (bloating file size), especially when the tables involved are large.

So here's a formula that allows you to grab the value from the Unit Price column without first establishing a relationship:

```
=LOOKUPVALUE(Prices[Unit Price], Prices[Date], Sales[Date],
    Prices[Product], Sales[Product])
```

It's very simple. LOOKUPVALUE()'s first argument asks what column's value you want to fetch. Then you specify pairs of columns—first the column in the "fetch *from*" table and the matching column in the "fetch *into*" table. You can have as many pairs as you like, practically speaking. And it works:

Date	Product	Quantity	Effective Unit Price
1/1/2014	A	33	$1.50
1/1/2014	B	39	$3.10
1/1/2014	A	40	$1.50
1/1/2014	B	36	$3.10
1/2/2014	A	49	$1.60
1/2/2014	B	30	$3.25
1/2/2014	A	27	$1.60
1/2/2014	B	38	$3.25
1/3/2014	A	27	$2.00
1/3/2014	B	41	$2.75
1/3/2014	A	44	$2.00
1/3/2014	B	28	$2.75

Figure 3.12

What Happens if LOOKUPVALUE() Finds More Than One Match?

Hey, great question. To see this in action, introduce another row into the Prices table, for Product A on January 1. This time, give it the same price ($1.50) as in the original January 1/Product A row:

Date	Product	Unit Price
1/1/2014	A	$1.50
1/1/2014	B	$3.10
1/1/2014	A	$1.50

Figure 3.13

Next, check in on the `LOOKUPVALUE()` calc column:

Date	Product	Quantity	Effective Unit Price
1/1/2014	A	33	$1.50
1/1/2014	B	39	$3.10
1/1/2014	A	40	$1.50
1/1/2014	B	36	$3.10
1/2/2014	A	49	$1.60
1/2/2014	B	30	$3.25
1/2/2014	A	27	$1.60
1/2/2014	B	38	$3.25
1/3/2014	A	27	$2.00
1/3/2014	B	41	$2.75
1/3/2014	A	44	$2.00
1/3/2014	B	28	$2.75

Figure 3.14

Hey, it still works! Cool, so it detected that, even though it found multiple rows, they all returned the same value ($1.50), and it didn't raise an error. We salute such robustness!

If you then go back and change that "new" row to be $1.60, which creates a conflict, you do indeed get an error:

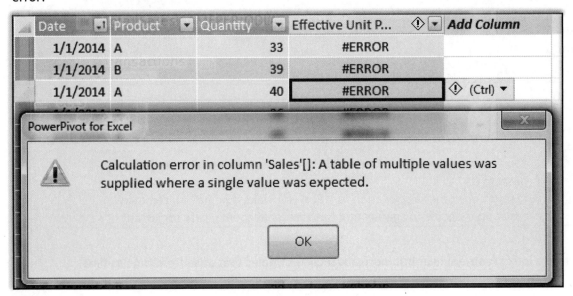

Figure 3.15

What if LOOKUPVALUE() Doesn't Address Your Need?

What if that prior example—with two Prices table rows for the same Day/Product pair, with different price values—is completely legitimate? What do you do then? Well, it's back to our old friends CALCULATE() and FILTER():

```
=CALCULATE(AVERAGE(Prices[Unit Price]),
           FILTER(Prices,
                  Prices[Date]=Sales[Date] &&
                  Prices[Product]=Sales[Product]
                  )
           )
```

This works like a charm:

Date	Product	Quantity	Effective Unit Price	⚠	Effective Avg Unit Price
1/1/2014	A	33	#ERROR		$1.55
1/1/2014	B	39	#ERROR		$3.10
1/1/2014	A	40	#ERROR		$1.55
1/1/2014	B	36	#ERROR		$3.10
1/2/2014	A	49	#ERROR		$1.60
1/2/2014	B	30	#ERROR		$3.25
1/2/2014	A	27	#ERROR		$1.60
1/2/2014	B	38	#ERROR		$3.25
1/3/2014	A	27	#ERROR		$2.00
1/3/2014	B	41	#ERROR		$2.75
1/3/2014	A	44	#ERROR		$2.00
1/3/2014	B	28	#ERROR		$2.75

Average of $1.60 and $1.50

Figure 3.16

> **Note**
>
> You are *not* required to use the AVERAGE() function as the first argument to CALCULATE(). You can use MIN(), MAX(), SUM(), or pretty much any other aggregation function you want. And in "multi-match" cases, your choice of aggregation function is, of course, *very* important.

Now let's take a look at some similar but more advanced examples that arise from time to time.

Lookups Based on Start and End Dates

Common conundrums is the theme of this chapter, and this problem definitely qualifies. Here's a Schedule table with lots of dates in it:

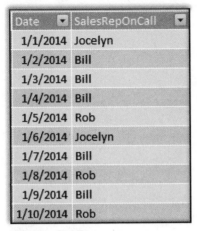

Date	SalesRepOnCall
1/1/2014	Jocelyn
1/2/2014	Bill
1/3/2014	Bill
1/4/2014	Bill
1/5/2014	Rob
1/6/2014	Jocelyn
1/7/2014	Bill
1/8/2014	Rob
1/9/2014	Bill
1/10/2014	Rob

Figure 3.17

And then here's a different kind of pricing table. This Prices2 table, rather than specifying the effective price on every single day, uses Start and End columns to indicate a time frame in which a given price is active:

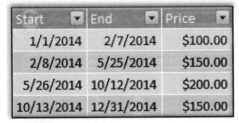

Start	End	Price
1/1/2014	2/7/2014	$100.00
2/8/2014	5/25/2014	$150.00
5/26/2014	10/12/2014	$200.00
10/13/2014	12/31/2014	$150.00

Figure 3.18

To add an effective price column to the Schedule table, use this formula:

```
=CALCULATE(MAX(Prices2[Price]),
        FILTER(Prices2,
                Prices2[Start]<= Schedule[Date] &&
                Prices2[End]>=Schedule[Date]
                )
            )
```

Here's the result:

Date	SalesRepOnCall	CalculatedColumn1
2/4/2014	Rob	$100.00
2/5/2014	Bill	$100.00
2/6/2014	Jocelyn	$100.00
2/7/2014	Bill	$100.00
2/8/2014	Rob	$150.00
2/9/2014	Bill	$150.00
2/10/2014	Jocelyn	$150.00
2/11/2014	Rob	$150.00
2/12/2014	Bill	$150.00

Price changes on Feb 8

Figure 3.19

The price changing on February 8 is precisely correct. Your work here is done.

Lookups Based on Start Date Only

Now say that you have this same problem, but now you have only a Start column, and no End column. For example, say that you have the Prices3 table pictured here, which is really just the Prices2 table with the End column removed:

Start	Price
1/1/2014	$100.00
2/8/2014	$150.00
5/26/2014	$200.00
10/13/2...	$150.00

Figure 3.20

Now what? Basically, you want to find the "most recent" row from this table that has happened on or before the current date. This is tricky. One approach would be to re-create the End column with a calc column, like this, in Prices3:

```
=CALCULATE(MIN(Prices3[Start]),
           FILTER(Prices3,
                  Prices3[Start]>
                        EARLIER(Prices3[Start]))
           )-1
```

Here's the result:

Start	Price	End
1/1/2014	$100.00	2/7/2014
2/8/2014	$150.00	5/25/2014
5/26/2014	$200.00	10/12/2014
10/13/2...	$150.00	12/29/1899

Figure 3.21

Now, re-equipped with the End column, you can apply the previous section's technique. But for completeness, here you'll solve the problem without re-creating the End column. Back in Schedule, you add the following calc column:

```
=CALCULATE(MAX(Prices3[Price]),
          TOPN(1,FILTER(Prices3,
               Prices3[Start]<=Schedule[Date]),
               Prices3[Start]
               )
          )
```

This calc column does not reference the End column at all! `FILTER()` removes all Prices3 rows that happened after the current `Schedule[Date]`, and then `TOPN()` grabs the latest of all those rows! And yes, it returns the same results as the previous examples:

Date	SalesRepOnCall	Price from Prices2	Price from Prices3 No Cheating
2/3/2014	Rob	$100.00	$100.00
2/4/2014	Rob	$100.00	$100.00
2/5/2014	Bill	$100.00	$100.00
2/6/2014	Jocelyn	$100.00	$100.00
2/7/2014	Bill	$100.00	$100.00
2/8/2014	Rob	$150.00	$150.00
2/9/2014	Bill	$150.00	$150.00
2/10/2014	Jocelyn	$150.00	$150.00
2/11/2014	Rob	$150.00	$150.00

Figure 3.22

> **Note**
>
> This use of `FILTER()` nested inside `TOPN()` might be blowing your mind—and we get that! "Normally" we use the `FILTER()` function as a direct argument to `CALCULATE()`, but here we are using it in a place where `TOPN()` asks for a table. There's a moment when you realize that functions like `FILTER()` (and `TOPN()` and `DATESYTD()` and many others) serve two different yet related purposes in DAX: They have a filter purpose (when used as a direct argument to `CALCULATE()`) and a table purpose (when used as the table argument to another function).
>
> The moment you realize this, we challenge you to resist giggling with glee (or cackling maniacally). It's a moment when you feel nearly unlimited power—and not only regarding calc columns. In fact, it's even more useful with measures! You will know this moment when you experience it; trust us. It is unmistakable. Everyone in the office turns and looks at you, and you don't care.

Basically, when you want to fetch cross-table values, `LOOKUPVALUE()` is a great place to start (assuming that using `RELATED()` isn't possible or practical). Failing that, you can move on to `CALCULATE()` and `FILTER()`, and maybe even things like `CALCULATE(.., TOPN(…, FILTER(…)))`.

> **Note**
>
> This is a topic where "moving pictures" are worth a thousand pictures, and thus a million words. We're going to skip those million words here and move on. If you want more coverage of this topic, go to PowerPivotPro University, where you'll find this and many other things illustrated and explained using animated visuals.

Totaling Data Table Values in Lookup Tables

Here's another common conundrum. Say that you have the same Sales table from earlier in this chapter, and it's not related to a Products table. Sales is a data table, and Products is a lookup table.

> **Note**
>
> For further explanation of data versus lookup tables, see *DAX Formulas for Power Pivot* or PowerPivotPro University.

As per our normal convention, the lookup table is arranged vertically above the data table in diagram view:

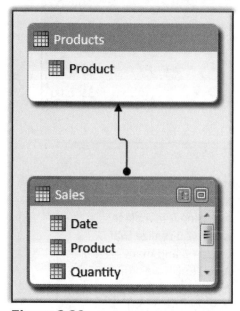

Figure 3.23

And here are those two tables in data view. First you see Products, which is very simple, with just two rows:

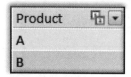

Figure 3.24

And here again for reference is the Sales table:

Date	Product	Quantity
1/1/2014	A	33
1/1/2014	B	39
1/1/2014	A	40
1/1/2014	B	36
1/2/2014	A	49
1/2/2014	B	30
1/2/2014	A	27
1/2/2014	B	38
1/3/2014	A	27
1/3/2014	B	41
1/3/2014	A	44
1/3/2014	B	28

Figure 3.25

The desired result is a Total Quantity Sold column in the Products table, like this:

Product	Total Quantity Sold
A	220
B	212

Figure 3.26

There are a number of ways to fail at this and a number of ways to succeed. Here's one successful formula:

```
=CALCULATE(SUM(Sales[Quantity]))
```

What? A CALCULATE() with only one argument? What the heck? We could burn a bunch of pages on that. Or we could just tell you that the CALCULATE function takes a row context and promotes it to become a filter context. That is the "right" explanation, but again, this is one of those places where we must choose between a million words and animations. Or, pragmatically speaking, you can just take this as a pattern and not worry about the inner workings.

It turns out, by the way, that in this case, a SUM() without a CALCULATE() may also be useful:

```
=SUM(Sales[Quantity])
```

Here's the result:

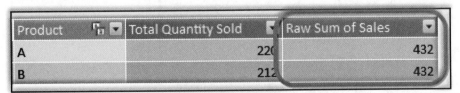

Product	Total Quantity Sold	Raw Sum of Sales
A	220	432
B	212	432

Figure 3.27

This is pretty nifty. Maybe you want to use this as a denominator sometimes. Also, this "raw sum" formula does *not* rely on a relationship being in place. It *always* sums up *all* the rows in the other table. (In fact, we often find it useful to take MAX() of the date column in a data table; see the section "Common Calendar Conundrums," later in this chapter.)

For completeness, here is another way to write the first (successful) formula:

```
=SUMX(RELATEDTABLE(Sales), Sales[Quantity])
```

`RELATEDTABLE()` is essentially the "opposite" of `RELATED()`, since it traverses the relationship in the opposite direction. Whereas `RELATED()` always fetches a single lookup table value into a data table, `RELATEDTABLE()` fetches all related rows from a data table to make them available for an aggregation in a lookup table.

Notice that the formula above returns the same results as the first formula:

Product	Total Quantity Sold	Raw Sum of Sales	SUMX RELATEDTABLE Method
A	220	432	220
B	212	432	212

Figure 3.28

It's important to understand that subtotal calculations like this in a lookup table are *very* often better implemented as measures. The most common "valid" reason to do this in a calc column is to create a "grouping" column—like High/Low/Medium—that groups products (or other entities) into categories. You can then place the grouping column in the Rows, Columns, Slicers, or Report Filters drop zone of your Pivot and view results accordingly.

CONTAINSX: Finding Matching Values in Two Tables

Rather than look up or aggregate values across tables, you may at some point want to find whether a value in one table has a matching value in another table. For example, here you want to flag rows in the Companies table on the left when they contain a keyword from the MatchList table on the right:

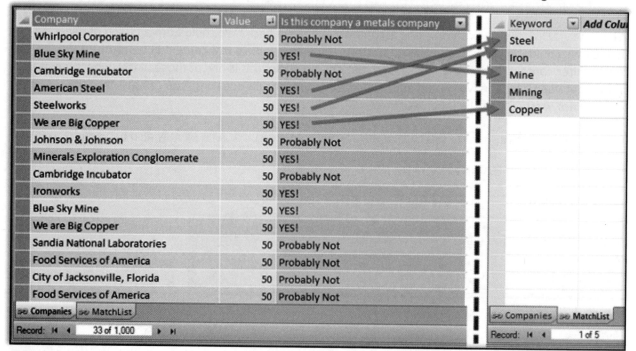

Figure 3.29

Finding matching values in two tables is a pretty common need. Sometimes you can do this very quickly in Power Pivot by relating the two tables and then writing a =RELATED calculated column in one table to see if it has a matching value in another table. But there are times when this doesn't work—for instance, when you're not looking for an exact match but a "contains" match.

Rolling Your Own X Functions

Perhaps the only thing that makes me (Rob) happier than a new X function is "inventing" a new one (such as PRODUCTX(); see http://ppvt.pro/PRODUCTX).

> **Note**
>
> I (Bill) still badly want a CONCATENATEX() or perhaps ROMANX() function!

The other day, I was looking at a Power Pivot model and thinking "Gee, it sure would be nice to have a CONTAINSX()." Turns out you can "make" your own CONTAINSX() by using SUMX().

The Formula for Matching Table Values

Here's one formula you can use to determine whether the same value appears in two tables:

```
[Is this company a metals company] =
=IF(
    SUMX(MatchList,
        FIND(
            UPPER(MatchList[Keyword]),
            UPPER(Companies[Company])
            ,,0
            )
        ) > 0,
    "YES!",
    "Probably Not"
    )
```

> **Note**
>
> There are definitely other ways to do this.

Here's what the formula does:

- SUMX() steps through every row in MatchList. For each row in MatchList, it evaluates the FIND() function. FIND() returns a number. SUMX() then sums up all the values from FIND(). (There will be five values to sum up because there are five rows in MatchList.)

- For the FIND() row of MatchList, it looks to see if that substring also appears in the current row of Companies. If it does, FIND() returns the number of the position where that substring is found, as it always does. If it doesn't find a substring match, it returns 0.

- The UPPER() functions make the FIND() case-insensitive. If you want it to be case-sensitive, remove the UPPER() functions.

- If you get 0 back from SUMX(), no matches were found, so IF() returns Probably Not. If anything other than 0 comes back, there was at least one match (maybe more!), and IF() returns YES!.

No Relationships Needed

No relationships are required for this technique:

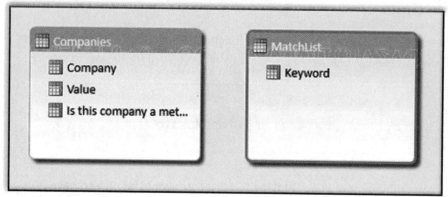

Figure 3.30

A Million Variations

You could twist this example in many practical ways: You could return the number of matches rather than `Yes/No`. You could make the search case-sensitive rather than case-insensitive. You could look for "begins with," "ends with," or an exact match.

CONTAINSX Revisited: What Is the Match?

You just learned how to find whether there's a match between two tables. You might also want to find out what the match *is*:

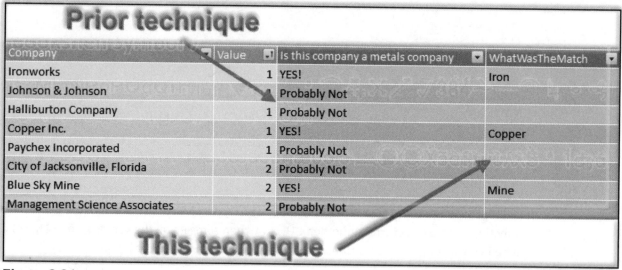

Figure 3.31

You've seen that it's pretty easy to write a formula that reports whether there is a match. But what if you want to know what the matching keyword actually is? It's pretty easy to write a formula for this, too, especially if you're using Power Pivot.

> **Note**
>
> Determining what keywords match is an example of something that is easier in Power Pivot calculated columns than in regular Excel. Once you get used to calculated columns in Power Pivot, you'll actually start to realize that handling those same problems in normal Excel is clumsier. At the beginning of this chapter, we mentioned that using `RELATED()` is easier than using `VLOOKUP()`. Here you are essentially doing a `VLOOKUP()` for a wildcard. Sure, this is possible in regular Excel with `=VLOOKUP("*"&A1&"*"...)`, but 99.9% of people using Excel have never seen this use of `VLOOKUP()`.

To determine what the matching keyword is, you can create a WhatWasTheMatch column:

Company	Value	Is this company a metals company	WhatWasTheMatch
Latrobe University	40	Probably Not	
International Mining Corp	40	YES!	Mining
Ironworks	40	YES!	Iron
Whirlpool Corporation	40	Probably Not	
Whirlpool Corporation	40	Probably Not	
Minerals Exploration Conglomerate	40	YES!	Mine
Whirlpool Corporation	40	Probably Not	
Copper Inc.	40	YES!	Copper

Figure 3.32

Here's the formula for that column:

```
[WhatWasTheMatch] =
=FIRSTNONBLANK(FILTER(
                    VALUES(MatchList[Keyword]),
                    SEARCH(
                          MatchList[Keyword],
                          Companies[Company],
                          1,
                          0
                          )
                    )
            ,1
            )
```

Look at the `FIRSTNONBLANK()` part of this formula (boldfaced). This is a nonstandard use of `FIRSTNONBLANK()`. You can often "misuse" `FIRSTNONBLANK()` in useful ways like this.

See the boldfaced `,1` in the formula? That is the second input to `FIRSTNONBLANK()`, and in "standard" uses, it is typically a measure. For example, you might be trying to find the first time a customer *ever* bought something, which happens when the sales measure first returns a nonblank value. In this case, using `1` as the last input short-circuits the "Is it blank?" test (the `NONBLANK()` part) and grabs the first value found. In other words, `FIRSTNONBLANK()` with a `1` as the last input is a makeshift "first text value we find" function.

In the formula above, the `FILTER(VALUES(SEARCH(...)))` part (between the boldfaced portions) has only one purpose: to return a single column of text values from the `MatchList[Keyword]` column. But it returns only values from that column that actually were found in the current row of `Companies[Company]`. In other words, it only returns keywords that were found.

It all starts with `VALUES(MatchList[Keyword])`. And because there is no relationship or other dependency between the Companies table and the MatchList table, this will *always* start out with *every* distinct value from the `MatchList[Keyword]` column:

Figure 3.33

In this particular calculated column formula, `VALUES(MatchList[Keyword])` *always* starts with the unfiltered list of all values in that column. Then `FILTER()` kicks in and only keeps rows/values where `<filter expr>` evaluates to `TRUE`.

The formula then uses the `SEARCH()` function as the `<filter expr>` test to `FILTER()`. Since `SEARCH()` returns a nonzero number whenever it finds something, and `FILTER()` treats nonzero numbers as `TRUE`, well, `FILTER()` only keeps values that it finds.

Where Can You Use This Trick?

What would you *do* with a column like the calculated column shown in this trick? Well, how about slapping the new column in the Rows drop zone of a Pivot, with a couple measures? This new column works pretty well in Rows:

Industry ↵	Company Entries	Average Value
Mine	61	27.8
Mining	42	25.9
<unknown>	672	25.5
Copper	94	25.2
Iron	36	25.1
Steel	95	24.6
Grand Total	**1000**	25.5

Figure 3.34

Note here that we typed over the Row Labels cell in the Pivot and called it Industry, and we typed over the blank cell and called it <unknown>. You could do a bunch of other things, too:

- Use the new column as a slicer instead of in the Rows drop zone.

- Use the new column as a `<filter>` input to a `CALCULATE()`. You could use a new measure called `[Average Value of Copper Companies]`, for instance, with the formula `CALCULATE([Average Value], Companies[WhatWasTheMatch]="Copper")`.

- Write another calculated column that groups "Mine" and "Mining" into a single value, like, um, "Mining." And then you could maybe use *that* new column for any of the purposes just mentioned.

Common Calendar Conundrums

A tour of common calc column scenarios would not be complete without some time in calendar land, so that's our last stop in this chapter.

Using an IsFutureDate Column

Here you see that the most recent date in the ServiceCalls table is 6/1/2004:

CallDate	ProductID	CustomerID	SalesTerrit
6/1/2004	371	25407	
6/1/2004	535	25910	
6/1/2004	467	21339	
6/1/2004	541	20976	
6/1/2004	354	14654	
6/1/2004	594	11894	

Figure 3.35

But the Calendar table extends beyond that, into August 2004:

Date	DayNumberOfWeek	EnglishDayNameC
8/31/2004	3	Tuesday
8/30/2004	2	Monday
8/29/2004	1	Sunday
8/28/2004	7	Saturday
8/27/2004	6	Friday
8/26/2004	5	Thursday

Figure 3.36

It is often very helpful to have a calculated column in a Calendar table that flags dates as being in the future, from the perspective of your data tables. Here is one such formula:

```
=IF(Calendar[Date]>MAX(ServiceCalls[CallDate]),"Yes","No")
```

When you add this formula to the Calendar table, it starts returning "Yes" on 6/2/2004:

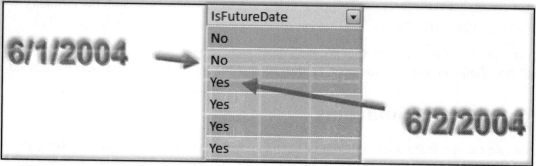

Figure 3.37

Using a DayOfWeekName Column

You already have a column, DayNumberOfWeek, that is a number from 1 to 7. But now you want the names of those days. Here's an incredibly simple formula for that:

```
=FORMAT([DayNumberOfWeek], "dddd")
```

The result is crazy cool:

Figure 3.38

Using a YearMonth Column

Now that you've seen the basic pattern involved in handling calendar conundrums, we'll start moving in rapid fashion, providing just a formula and then an image of the result. Here are the YearMonth formula and result:

```
=[CalendarYear]&FORMAT([MonthNumberOfYear], "00")
```

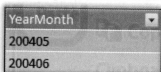

Figure 3.39

Using an IsWknd Column

Here are the IsWknd formula and result:

```
=SWITCH([DayNumberOfWeek],1,"Weekend",7,"Weekend","Weekday")
```

Figure 3.40

> **Note**
>
> Obviously, this formula uses a U.S.-centric definition of "weekend" being Saturday and Sunday.

Using a Quarter Year Column

Here are the Quarter Year formula and result:

```
=[CalendarYear]*10 + [CalendarQuarter]
```

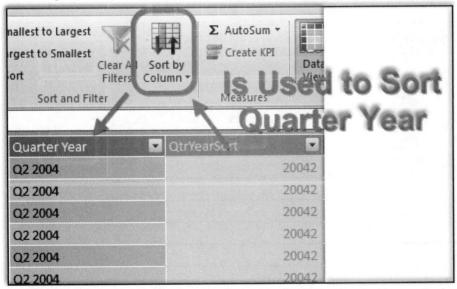

Figure 3.41

An exceedingly common problem is that periods of time bigger than a single day (week, month, quarter, etc.) that also "bake in" a particular year (like Q2 2004) cannot be sorted by any column you typically have in your Calendar table by default.

We think we should be allowed to sort by date, but Power Pivot doesn't like that. And you certainly can't sort by Quarter Number of Year, since that fails to account for different years.

So we often find ourselves implementing a workaround: We multiply the year number by 10 to "make room" for the single-digit quarter number and then add that in. Who cares that "20042" is relatively useless and will never be used on a Pivot? The point is that it *sorts* properly. We then hide that column from client tools and forget about it.

> **Note**
>
> You can use the same technique for Year Month, except in that case, you multiply Year by 100 because you need two digits to accommodate Month Number.

Custom Calendar Conundrums

All of the previous examples deal with what we call "standard calendars": calendars in which a month is defined strictly by the calendar on the wall.

In many businesses, including retail, a standard calendar is nearly worthless. All time period comparisons are performed on the basis of custom-defined calendars. Very often, these are of the form "445," in which months consist of 4 weeks, 4 weeks, and then 5 weeks (and then the pattern repeats).

Some of the columns usually required in those tables can get quite sticky, so this trick provides a few examples.

Finding the Day of the Period

Let's say you have a 445-style calendar table named HybridCal. Among other columns, it already contains DateID and 445MonthID:

DateID	445MonthID
7/25/2001	1
7/26/2001	1
7/27/2001	1
7/28/2001	1
7/29/2001	2
7/30/2001	2
7/31/2001	2
8/1/2001	2
8/2/2001	2

Figure 3.42

445MonthID is integral to all month-level calculations; in order to go back and look at last month, you perform simple −1 arithmetic, based on that column.

But you quickly find, when writing your 445-based time comparison measures, that you need to know what day of the period you are currently "in." This number should go from 1 to 28, then 1 to 28 again, then 1 to 35 (the 5-week month/period), and then repeat. That results in some head scratching.

To save your scalp, here is an example of a formula that works:

```
=INT([DateID] -
        CALCULATE(FIRSTDATE(HybridCal[DateID]),
                    FILTER(HybridCal,
                        HybridCal[445MonthID]=
                            EARLIER(
                                HybridCal[445MonthID])
                                )
                            )
                        )
            + 1
            )
```

And here's the result:

DateID	445MonthID	DayOfPeriod
7/23/2001	1	23
7/24/2001	1	24
7/25/2001	1	25
7/26/2001	1	26
7/27/2001	1	27
7/28/2001	1	28
7/29/2001	2	1
7/30/2001	2	2
7/31/2001	2	3
8/1/2001	2	4
8/2/2001	2	5
8/3/2001	2	6

Figure 3.43

Finding the Week of the Period

Another common question is "What week are we in within the current period?" This should go 1 through 4, 1 through 4, then 1 through 5.

This problem is simpler than finding the day of the period but still can cause an embarrassing amount of head-scratching when someone is watching you. Here's the formula:

```
=CEILING([DayOfPeriod]/7,1)
```

The Ever-Increasing and "Smooth" WeekID

"Prior week"–style measures quickly inform you that you need a column like the one pictured below, which "goes up" by 1 for every week that goes by but never "resets" (back to 1) when you roll over to a new year. It also never has gaps. (In other words, you need the first week of year 2 to be exactly 1 number higher than the last week of year 1.)

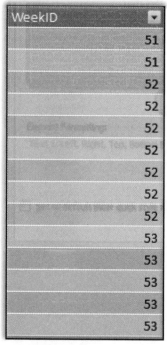

Figure 3.44

This is a surprisingly difficult formula to write—not because it's Power Pivot, but because the math itself tends to tie our brains in knots. But here's what you do:

```
=ROUNDDOWN(([445MonthID]-1)/3,0)*13  + MOD([445MonthID]-1,3)*4 +
[WeekOfPeriod]
```

If we went any further down this road, we would exhaust authors and readers alike. So instead we'll change gears and have some fun with portable formulas in Chapter 4.

Chapter 4: Modeling and Portable Formulas

Here's a "story" that I (Rob) tell everywhere I go, and it's about you (the Excel pro): You're tasked with solving an analytical/reporting problem. The people awaiting the results are not Excel pros (they aren't data people!), and they underestimate how much work it is because the problem *sounds* simple: "We need to see how we're doing, sales-wise, versus our budget, for every month this year and for every product line." So they set an unrealistic deadline: "We need it for the meeting first thing in the morning."

Here's what happens next in the land of traditional Excel: You create two Pivots—one against the sales data, and one against the budget data. Both Pivots are broken out by month and product line. Then, on a different worksheet, you start creating your report. The methodology you use to create this report is something we euphemistically refer to as "formula surgery." You write formulas using functions like VLOOKUP(), HLOOKUP(), INDEX(), MATCH(), etc. to fetch values from the Sales and Budget tables, and you compare the "fetched" values within those same formulas to create the report. It's very tedious and error-prone work, but you work diligently into the night and get it done *just* in time for the big meeting.

When you present your work at the meeting, it only takes about five seconds before you hear the dreaded words: "Oh, this is great, but we also need to see it subdivided by region." None of your colleagues understand that what they are asking for is a complete "do-over." Again, it sounds so *simple* to them. The simplicity of their question (which is *indeed* simple) and their blissful ignorance of your spreadsheet world combine to create a perfect storm in which they don't see the difficulty of their last-minute changed requirements but instead focus on your seeming inability to magically conjure the new answers in a timely manner.

You, the unsung, toiling hero in this story, end up looking *bad*, and now your day is being hijacked to repeat the exercise that you performed the night before—an exercise that involved the sacrifice of sleep and your personal life. How did this *happen*, exactly? And once you eventually get the report "right," what is the reward for your success? You get to babysit that black hole of formulas for the rest of your time in that organization. You know...show up early to work every day to "turn the crank" on your portfolio of spreadsheets so that everyone else can start their days properly informed. Even your *successes* become things that you carry around with you like luggage.

Every time I tell this story, people come up to me and say something to the effect of "How did you know about that? I thought I was the only one experiencing that nightmare."

Well, if this story resonates with you, good news is at hand: You are far from alone. There are about 30 million people experiencing this worldwide. It's just that there's really no mechanism for you to meet each other today. Also, thanks to Power Pivot, your days of living that nightmare will soon be over.

A New and Better Reality

Here's a chart that illustrates the problem described above:

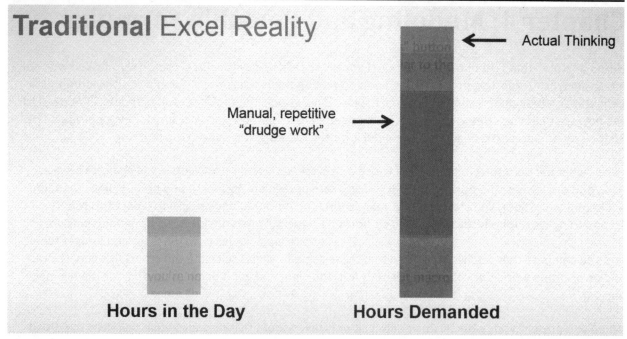

Figure 4.1

Now, remember: We are *huge* Excel fans! We are not denigrating the world's greatest data tool. Far from it. The fact is, you can solve nearly *any* data problem with traditional Excel. How many tools can claim that? (Answer: None of them can, which is why every other data tool on the planet prominently features Export to Excel as its third-most-common button, after OK and Cancel.) With Excel, generally speaking, you will eventually get an answer to even the most complex of questions. There is no denying the reality, however, that those complex reporting and analysis problems require a large proportion of repetitive, manual work.

Now imagine what you can do in Excel once the "manual/repetitive" walls come down. We say "imagine" because until those walls *do* come down, you cannot see what's on the other side! Turns out there's a *massive* world of possibility out there!

Once you add Power Pivot's modeling and calculation engine into your Excel workflow, the chart above starts to look like this:

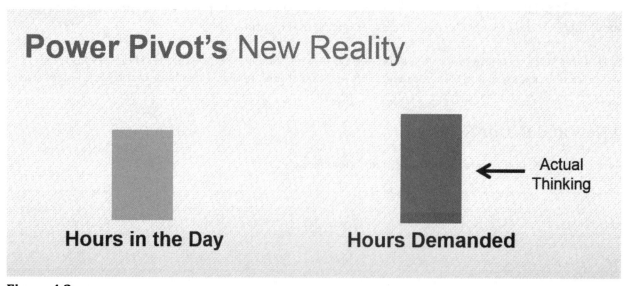

Figure 4.2

Yes, there will *always* be more work to do than hours in which to do it; this is pretty much true in any profession. But for a very long time our jobs as Excel pros have quietly been *much* harder than most people's jobs, in terms of hours demanded versus available. But that long era is coming to a close. Our jobs are now changing to resemble those of other "information workers"—only *slightly* more work to do than time in which to do it and lots of thinking about what the right thing should be and how to do it. Going and *building* that right thing becomes merely the last step, a natural extension of the thinking process. Practically speaking, what does this mean? It means a *bunch* of good things:

- The questions you were struggling to answer yesterday (due to lack of time) will all get answered. Period.

- Those questions will *stay* answered, without requiring you to babysit them.

- The "stretch questions" that you and/or your colleagues have been talking about but never gotten around to—"What we really need to be able to see is *X*"—will now *also* get answered.

- Variations on all of these questions—things that *used* to take hours or days to address, even after you'd answered their original flavors—will now be answered in seconds or minutes.

- On top of all this other productivity, you will have capacity to do more! You will start identifying, either on your own or collectively with colleagues, questions that you had *never* asked before. *Better* questions. Questions that were hidden behind the blinding "manual/repetitive" walls.

- The occurrences where you appear unable to do things will dwindle into distant memory. The days of being known as a Can-Do Data Monster? Those begin now.

- Along with all this comes the opportunity for greater compensation and brand-new career opportunities. And you will start to *enjoy* your job immensely. The next time a stranger asks you what you do for a living, you will smile and gush about how cool your job is rather than shyly try to hide that you spend your days tied to Excel.

What's "Portable Formulas" Got to Do With It?

With apologies to Tina Turner, portable formulas have got *everything* to do with it. The "manual/tedious" walls in traditional Excel exist primarily because, until now, Excel has lacked two particularly important capabilities:

- The ability to quickly integrate different data sources into a cohesive picture

- The ability to write formulas that keep working when you change the shape of a report in order to look at the data in a slightly different manner

Power Pivot adds both of these capabilities. First, you can now import multiple tables, quickly link them via relationships, and then "deploy" that data (from multiple sources!) into a single cohesive report/dashboard/analysis. Second, you can use measures (which were unfortunately renamed *calculated fields* in Excel 2013). Collectively, we refer to these two activities as *modeling*.

Measures *are* portable formulas. So whenever you see us say "maybe you should consider using a measure rather than a calc column in this case," it's primarily because we are encouraging you to write formulas that you can reuse in multiple circumstances. And when we say *reuse*, we *don't* mean copy/paste. We literally mean that you write a measure once and use it all over the place. Let's start with a simple example.

A Simple Example of Portability

In Chapter 3, we presented an example of a data table called Sales:

Date	Product	Quantity
1/1/2014	A	33
1/1/2014	B	39
1/1/2014	A	40
1/1/2014	B	36
1/2/2014	A	49
1/2/2014	B	30
1/2/2014	A	27
1/2/2014	B	38
1/3/2014	A	27
1/3/2014	B	41
1/3/2014	A	44
1/3/2014	B	28

Figure 4.3

That example also features a lookup table, Products, which is related to Sales:

Product	Total Quantity Sold
A	220
B	212

Figure 4.4

In that example, we wrote the calc column formula for Total Quantity Sold, the column on the right in the figure above. But we hinted, at the time, that most often, you should use a measure in such a case instead of a calc column. To see why we made that recommendation, create a Pivot, with Products[Product] in the Rows drop zone and Sum of [Total Quantity Sold] (the calc column in the Products table) in the Values drop zone:

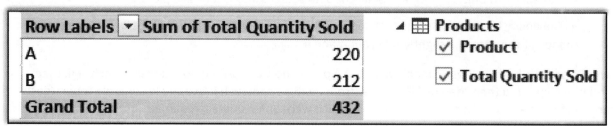

Row Labels	Sum of Total Quantity Sold
A	220
B	212
Grand Total	432

◢ ▦ **Products**
   ✓ **Product**
   ✓ **Total Quantity Sold**

Figure 4.5

There's nothing wrong there; the numbers are correct.

But now you put Sales[Date] in the Columns drop zone, and you get:

◢ ▦ **Products**
     ☑ **Product**
     ☑ **Total Quantity Sold**

◢ ▦ **Sales**
     ☑ **Date**

Sum of Total Quantity Sold	Column Labels ▼			
Row Labels ▼	**1/1/2014**	**1/2/2014**	**1/3/2014**	**Grand Total**
A	220	220	220	220
B	212	212	212	212
Grand Total	**432**	**432**	**432**	**432**

Figure 4.6

When it comes to the Products[Total Quantity Sold] column, you can get any value you want in your Pivot... as long as it's precisely the same fixed value you see in the calc column.

Like Excel formulas, calc columns do not "respond" to changes made in the Pivot. The calc column has 220 for Product A's [Total Quantity Sold] value, and that's what is going to display on the Pivot—everywhere and at all times.

If you just use the "raw" Sales[Quantity] column on the Pivot instead, you get the right results:

Sum of Quantity	Column Labels ▼			
Row Labels ▼	**1/1/2014**	**1/2/2014**	**1/3/2014**	**Grand Total**
A	73	76	71	220
B	75	68	69	212
Grand Total	**148**	**144**	**140**	**432**

Figure 4.7

But, hey, that's not even a measure yet! The point is, aggregate calculations like quantity sold don't *typically* "belong" in calc columns.

Next, you'll do a percentage-of-sales calculation—both as a calc column and as a measure. Here's the calc column:

[Pct of Sales] ▼	f_x =[Total Quantity Sold]/[Raw Sum of Sales]		
Product ▼	Total Quantity Sold ▼	Raw Sum of Sales ▼	Pct of Sales ▼
A	220	432	50.93 %
B	212	432	49.07 %

Figure 4.8

And here's what that calc column looks like when you put it on the Product/Date Pivot:

Sum of Pct of Sales	Column Labels			
Row Labels	1/1/2014	1/2/2014	1/3/2014	Grand Total
A	50.93 %	50.93 %	50.93 %	50.93 %
B	49.07 %	49.07 %	49.07 %	49.07 %
Grand Total	100.00 %	100.00 %	100.00 %	100.00 %

Figure 4.9

Once again, the Pivot is giving the same number over and over again, which is clearly incorrect.

So write the calc column as a measure instead:

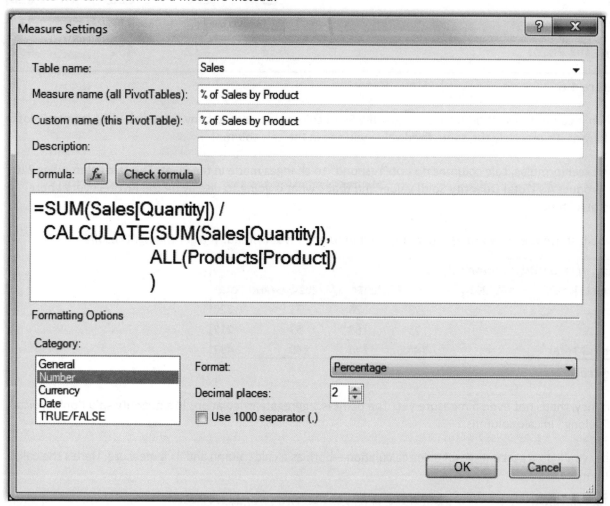

Figure 4.10

And then use *it* on the Pivot:

% of Sales by Product	Column Labels			
Row Labels	1/1/2014	1/2/2014	1/3/2014	Grand Total
A	49.32 %	52.78 %	50.71 %	50.93 %
B	50.68 %	47.22 %	49.29 %	49.07 %
Grand Total	100.00 %	100.00 %	100.00 %	100.00 %

Figure 4.11

Excellent! Now the numbers vary depending on the date, which is what you expect.

So, to recap: The calc column values are correct for exactly *one* "flavor" of report (when you are looking only at totals by product, without any additional detail, filtering, or grouping). But measures are "portable"—that is, they respond to different report layouts and still keep working. Think of them as being ready for any question you throw at them. Of course, this is a very simple example. Now let's have some *real* fun.

Integrating Data of Different "Grains"

Imagine a national convention of managerial accountants. Now imagine Microsoft getting on stage at this conference and unveiling a new product to solve the problem of matching a top-level "budget" data set with a detailed "actuals" data set. The entire audience would begin doing cartwheels and singing in unison. Every accounting department would be writing checks, on the spot, in exchange for the ability to finally solve this problem. The bad news is that Microsoft hasn't unveiled that particular product at that particular convention. The good news is that it doesn't matter: You are already in possession of such a miracle tool.

> **Note**
>
> This technique also briefly appears in *DAX Formulas for Power Pivot*. This is such a serious game changer that it's worth including here as well.
> In fact, we should write a 100-page book that promises to solve this problem. This technique would be first, followed by 70+ pages of blank paper, and people would still be thrilled with the book.

Say that you have a Sales table with 60,000 sales rows:

OrderDate	ProductKey	OrderQuantity	UnitPrice	ExtendedAmount
7/24/2004	528	1	4.99	4.99
10/15/2003	529	1	3.99	3.99
7/24/2004	537	1	35	35
11/1/2003	465	1	24.49	24.49
11/1/2003	217	1	34.99	34.99
9/24/2003	217	1	34.99	34.99
11/1/2003	528	1	4.99	4.99
9/24/2003	529	1	3.99	3.99
11/1/2003	537	1	35	35

Sales | Customers | Calendar | Promotions | Territories | Products | Budget | ProdSubCategories | Periods

Record: 1 of 60,398 ←——— More than 60k transactions

Figure 4.12

You also have a Budget table with 2,000 budget rows:

CalendarYear	MonthNum...	SalesTerrit...	Englis...	Budget...
2001	7	Australia	Mountain Bi...	71510
2001	7	Australia	Road Bikes	190248
2001	7	Canada	Mountain Bi...	4183
2001	7	Canada	Road Bikes	15429
2001	7	France	Mountain Bi...	7916
2001	7	France	Road Bikes	31825
2001	7	Germany	Mountain Bi...	4384
2001	7	Germany	Road Bikes	36068
2001	7	Northwest	Mountain Bi...	12058

Sales | Customers | Calendar | Promotions | Territories | Products | **Budget** | ProdSubCategories | Periods

Record: ◄ 1 of 1,877 ◄— Less than 2k rows

Figure 4.13

In this case, you want a single unified report. Power Pivot can help you easily solve a "budget versus ac-tuals" problem or any other problem where you have data sets of different granularities that you want to compare in a single report.

The crux of the current problem is that the Budget table only budgets down to the month level, whereas the Sales table goes down to the day level. To solve this problem, you create a separate Periods table that contains only months (no sales or budget data—just months) and assign a PeriodID (or MonthID) to each month:

PeriodID	Year	Month	EnglishMonthName
200107	2001	7	July
200108	2001	8	August
200109	2001	9	September
200110	2001	10	October
200111	2001	11	November
200112	2001	12	December
200201	2002	1	January
200202	2002	2	February
200203	2002	3	March

Sales | Customers | Calendar | Promotions | Territories | Products | Budget |

Record: ◄ 3 of 39 ◄— 39 Year-Month Rows

Figure 4.14

You then link that PeriodID column to the PeriodID column that already exists in the Budget table:

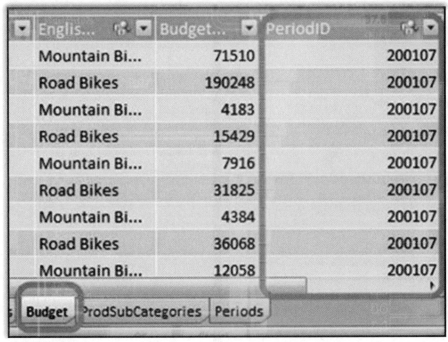

Figure 4.15

Then you create a new PeriodID column in the Sales table by using a formula:

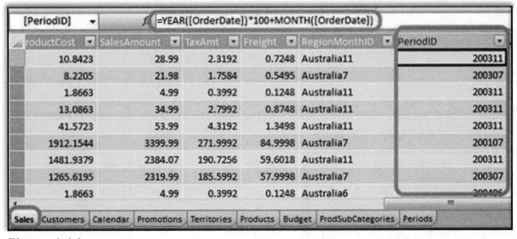

Figure 4.16

You end up with a three-table setup that looks like this:

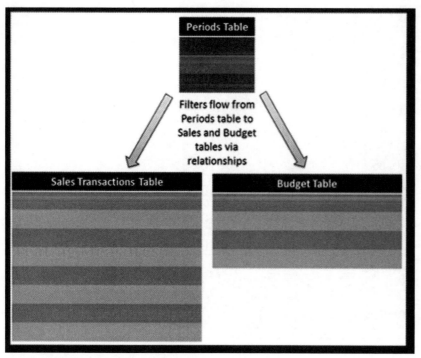

Figure 4.17

> **Note**
>
> To read the full (short) article and see the details of how to create the link between the two tables, see http://ppvt.pro/CIMABUDACT.

You can then use fields from that Periods table on slicers (or in the Rows or Columns drop zones) while using measures from both Sales and Budget in the same Pivot:

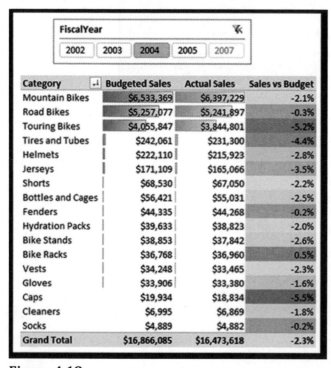

Category	Budgeted Sales	Actual Sales	Sales vs Budget
Mountain Bikes	$6,533,369	$6,397,229	-2.1%
Road Bikes	$5,257,077	$5,241,897	-0.3%
Touring Bikes	$4,055,847	$3,844,801	-5.2%
Tires and Tubes	$242,061	$231,300	-4.4%
Helmets	$222,110	$215,923	-2.8%
Jerseys	$171,109	$165,066	-3.5%
Shorts	$68,530	$67,050	-2.2%
Bottles and Cages	$56,421	$55,031	-2.5%
Fenders	$44,335	$44,268	-0.2%
Hydration Packs	$39,633	$38,823	-2.0%
Bike Stands	$38,853	$37,842	-2.6%
Bike Racks	$36,768	$36,960	0.5%
Vests	$34,248	$33,465	-2.3%
Gloves	$33,906	$33,380	-1.6%
Caps	$19,934	$18,834	-5.5%
Cleaners	$6,995	$6,869	-1.8%
Socks	$4,889	$4,882	-0.2%
Grand Total	$16,866,085	$16,473,618	-2.3%

Figure 4.18

And this, friends, is a very useful thing indeed!

Can You Add the PeriodID Column to Sales and Then Stop?

This is an important question to consider. Once you have a PeriodID column in both Sales and Budget, can you skip the creation of the Periods table and just move on? No, you can't—for two reasons.

First, you can't create a relationship between Sales and Budget because each PeriodID appears more than once in each table:

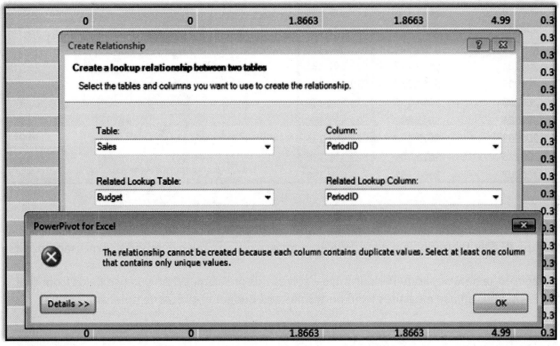

Figure 4.19

With relationships, the matching column needs to be unique (that is, no value can appear more than once) in at least one of the two tables. There's no need to really worry about why, but if you think about how VLOOKUP() works when you set the last argument to FALSE, you see that this is pretty similar.

Here's the second reason you can't skip the creation of the Periods table and just move on: Without a relationship, PeriodID from one table doesn't work with measures from the other.

Look what happens to Budget table measures if you use PeriodID from the Sales table:

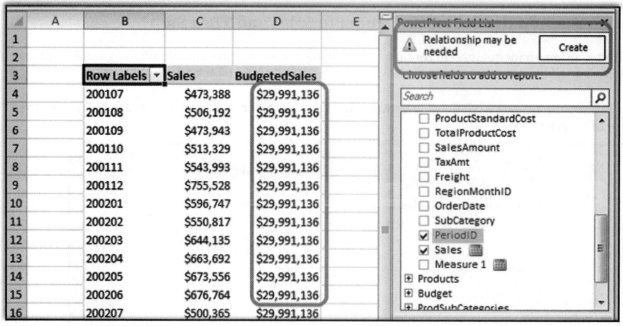

Figure 4.20

Yep, it's all busted: The budget measures are broken, and you get a relationship warning. If you use PeriodID from the Budget table, you get good budget numbers, but the sales numbers are messed up.

Using a third table—the new, separate Periods table—solves this problem. When you use fields from that table on your Pivot, you can use measures from both Sales and Budget at the same time, and nothing breaks.

So you use the Periods table as a master filter of sorts—a filter that can drive filters down into both Sales and Budget.

> **Note**
>
> I (Rob) debated using a bridge metaphor rather than the master filter idea to describe the role of the Periods table, but I think that's misleading. A bridge helps you travel from point A to point B: A –> Bridge –> B. This could imply "starting" on the Sales table and "traversing" the Periods table to get to the Budget table. But that's not how it works. Neither Sales nor Budget is "in charge" here, and neither one is a starting point. There are two separate paths here: Periods –> Sales and Periods –> Budget. The diagram in Figure 4.17 drives that home.
>
> You can think of the Periods table as being "in charge" here. This makes sense because you have to use it on the Pivot and can't use PeriodID from either Sales or Budget.

Extending the Rule to Fields Other Than PeriodID

You need to understand an important rule here: When you have separate data tables that cannot be combined into a single table (as is the case with Sales and Budget), you *cannot* use row/column/slicer fields from one table in a Pivot with measures from the other table. You *must* have a separate master filter table and use fields from *that* table in your Pivot.

So does this apply to fields other than PeriodID? You betcha. Guess what happens if you use a Product Subcategory or similar field from the Budget table in a Pivot that contains a Sales measure (or vice versa)? Yep, you get the same problem you got earlier, when you tried to use PeriodID from Sales:

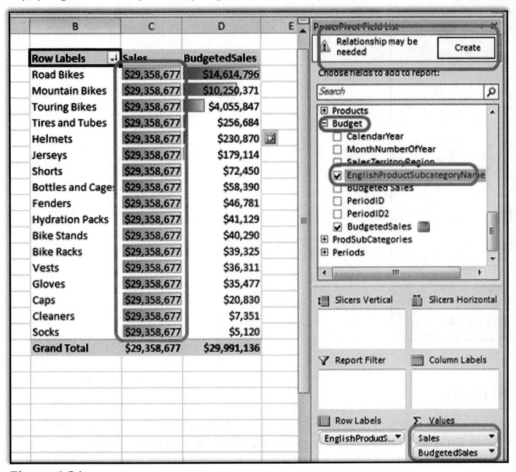

Figure 4.21

What's the solution? You need a separate master filter table for products! And this may be as simple as a single column:

Figure 4.22

Lather, Rinse, Repeat

Once you have measures from two different data tables, every row/column/slicer field you use requires a separate master filter table. Creating all these tables may sound tedious, but it's actually quite quick. To easily create such a table, you can just use a Pivot:

1. Put the ProductSubCat field from either Sales or Budget in the Rows drop zone.

2. Copy/paste that column of unique values into Power Pivot as a new table. (It's even better to get someone to add a new view or table to a database for you if that's available, but copy/paste works well otherwise.)

3. Create the relationships to Sales and Budget.

4. Use fields from the newly created master filter table in your Pivot. Done.

Using Master Filter Tables in Single-Table Situations

This might blow your mind, but even when you have only a single table of data, like Sales, it's often still quite useful to create separate master filter tables. Why? Because creating master filter tables gives you an opportunity to remove lots of columns from your "big" table.

Imagine a Sales table that, in addition to having columns like Quantity and Amount, also contains columns like CustomerID, CustomerGender, CustomerAge, CustomerAddress1, and CustomerAddress2. If you leave CustomerID in the Sales table but "move" all the other customer columns into a separate Customer table and then link the two tables by CustomerID, you can reduce the number of columns in your Sales table by a significant number. Doing this could shrink your files dramatically—and speed them up. (See the post http://www.powerpivotpro.com/2011/08/less-columns-more-rows-more-speed/ for an example.)

A Mystifying and Awesome Solution for the Many-to-Many Problem

When I (Rob) was at a SharePoint conference, one night I went to Ask the Experts. If you're a speaker at the conference, they put a tacky t-shirt on you that says EXPERT on it, and then they send waves of people to ask you questions. In this case, they came asking about Reporting Services—which I know nothing about. I tried to divert them to a real Reporting Services expert, but he was busy with someone else (who was probably asking Power Pivot questions).

At some point, though, I started to get Power Pivot questions. One guy asked me this: "We have a lot of many-to-many relationships in our business. If we adopt Power Pivot, can Excel pros handle many-to-many?" So I answered honestly and humbly: "No. It's too complex to grasp for most...even I dread it...and it makes your formulas too complex. M2M is something I encourage people to avoid. It is not the simple part of Power Pivot."

What Is the Dreaded Many-to-Many Problem?

Here's an example of the many-to-many problem:

Customer	LikesColor		Product	Color	Price	
Jim	Blue		1	Blue	$	741
Jim	Red		2	Red	$	503
Jim	Yellow		3	Yellow	$	558
Pat	Green		4	Green	$	969
Pat	Orange		5	Orange	$	989
Alice	Blue		6	Blue	$	956
Alice	Green		7	Red	$	835
Alice	Orange		8	Yellow	$	894
			9	Green	$	538
			10	Orange	$	532

Figure 4.23

In this example, each customer likes more than one color, and there is more than one product of each color. If you sell each customer all of the products from all of the colors that they like, how much money do you make?

If you try to relate these tables to each other in Power Pivot, using Color as the link, you get an error:

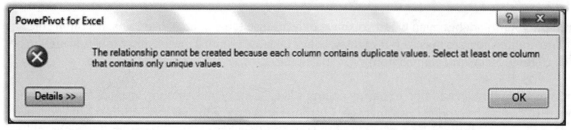

Figure 4.24

You can see that this is a bad case of the many-to-manies. Your prognosis is not good. However, you *can* solve this problem by using DAX measures and a few extra steps, but the DAX ends up being kinda scary.

Greetings, Gerhard Brueckl!

When I got home from the SharePoint conference, I continued thinking about this problem and began to wonder if the state of the art had advanced while I'd been busy avoiding the issue. So off I went to Google, which gave me this article
(http://ppvt.pro/GERHARD1):

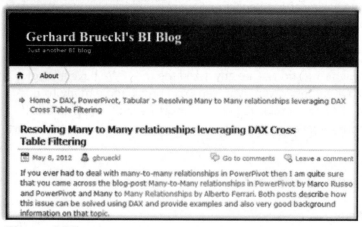

Figure 4.25

Gerhard is a thinker. He did some serious sleuthing, some reading of Jeffery Wang's blog (see http://mdxdax.blogspot.com/2011/03/logic-behind-magic-of-dax-cross-table.html), some thinking, and some testing. And then probably some more thinking.

Gerhard offers up a solution to the many-to-many problem that's brilliant—so brilliant that I still don't completely understand how or why it works. But his solution is so simple to use that it's one of those patterns I can happily reuse many times over. Because for now it's just a pattern to me rather than something I understand at the atomic level, I make it very simple here. Please read Gerhard's article if you want to understand more deeply. And if I've botched something here, please let me know.

Gerhard's Solution to the Many-to-Many Problem

To begin addressing this problem, you need two new tables, JustColors and JustCustomers. They should both be single-column tables that contain only the unique values from the column you'd like to relate on (Color) and from the column you want to use in the Rows drop zone of your Pivot (Customer):

Figure 4.26

Next, you need to set up relationships so that your model looks like this:

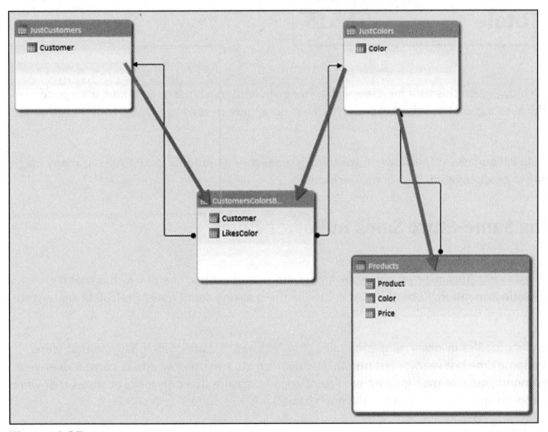

Figure 4.27

> **Note**
>
> The arrows in this figure indicate the direction that filters flow, but in this case, it's harder than usual to understand why the filter flows actually help.

Here's the magic:

```
[Potential Sales] =
CALCULATE(SUM(Products[Price]),
          CustomersColorsBridge
          )
```

You just do a simple CALCULATE() over a SUM() and then list the name of the bridge table. Is this really it? Well, it works:

Customer ▼	Potential Sales
Alice	$4,725
Jim	$4,487
Pat	$3,028
Grand Total	$7,515

Figure 4.28

Listen, I've been blogging on this stuff for a few years. I've even written a book on it. I think it's a good book. Others think it's a good book. But what Gerhard has done here never, *ever*, would have occurred to me.

None of us should kid ourselves: This Power Pivot thing is a deep, deep product, and it still has many magical things lurking to be discovered. Well done, Gerhard!

Calculating Same-Store Sales in Power Pivot

I (Rob) love the Power Pivot forum over at MrExcel (http://www.mrexcel.com/forum/powerpivot-questions/) for many reasons, one of which is that it gives me useful, real-world inspiration. Recently, I saw someone there asking about how to calculate same-store sales.

Simply put, same-store sales involves comparing sales of *only* stores that are open today and that were also open at the same time last year (or last month, last quarter, etc.). In other words, it's a year-over-year (or month-over-month, quarter-over-quarter, etc.) comparison measure that only looks at stores that were open last year (month, quarter, etc.) and are still open today.

Creating a Stores Table

To begin tackling the same-store sales calculation, you should import or create a Stores table. It doesn't have to be fancy—and can even be a single column, like this:

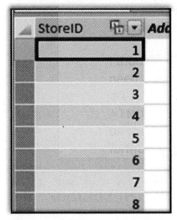

Figure 4.29

After you find or create this table, you relate it to your Sales table.

The "Raw" Formulas

Here are the measures you use to calculate the raw (unfiltered, all-stores) sales:

```
[Units Sold] = SUM(Sales[QtySold])

[Units Sold Last Year] =
CALCULATE([Units Sold],SAMEPERIODLASTYEAR(Calendar[Date]))
```

> **Note**
>
> You could calculate raw sales in *many* different ways, including using the greatest formula in the world (see http://ppvt.pro/GFITW1).

```
[Raw Growth vs last Year] =
IF([Units Sold Last Year]=0,BLANK(),
    ([Units Sold]-[Units Sold Last Year])/[Units Sold Last Year]
)
```

Getting a Transaction Count

One way to determine whether a store was open last year is to determine whether it had any transactions. This is slightly more reliable than testing for [Units Sold] > 0 because in rare cases, you might have returns (refunds/exchanges) that offset all the products you sold. If the following measure returns 0 or BLANK for a store, you can assume that the store was not open last year:

```
[Transactions] =
COUNTROWS(Sales)

[Transactions Last Year] =
CALCULATE([Transactions],SAMEPERIODLASTYEAR(Calendar[Date]))
```

There are alternatives, of course, but this is a great place to start.

Filtering Sales

You need to filter sales to stores that were open before and that remain open today. If both `[Transactions] > 0` *and* `[Transaction Last Year] > 0` for a particular store, you know this is a store that you want to count. So you use that to generate new versions of `Current Sales` and `Sales Last Yr`:

```
[Current Sales - Stores Active Today and Last Yr] =
CALCULATE([Units Sold],
    FILTER(Stores,
        [Transactions Year Ago]>0 && [Transactions] >0
    )
)

[Sales Last Yr - Stores Active Today and Last Year] =
CALCULATE([Units Sold Last Year],
    FILTER(Stores,
        [Transactions Year Ago]>0 && [Transactions] >0
    )
)
```

Make sense? You filter the Stores table to only include rows (stores) for which both current transactions and last year's transactions are greater than 0.

Implementing the Final Measure

The next step is really straightforward:

```
[Same Store Sales vs Last Yr] =
([Current Sales - Stores Active Today and Last Yr]
  - [Sales Last Yr - Stores Active Today and Last Year]
)
/[Sales Last Yr - Stores Active Today and Last Year]
```

You can see here that growth looks much worse when you compare same-store sales than it does when you look at year-over-year sales:

Row Labels	Units Sold	Units Sold Last Year	Raw Growth vs Last Yr	Same Store Sales vs Last Yr
2001				
Apples	400			
Oranges	425			
Peaches	496			
Pears	426			
2002				
Apples	458	400	14.5%	0.5%
Oranges	471	425	10.8%	0.0%
Peaches	391	496	-21.2%	-31.0%
Pears	454	426	6.6%	-3.8%
2003				
Apples	425	458	-7.2%	-12.0%
Oranges	484	471	2.8%	-4.0%
Peaches	504	391	28.9%	18.7%
Pears	482	454	6.2%	1.5%

Figure 4.30

The raw growth and same-store growth measures tell very different stories. In this case, that's due to the way I (Rob) manufactured data for this example (using functions like RANDBETWEEN ()). In the real world, of course, this type of thing can happen when you open a bunch of new stores—which skews your overall numbers higher. In that case, same-store sales can show you that per-store sales have been falling, a fact that is masked by the broader totals.

Same-Store Sales Continued: Using Store Open/Close Dates

You've just learned how to calculate same-store sales. What if you want to use precise open/close dates for your stores rather than simply indicate whether there were sales? For example, say that a store must be open for at least a year before it is included in a same-store sales total.

Remember that in the preceding trick, if a store had sales last year and this year, you included it in the same-store sales calculation. But if you have columns in your data indicating the date a store opened (and when it closed), it's a very rational thing to want to use that instead.

To handle this situation, you can invent some new columns for your Stores table:

StoreID	OpenDate	CloseDate
1	6/30/2001	2/28/2009
2	1/16/2002	9/16/2009
3	8/24/2002	4/24/2010
4	5/11/2003	1/9/2011
5	2/15/2004	10/16/2011
6	1/10/2005	9/10/2012
7	1/25/2006	9/25/2013
8	3/31/2007	11/29/2014
9	6/3/2008	2/2/2016
10	1/1/2001	9/1/2008
11	6/30/2001	2/28/2009

Figure 4.31

You can use these (fictional) store open and close dates to drive your Power Pivot same-store sales calculation.

Creating the Measures

You need to create a measure to calculate when a store opened, and you add it to the Stores table:

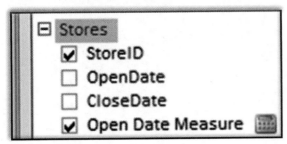

Figure 4.32

The formula is quite straightforward:

```
[Open Date Measure] =
LASTDATE(Stores[OpenDate])
```

> **Note**
>
> You could use `FIRSTDATE()` just as easily as `LASTDATE()`, since this measure only makes sense in the context of a single store. And in that case, the two functions will return the same date, since you'll only have one row of the Stores table in that context.

`LASTDATE()` does what you need it to do when you put `StoreID` in the Rows drop zone:

Store ID	Open Date Measure
1	6/30/2001 0:00
2	1/16/2002 0:00
3	8/24/2002 0:00
4	5/11/2003 0:00
5	2/15/2004 0:00
6	1/10/2005 0:00
7	1/25/2006 0:00
8	3/31/2007 0:00
9	6/3/2008 0:00
10	1/1/2001 0:00
11	6/30/2001 0:00
12	1/16/2002 0:00

Figure 4.33

Then you create a measure that calculates how many days a store has been open:

```
[Store Age at Period Start] =
INT(FIRSTDATE(Calendar[Date])-[Open Date Measure])
```

> **Note**
>
> You wrap the `INT()` function around `FIRSTDATE()` because otherwise Excel will try to format the result as a date rather than as an integer.

For this to make sense, you need to have something from the Calendar table on the Pivot, so for now, here's Year Month on a slicer:

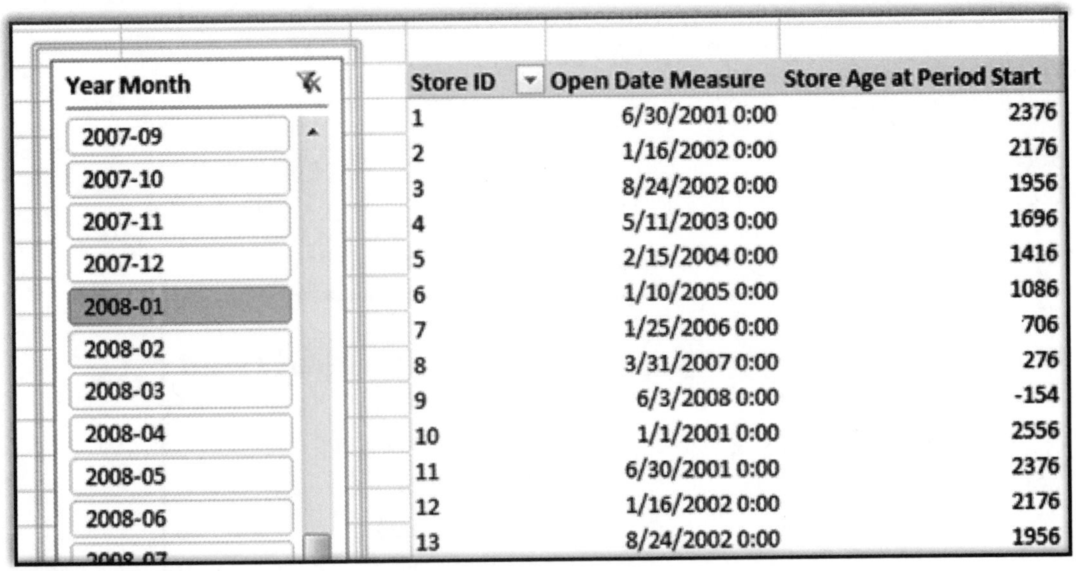

Store ID	Open Date Measure	Store Age at Period Start
1	6/30/2001 0:00	2376
2	1/16/2002 0:00	2176
3	8/24/2002 0:00	1956
4	5/11/2003 0:00	1696
5	2/15/2004 0:00	1416
6	1/10/2005 0:00	1086
7	1/25/2006 0:00	706
8	3/31/2007 0:00	276
9	6/3/2008 0:00	-154
10	1/1/2001 0:00	2556
11	6/30/2001 0:00	2376
12	1/16/2002 0:00	2176
13	8/24/2002 0:00	1956

Figure 4.34

Here you can see that in January 2008 (2008-01 on the slicer), store 1 had been open 2376 days, and store 9 had an age of –154, meaning that it was still 154 days away from opening.

Now, to determine whether the store was open last year at this time, you add another measure:

```
[Was Store Open Last Year] =
IF([Store Age at Period Start]>365,1,0)
```

In this figure, the two circled zeros indicate stores that were *not* open a year prior to August 2008:

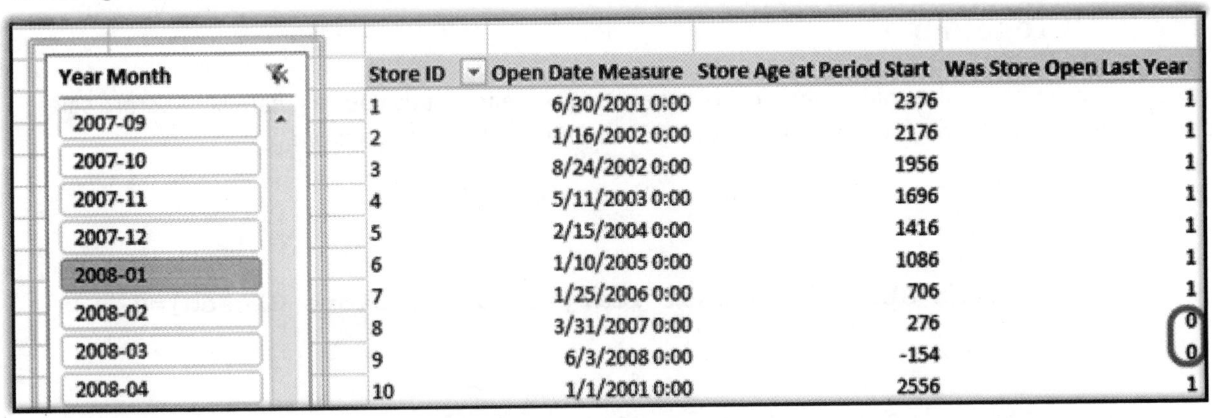

Store ID	Open Date Measure	Store Age at Period Start	Was Store Open Last Year
1	6/30/2001 0:00	2376	1
2	1/16/2002 0:00	2176	1
3	8/24/2002 0:00	1956	1
4	5/11/2003 0:00	1696	1
5	2/15/2004 0:00	1416	1
6	1/10/2005 0:00	1086	1
7	1/25/2006 0:00	706	1
8	3/31/2007 0:00	276	0
9	6/3/2008 0:00	-154	0
10	1/1/2001 0:00	2556	1

Figure 4.35

> **Note**
>
> In this measure, it might be safer to use 366 or 367 rather than 365 to account for leap years and those rare "off by one" problems.
>
> If you require that a store be open for a full 15 months, and not merely open 12 months ago, you can change that number to be 365+92 or something similar.

Calculating the Store Close Date

Now you add two more measures to deal with the close date:

```
[Close Date Measure] =
LASTDATE(Stores[CloseDate])

[Is Store Closed] =
IF(LASTDATE(Calendar[Date])>=[Close Date Measure],1,0)
```

You can see here that in July 2009, three of the fictional stores had closed:

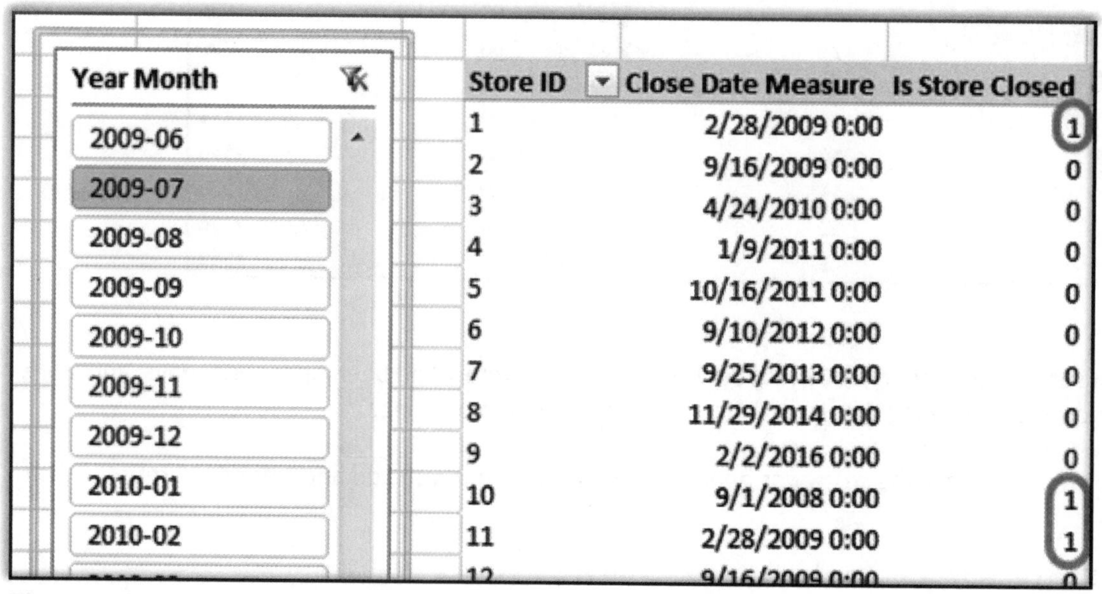

Year Month	Store ID	Close Date Measure	Is Store Closed
2009-06	1	2/28/2009 0:00	1
2009-07	2	9/16/2009 0:00	0
2009-08	3	4/24/2010 0:00	0
2009-09	4	1/9/2011 0:00	0
2009-10	5	10/16/2011 0:00	0
2009-11	6	9/10/2012 0:00	0
2009-12	7	9/25/2013 0:00	0
2010-01	8	11/29/2014 0:00	0
2010-02	9	2/2/2016 0:00	0
	10	9/1/2008 0:00	1
	11	2/28/2009 0:00	1
	12	9/16/2009 0:00	0

Figure 4.36

Tying It All Together

Now you can calculate "sales that count" for this year and last year, just as you calculate same-store sales in general, but this time you use a different set of tests in the FILTER() function:

```
[Current Sales - Respect Open Close Dates] =
CALCULATE([Units Sold],
    FILTER(Stores,
        [Was Store Open Last Year]=1 && [Is Store Closed]=0
    )
)

[Same Store Sales Last Yr - Respect Open Close Dates] =
CALCULATE([Units Sold Last Yr],
    FILTER(Stores,
        [Was Store Open Last Year]=1 && [Is Store Closed]=0
    )
)
```

Only the boldfaced portions here differ from the original method used in the preceding trick.

Now you use a simple "(New – Old) / Old" measure:

```
[Same Store Sales vs Last Yr - Respect Open Close Dates] =
(
    [Current Sales - Respect Open Close Dates]-
    [Same Store Sales Last Yr - Respect Open Close Dates]
) /
[Same Store Sales Last Yr - Respect Open Close Dates]
```

And you test it in a new Pivot that just has Year-Month in the Rows drop zone:

Year - Month	Same Store Sales vs Last Yr - Respect Open Close Dates
2002-02	-10.0%
2002-03	-78.9%
2002-04	20.0%
2002-05	0.0%
2002-06	-61.9%
2002-07	-42.0%
2002-08	5.1%
2002-09	28.1%
2002-10	63.6%
2002-11	3.4%
2002-12	-55.3%
2003-01	-68.9%
2003-02	88.0%

Figure 4.37

Hey That's a *Long* Measure Name!

Yes, `Same Store Sales vs Last Yr - Respect Open Close Dates` certainly is a long measure name. We prefer to give measures *very* descriptive names so that in six months, we know what a measure actually *does*. But these longs names make Pivots unwieldy to look at.

No worries. You can change a measure header in a Pivot by just selecting its cell in the Pivot and typing over it:

Year - Month	Same Store Sales
2002-02	-10.0%
2002-03	-78.9%
2002-04	20.0%
2002-05	0.0%
2002-06	-61.9%
2002-07	-42.0%
2002-08	5.1%

Figure 4.38

The field list changes to reflect your change, but only in one place:

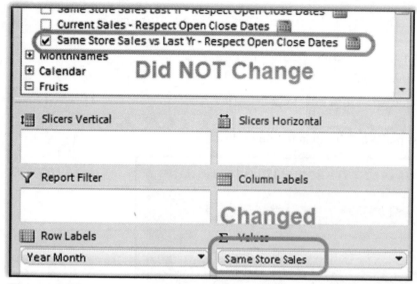

Figure 4.39

The custom measure name appears in the drop zone but not in the measure list. Genius! WE LOVE THIS. We can quickly tell what's what this way. We could write pages on how much we like this, but we'll skip that and just leave it at "We really think this was a great design decision."

One Advantage of the "Did We Have Sales?" Approach

Earlier in this chapter, if a store was open last year but didn't even have a department that sold fruit until last month, the open/close date method would tell you that the store should "count" when it really shouldn't. The "Did we have sales?" method, however, automatically accounts for this, on a per-product basis. That's pretty cool.

Of course, if certain products don't sell very often even when they *are* offered for sale, the "Did we have sales?" method can again be misleading because sometimes not selling something does *not* mean that you weren't *trying* to sell something.

Every business situation is different, and it's therefore good to have many different methodologies to choose from. There is no "one size fits all"; you have to choose the alternative that works best for you, given the trade-offs.

Campaign Analysis: Seasonally Adjusted Measures

An age-old problem is determining what caused a change. It's easy to address this problem with Power Pivot. There isn't much complexity to this trick, and yet it's much more useful and reusable than anything you can do with Excel alone.

Let's say you work for the fictional AdventureWorks bicycle company. For the past few weeks, you've been running a special promotion: "Buy a Bike, Get a Free Water Bottle." So far, it's looking pretty successful, as evidenced by the circled region on this chart:

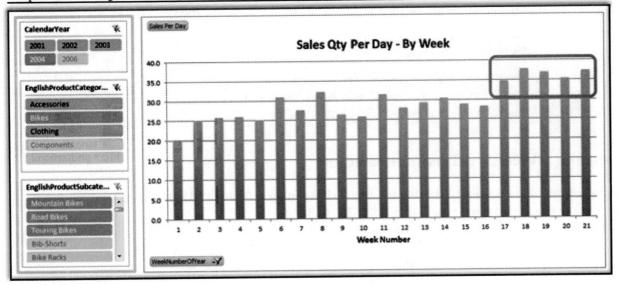

Figure 4.40

But, hey, those giveaway water bottles are expensive and cut into your profits. So if you want to be truly responsible, you need to make sure there aren't other variables driving this bump instead.

The most common source of "noise" in sales like this is normal seasonal fluctuation. Look at weeks 17 thru 21 in Figure 4.40. Are those normally hot weeks for bike sales every year, whether there are promotions running or not? This trick shows just one technique for getting a baseline from prior years. There are many others, but this should get you thinking.

Creating a Baseline PivotTable

The chart above looks at bike sales in 2004. To get a baseline, you should look at the three prior years:

Week Number	Sales Per Day
1	6.7
2	7.0
3	7.6
4	6.9
5	6.7
6	8.6
7	8.1
8	7.6
9	7.4
10	8.4
11	7.1
12	7.9
13	6.9
14	7.8
15	7.8
16	9.3
17	7.8

CalendarYear
2001 2002 2003
2004 2006

EnglishProductCategoryN...
Accessories
Bikes
Clothing
Components

Figure 4.41

Here you see that the numbers are smaller in prior years than they are in 2004.

> **Note**
>
> The data from a sample data set like AdventureWorks isn't always re-
> alistic. But the technique here is the important thing, not whether the
> sample data set is realistic.

Creating a Weekly Adjustment Factor

At the bottom of the baseline Pivot (the top of which is shown in Figure 4.41), the grand total represents
the average sales per day over the entire 2001–2003 period:

49	18.1
50	18.0
51	17.5
52	16.1
53	19.6
Grand Total	10.3

Figure 4.42

The ratio of a given week's sales per day versus that grand total is an excellent indicator of how active that
week of the year tends to be.

You can calculate the seasonal adjustment ratio for each week as one-time fixed values, and you can use
normal Excel formulas to do it (as opposed to creating measures):

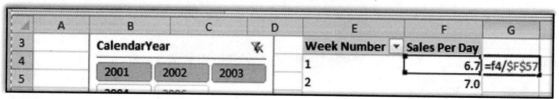

Figure 4.43

Here F57 is a fixed reference to the grand total cell. If you fill that formula down for all weeks, you get this:

Week Number ▾	Sales Per Day	Seasonal Adj Factor
1	6.7	0.646099291
2	7.0	0.678404255
3	7.6	0.733784195
4	6.9	0.664559271
5	6.7	0.650714286
6	8.6	0.830699088
7	8.1	0.789164134
8	7.6	0.733784195
9	7.4	0.713016717
10	8.4	0.809931611
11	7.1	0.69224924
12	7.9	0.768396657
13	6.9	0.671481763

Figure 4.44

Note

It pays to think about the makeup of your reference Pivot. What measure should you use? For instance, if the price you charge for your products fluctuates a lot for random reasons (for example, if you sell farm produce, which is subject to worldwide random price changes), then a pure dollar figure measure may not be a clean baseline. A Qty per Day measure would be better in this situation.

Similarly, if your company acquired another company in June 2003, and its product line merged into yours in that month, effectively doubling your sales, that would also skew your baseline higher for the second half of the year. In this case, the Qty per Day measure would *not* be immune to that problem. So here you might prefer to slice the baseline Pivot to *only* include the original company's product line.

The point is that it takes business-specific expertise to define your cleanest baseline.

Importing the Adjustment Factors into the Power Pivot Model

Once you have the adjustment factors, you need to get them into Power Pivot so you can apply them all over the place. Using Copy and Paste Values gets you this two-column table in Excel:

Week Number	Seasonal Adj Factor
1	0.646099291
2	0.678404255
3	0.733784195
4	0.664559271
5	0.650714286
6	0.830699088
7	0.789164134
8	0.733784195
9	0.713016717
10	0.809931611
11	0.69224924

Figure 4.45

From here, you can copy and paste the table into the Power Pivot window as a brand-new table:

Week Number	Seasonal Adj Factor
1	0.646099290780142
2	0.678404255319149
3	0.733784194528875
4	0.664559270516717
5	0.650714285714286
6	0.830699088145897
7	0.789164133738602
8	0.733784194528875
9	0.713016717325228
10	0.809931610942249
11	0.692249240121581
12	0.768396656534954

Figure 4.46

Relating the Table to the Rest of the Model

The next step is to create a relationship. In this particular model, you need to connect the new table to the existing date table, since that's the only place you have a Week Number column in the model:

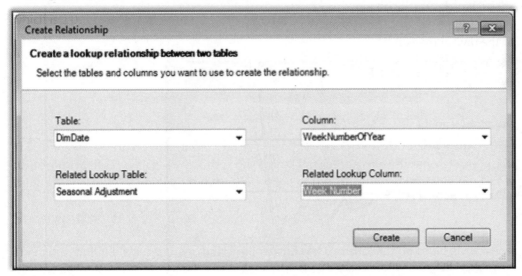

Figure 4.47

You don't want to put fields from this new Seasonal Adjustment table on any of your Pivots, and this means the table will never get filtered by anything (slicers, row fields, etc.). That's a problem because ultimately you will need filtering by week in order to make your measures work. So your need to get those values added to the date table because date table fields *will* be on your Pivots. A little =RELATED() is in order:

CalendarSemester	FiscalQuarter	FiscalYear	FiscalSemester	Seasonal Adj Factor
2003	2	1	2004	1	0.881464032421479
2003	2	1	2004	1	0.881464032421479
2003	2	1	2004	1	0.881464032421479
2003	2	1	2004	1	0.881464032421479
2003	2	1	2004	1	0.881464032421479
2003	2	1	2004	1	0.922998986828774
2003	2	1	2004	1	0.922998986828774
2003	2	1	2004	1	0.922998986828774
2003	2	1	2004	1	0.922998986828774
2003	2	1	2004	1	0.922998986828774

fx =RELATED('Seasonal Adjustment'[Seasonal Adj Factor])

Figure 4.48

Creating a Seasonal Adjustment Divisor Measure

Basically, you want a measure that, in the context of a specific week of the year, returns the corresponding adjustment factor from the date table. Once you have the measure, you can divide other measures by that measure to create seasonally adjusted versions.

Here's the formula for the divisor measure:

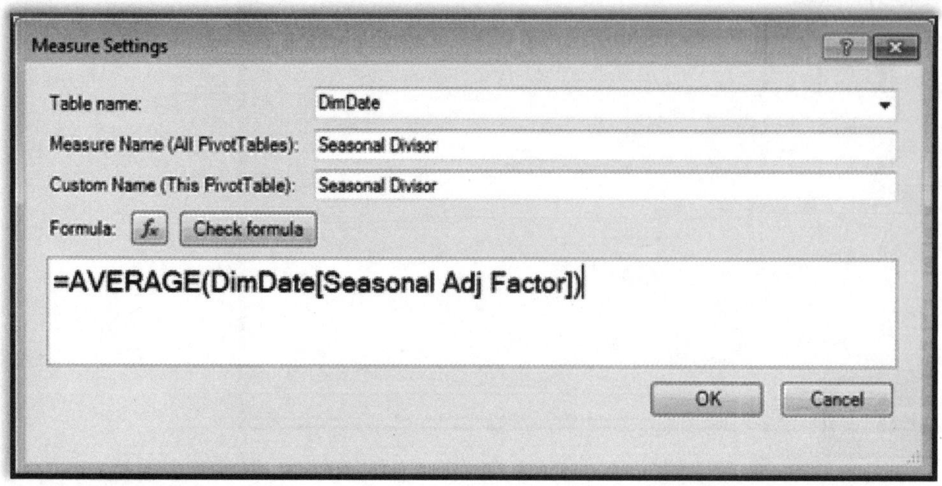

Figure 4.49

Were you expecting something more complex? Yeah, I (Rob) was, too. And to be fair, in a real-world example I am working on, it is a bit more complicated, but that has more to do with the data than with the basic approach.

To verify that the measure works, you can compare it side-by-side with the original seasonal table you built in Excel:

Week Number	Sales Per Day	Seasonal Divisor		Week Number	Seasonal Adj Factor
1	6.7	0.646099291		1	0.646099291
2	7.0	0.678404255		2	0.678404255
3	7.6	0.733784195		3	0.733784195
4	6.9	0.664559271		4	0.664559271
5	6.7	0.650714286		5	0.650714286
6	8.6	0.830699088		6	0.830699088
7	8.1	0.789164134		7	0.789164134
8	7.6	0.733784195		8	0.733784195
9	7.4	0.713016717		9	0.713016717
10	8.4	0.809931611		10	0.809931611
11	7.1	0.69224924		11	0.69224924

Figure 4.50

Bingo—a perfect match. Of course, given that you're just looking at single-week numbers here, you didn't have to use AVERAGE(). You could instead use MIN(), MAX(), or SUM() to get the same results. But AVERAGE() really does make a big difference at higher levels, like when you add month to the Pivot:

Week Number ▾	Sales Per Day	Seasonal Divisor
⊟ April	8.4	0.813508232
14	7.7	0.754551672
15	7.8	0.754551672
16	9.3	0.899924012
17	7.8	0.754551672
18	9.7	0.969148936
⊟ August	10.1	0.98793395
31	6.7	0.881464032
32	10.1	0.982993921
33	9.6	0.925537234
34	10.6	1.024528875
35	11.4	1.070678825
36	18.0	0.936843972
⊟ December	17.5	1.705116569
48	5.0	1.296813576
49	17.9	1.75831307

Figure 4.51

So you can see that the month of April, for instance, typically moves about 81% as much product as the average month. Neat. And December, unsurprisingly, clocks in at 170% as much volume as the average month. (Hey, the AdventureWorks sample database *did* get that one right.)

Now you've finished the prep and can get to the payoff—the creation of seasonally adjusted versions of the core measures.

Seasonally Adjusted Sales Measures

All the work you've just done may seem like quite an investment, but trust us, it has taken you longer to read these instructions than it will take you to actually build the model; you'll spend 10 minutes, tops.

No matter what, though, the next step is as quick and as painless as it gets. Just start dividing existing measures by the divisor measure! For instance, at the beginning of this trick, you were using the `Qty per Day` measure. Here's the seasonally adjusted version:

Measure Settings

Table name:	FactInternetSales
Measure Name (All PivotTables):	Sales per Day - Season Adj
Custom Name (This PivotTable):	Sales per Day - Season Adj

Formula: *fx* Check formula

`=[Sales Per Day] / [Seasonal Divisor]`

OK Cancel

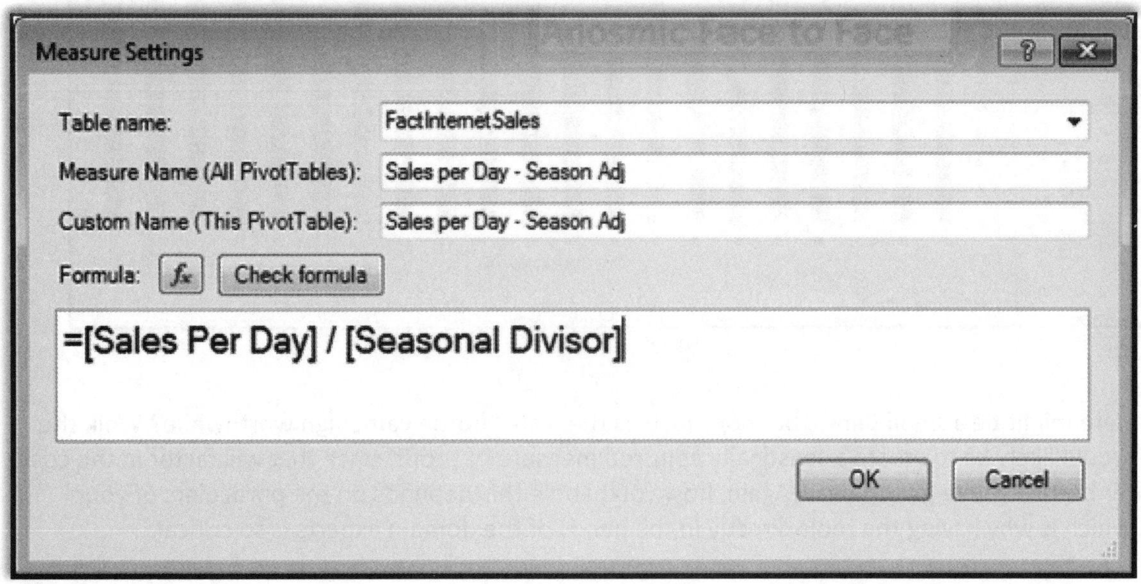

Figure 4.52

> **Note**
>
> How did we make the text in the measure dialog bigger? Well, it's as simple as holding down the Ctrl key and rolling the mouse wheel. Thanks to Alberto Ferrari (see http://ppvt.pro/MEASURE45) for this great tip.

It's time to test it. Go back to the original chart and add this seasonally adjusted measure side-by-side with the original measure:

Figure 4.53

When the chart is adjusted for seasonal trends, you see that sales activity was actually even higher...but then again, it was higher in all the other weeks on the chart, too.

In fact, after you adjust for seasonality, the "bump" from the promo campaign doesn't seem as large as it did before. Here's the chart again, this time with just the seasonally adjusted measure:

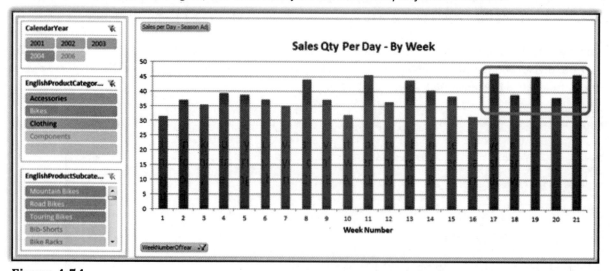

Figure 4.54

So yeah, there might be a small bump, but not much. Is the water bottle campaign worthwhile? Well, the next step would likely be to create a seasonally adjusted measure of profit, since that will factor in the cost of the water bottles you're giving away. Again, how you handle this depends on the particulars of your business, which is why having the tools directly in the hands of the domain experts is so critical.

Using Seasonally Adjusted Measures Elsewhere

Once you have a seasonal divisor measure, you can quickly create seasonally adjusted versions of as many measures as you need. One quick division, and you're done.

Also, if you ever want to adjust your definition of seasonality, all you have to do is change the formula for that one divisor measure, or the table that underlies it, and *all* of your seasonally adjusted measures respond accordingly. You don't get that kind of "one-touch update" in traditional Excel.

Finally, because you are creating measures rather than calculations that are fixed to the layout of a given sheet, you can easily reuse all your work in many different contexts: You can analyze by individual products or by entire categories, by city or by country, on a daily or monthly level....You get the idea.

Here are two more possibilities to get you imagination going:

- Define the Seasonal Adjustment table in SQL. Why not move the whole process, and the underlying logic, into SQL? That way, you'll get updated seasonality numbers over time, and you can probably get more sophisticated logic into the system. Sure, you'll need help from your DBA, unless you *are* the DBA. Cooperation with your DBA team is a prime attribute of an optimal Power Pivot system.

- Differentiate by other fields. Maybe accessories have a different seasonality pattern than bikes. And maybe the southwest region of the country doesn't show as much drop-off in January as the northeast does. You can absolutely factor such things into your divisor measure. You could even try to do it 100% dynamically, in the measure, without pre-calculating an adjustment table.

A/B Campaign Analysis with Start and End Date Slicers

You've just leaned a trick about promotional campaign analysis that involves seasonal trends. Now let's look at another flavor of campaign analysis: comparing results when a campaign is active versus when it was not. Sometimes this is referred to as *A/B testing*.

The results of A/B testing can look like this:

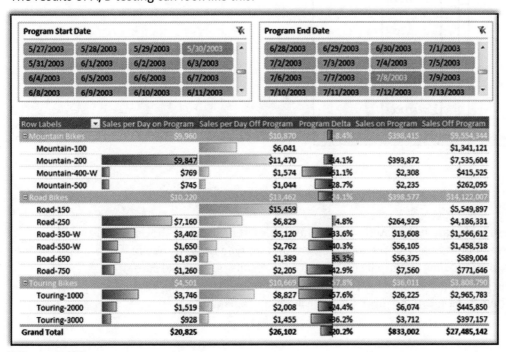

Figure 4.55

This report has two date slicers: one where you select the start date of a campaign, and another where you select the end date. This enables you to see sales results "on program," which means the sales that occurred between the start date and end date (inclusive) versus the sales results "off program," which means sales on all other dates.

Specifically, the report shows sales per day for on versus off program and then the percentage change in sales per day when on program versus off (labeled Program Delta above). (Because these programs run for short periods of time, sales per day is a much more "apples to apples" comparison than is total sales.)

> **Note**
>
> A quick glance at Program Delta shows that a really awful program ran from 5/20/03 to 7/8/03. That's what you get when you use AdventureWorks as the data set.

Creating Date Slicers and Date Measures

You need two single-column tables of dates to populate the start and end date slicers:

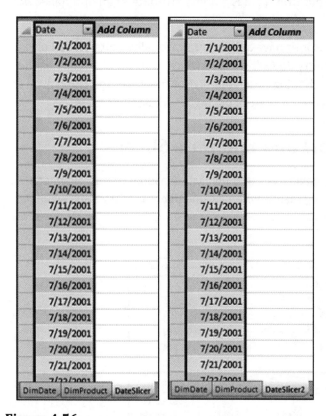

Figure 4.56

> **Note**
>
> These tables are *not* related to *any* other tables in the model. They stand alone—intentionally. *Make sure they are of data type Date!* If they're not, the following steps will give you strange results. Also, make sure none of the date columns in your model have time components lurking in them. (See http://ppvt.pro/DATETIME for an explanation.)

Next, you need to define a measure on each of these two tables. You use the same formula but name one Start Date and the other End Date and assign each one to a different table:

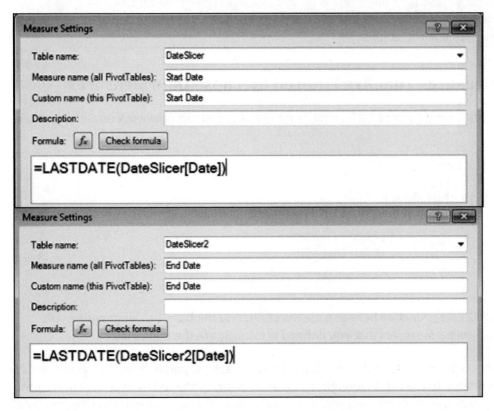

Figure 4.57

> **Note**
>
> The technique shown here is a variation of a technique that both Kasper de Jonge
> (http://ppvt.pro/KASPERSLICER) and Rob
> (http://ppvt.pro/FRESHNESS) have covered in blog posts. Read Kasper's in particular if we're moving a little too fast for your taste in this section.

For grins and to test this out, you can now slap both slicers and both measures on a Pivot and inspect what each of the measures returns:

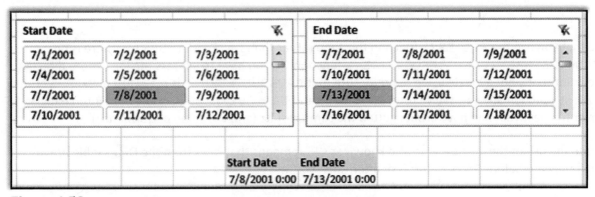

Figure 4.58

You'll never place these measures on an actual report, but it's good to see that they serve their purpose, which is to capture the dates that the user selects on the two slicers.

> **Note**
>
> Note that we changed the captions on each slicer to reflect their intend-
> ed use. Originally they both just had Date as a caption since that was the
> column name in each table.

Creating Sales Measures That Are Filtered by Those Date Measures

Assuming that you already have your base `Sales` measure defined, you can now work on `Sales on Program`:

```
[Sales on Program] =
 CALCULATE([Sales],
          DATESBETWEEN(
                       Dates[FullDate],
                       [Start Date],
                       [End Date]
                       )
          )
```

You use the `DATESBETWEEN()` function here as a means of filtering the base `Sales` measure; the `Start Date` and `End Date` measures that you defined previously are the end dates.

Note the use of the Dates table in the formula. That is a third date table, separate from the two slicer date tables, and this table is related to the Sales table. Here you are picking up the user's date selections from two tables that are not related to anything, and you're using the dates the user selected to filter the "real" Dates table. That filter then gets applied to the Sales table because it is related to the Sales table.

`Sales Off Program` is a bit trickier than `Sales On Program`. We suppose you *could* just subtract `Sales On Program` sales from `Sales`, but just in case someday you need to build some date sensitivity into the base `Sales` measure, you should define `Sales Off Program` to be `Sales` filtered to dates *outside* the selected date range:

```
[Sales Off Program] =
 CALCULATE([Sales],
          FILTER(Dates,
                 Dates[FullDate]<[Start Date] ||
                 Dates[FullDate]>[End Date]
                 )
          )
```

Notice that you use the `FILTER()` function this time rather than `DATESBETWEEN()`. There is no `DATESNOTBETWEEN()` or `DATESOUTSIDE()` function, so you have to express the logic more directly yourself. But that's not a big deal; we're pretty sure that `DATESBETWEEN()` is really just a "skin" over the `FILTER()` function anyway. We've used `FILTER()` and `DATESBETWEEN()` somewhat interchangeably over the past year and have always gotten the same results (and the same performance).

Also note the use of the `||` operator, also known as `OR`. It means that rows from the Dates table are included if they are before `Start Date` or after `End Date`.

> **Note**
>
> You always want to use `FILTER()` and `DATESBETWEEN()` against the smallest tables possible. Use them against your Dates table, for instance, rather than against the Date column in your Sales table. They are *much* slower against larger tables.

Here's what you get with those new measures on your Pivot and with some product hierarchy in the Rows drop zone:

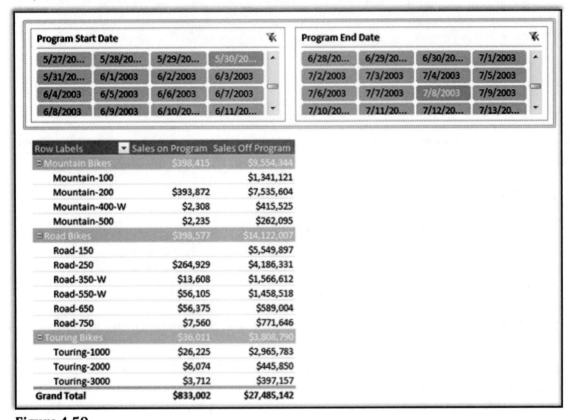

Figure 4.59

Now you see why "per day" versions of these measures are required: The programs are so short that they are dwarfed by the "off" dates.

> **Note**
>
> These two date slicers are great candidates for disabling cross-filtering and thereby improving the performance (update time) of this report.
> See
> http://ppvt.pro/SLICERPERF for an explanation.

Creating the Sales-per-Day Measures

You need a `Day Count` measure that you can use as a denominator:

```
[Day Count] = COUNTROWS(DISTINCT(Sales[OrderDate]))
```

> **Note**
>
> You explicitly count the Date column from the Sales table rather than
> the Dates table to account for product lines that did not exist for the
> duration of the entire Dates table and therefore did not sell at all. There
> are trade-offs here that we won't go into, but we think this is the right
> thing to do in most cases when calculating a per-day measure.

`Sales per Day`, then, is straightforward:

```
[Sales per Day] = [Sales] / [DayCount]
```

Now you need to create "on program" and "off program" versions of that measure. These formulas parallel
the on/off sales measures from above:

```
[Sales per Day on Program] =
 CALCULATE([Sales per Day],
           DATESBETWEEN(Dates[FullDate],
                        [Start Date],
                        [End Date]
                        )
            )"
```

Finally, you need to add the `Program Delta` measure, which is really percentage change in sales per
day:

```
[Sales per Day Off Program] =
CALCULATE([Sales per Day],
          FILTER(Dates,
                 Dates[FullDate]<[Start Date] ||
                 Dates[FullDate]>[End Date]
                 )
           )"
```

The `IF()` in here catches the case where a product did not sell during the selected dates. If you leave out
that `IF()`, the measure returns −100% for those cases. Sometimes that is what you want, and sometimes
it is not. You have to decide on a case-by-case basis.

Add some conditional formatting, and you get the report shown earlier, in Figure 4.55.

Alternative Approach: Using a Promotions Table

Rather than use two date slicers as you have here, you could have a single Promotions table that lists each promotion and its start and end dates, like this:

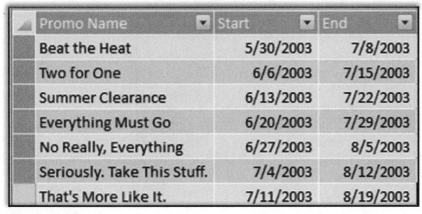

Figure 4.60

If you do this, you just have to go back to the Start Date and End Date measures and change their definitions to reference the Start and End columns in this table. Then you "attach" them to this table instead of to those slicer tables:

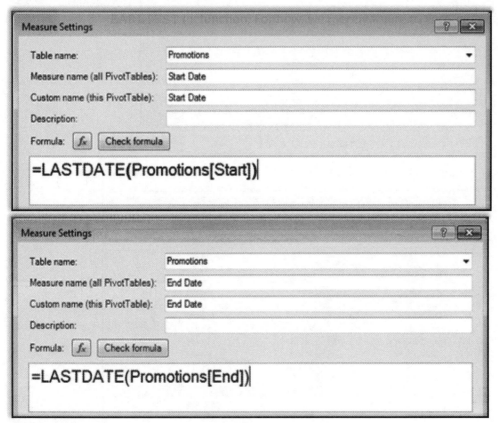

Figure 4.61

You don't have to make any other changes. Now you can remove the Start Date and End Date slicers and replace them with a single Promo Name slicer:

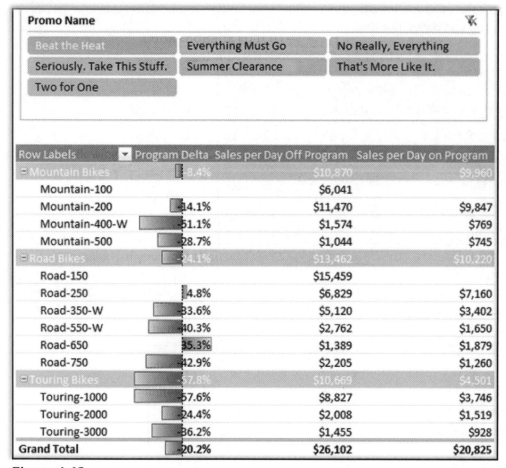

Figure 4.62

Or you can move the promo name to the Rows drop zone and some of the product stuff to slicers:

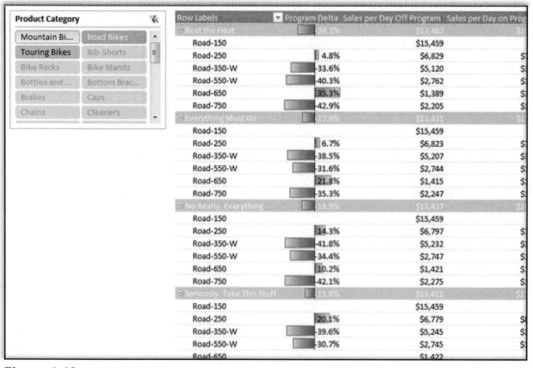

Figure 4.63

Other Fun Stuff

There are many other things you could do here. For instance, you could create a measure that calculates sales per day for the month leading up to the start of a promotion, or the month after it ends, or the same period a year earlier. PowerPivot truly opens doors that you'd never consider in traditional Excel (and probably would never get to in traditional BI).

Customers and Website Visitors: Percentage Who Return

Over breakfast at the Cozy Corner Cafe, Rob was showing Bill his "new customers per month (or year or day)" trick, and Bill pointed out that any manager would want to see the converse: Of the customers we had last year, how many came back? This trick, folks, tells you how to do it.

Finding out whether customers keep coming back is a lot of work in Excel alone, and the results are never quite flexible enough to answer the myriad inevitable follow-up questions. Power Pivot is, of course, a game changer for this kind of thing. Here we look at a handful of techniques that can help.

To determine how many of the customers who first "appeared" in one year returned a year later, you need to set up three tables: a data table (Sales) and two lookup tables (Customers and Calendar):

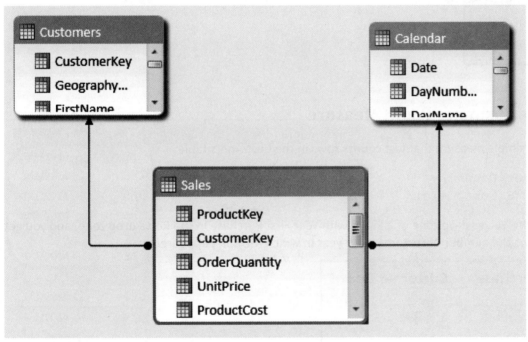

Figure 4.64

> **Note**
>
> In this example, you use Sales as the data table. But really, any "customer behavior" table will work. If you have website visits data, for instance, and a unique ID for each visitor (which is sometimes hard to come by in the web world, admittedly), you can substitute your Visits table for the Sales table. You use the same technique either way.

Adding the Year First Purchase Column in Customers

You need to add a calculated column in the Customers table that tells when a customer first "appeared" (that is, when the customer first purchased something):

```
[Year First Purchase] =
    YEAR(FIRSTDATE(Sales[OrderDate]))
```

This calculated column fetches the first year a customer appears in the related Sales table:

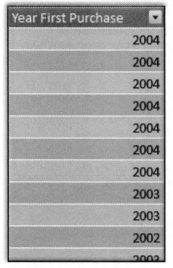

Figure 4.65

Creating the Customer Count Measure

You need a very simple measure that just counts rows in the Customers table:

```
[Customer Count] =
COUNTROWS(Customers)
```

You add this to the Values drop zone of a Pivot, with Year First Purchase in the Rows drop zone, and you get a table that shows the number of customers, by year in which they first appeared:

Year First Purchase	Customer Count
2001	1,013
2002	2,677
2003	7,698
2004	7,096
Grand Total	**18,484**

Figure 4.66

Creating the Active Customers Measure

Now you need a measure that actually counts unique customers as they show up in the sales data:

```
[Active Customers] =
DISTINCTCOUNT(Sales[CustomerKey])
```

For now, this measure and the `Customer Count` measure return identical results:

Year First Purchase ▾	Customer Count	Active Customers
2001	1,013	1,013
2002	2,677	2,677
2003	7,698	7,698
2004	7,096	7,096
Grand Total	**18,484**	**18,484**

Figure 4.67

Now you need to move Year First Purchase from the Rows drop zone to a slicer and add Calendar[YearMonth] to the Rows drop zone:

Figure 4.68

You can see that 7,698 customers first appeared in 2003, and 420 of those customers reappeared in January 2004.

Creating a Ratio/Percentage Measure

You need a measure to determine the ratio or percentage of customers who appeared in a selected year and returned later:

```
[% Customers Acquired in Selected Year Who Returned] =
DIVIDE([Active Customers], [Customer Count])
```

Add this to the Pivot and remove the intermediate measures, and you arrive at the originally desired result:

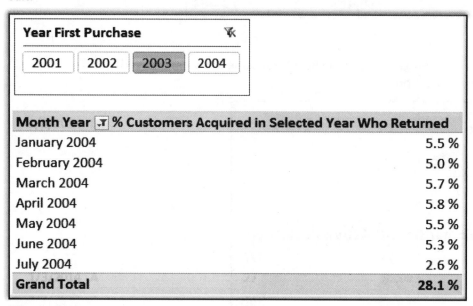

Month Year ⫶ % Customers Acquired in Selected Year Who Returned	
January 2004	5.5 %
February 2004	5.0 %
March 2004	5.7 %
April 2004	5.8 %
May 2004	5.5 %
June 2004	5.3 %
July 2004	2.6 %
Grand Total	**28.1 %**

Figure 4.69

Warning: Avoiding "Overlapping" Years

You cannot sensibly use the technique just described to measure the number of customers who returned in the same year in which they were acquired. If you try to do it, this is what you get:

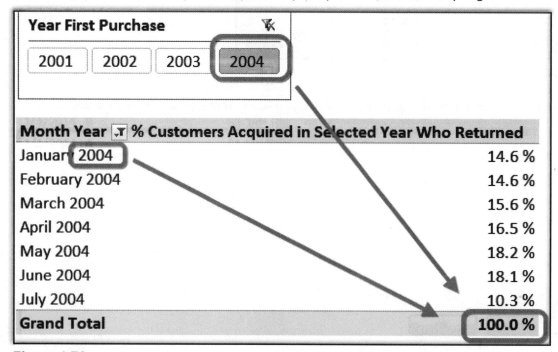

Figure 4.70

100% of all customers who first appeared in 2004 also came back in 2004? No, that is *not* what this Pivot is trying to tell you. Instead, it is saying that 100% of customers who were *first* seen in 2004 were *also* seen in 2004, which, um, is *always* true.

With this technique, the Year First Purchase selection *must* be prior to the Calendar values that are in play on the Pivot. This is why you have been slicing to 2003 on Year First Purchase and have the Row Labels area filtered to months in 2004.

If you want to perform "returning customer" analysis on a more granular basis, you need to write a differ-ent calculated column than `Year First Purchase`; for example, you could use `YearMonth First Purchase`.

Note that you *can* select multiple values on the slicer:

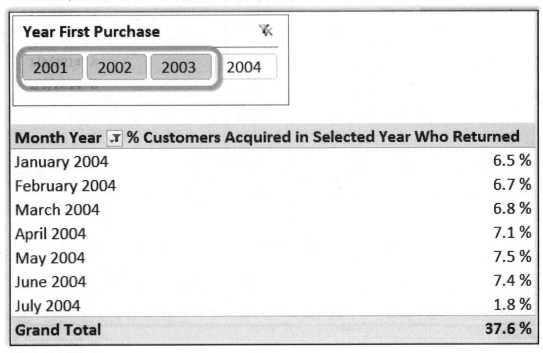

Month Year ⊤	% Customers Acquired in Selected Year Who Returned
January 2004	6.5 %
February 2004	6.7 %
March 2004	6.8 %
April 2004	7.1 %
May 2004	7.5 %
June 2004	7.4 %
July 2004	1.8 %
Grand Total	**37.6 %**

Figure 4.71

Now you can see that of all customers acquired in 2001–2003, 6.5% of them reappeared in January 2004.

Counting New Customers

The flip side of finding returning customers, of course, is identifying the number of customers who show up for the first time:

Figure 4.72

`Active Customers` is the same measure as before. But how do you calculate `New Customers`?

> **Note**
>
> Both `Active Customers` and `New Customers` work at multiple different calendar levels, including week of year.

A Measure Built on Intermediate Measures

The `New Customers` measure is built on two intermediate measures that are not displayed above. Here are the formulas for `New Customers` and its components:

```
[New Customers] =
COUNTROWS(FILTER(Customers,
          [Was Customer First Order In Period]=1))
```

The "smarts" are primarily encapsulated in `Was Customer First Order in Period`, which is merely a "true/false" type of measure that returns 1 or 0:

```
[Was Customer First Order in Period] =
IF(FIRSTDATE(Calendar[Date])<=[Customer First Order Date Ever],
   IF(LASTDATE(Calendar[Date])>=
      [Customer First Order Date Ever],
      1,
      0
    ),
   0
 )
```

In turn, `Customer First Order Date Ever` returns the date a customer first appears:

```
[Customer First Order Date Ever] =
FIRSTNONBLANK(ALL(Calendar[Date]),[Total Sales])
```

Calculating Average Customer Age

Here's another natural calculation in the vein of customer behavior metrics:

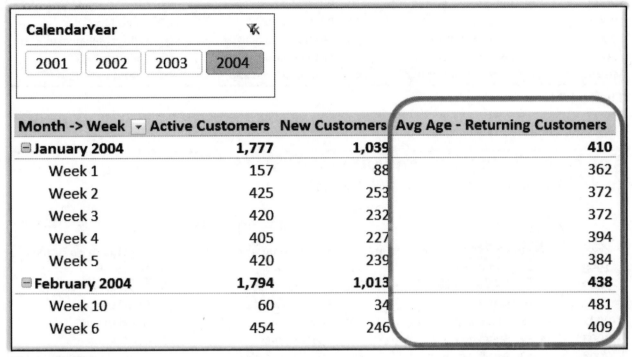

Figure 4.73

Here you determine customer "age" in days—the number of days elapsed between a customer's first-ever order and the last date in the selected time period:

```
[Avg Age - Returning Customers] =
AVERAGEX(
        FILTER(Customers,
              [Total Sales]>0 &&
              [Was Customer First Order In Period]=0
              ),
        LASTDATE(Calendar[Date]) -
              [Customer First Order Date Ever]
              )
```

Finding the Top-Performing "Thing"

This is a pretty nifty PivotTable:

Year	Pass TD Champ and Amount	Rush TD Champ and Amount	Rec TD Champ and Amount
1999	41: Kurt Warner	17: Stephen Davis	13: Cris Carter
2000	33: 2 Players Tied	18: Marshall Faulk	15: Randy Moss
2001	36: Kurt Warner	14: Shaun Alexander	16: Terrell Owens
2002	28: Tom Brady	21: Priest Holmes	13: Terrell Owens
2003	32: Brett Favre	27: Priest Holmes	17: Randy Moss
2004	49: Peyton Manning	17: LaDainian Tomlinson	16: Muhsin Muhammad
2005	32: Carson Palmer	27: Shaun Alexander	12: 2 Players Tied
Grand Total	218: Peyton Manning	89: Shaun Alexander	89: Marvin Harrison

Figure 4.74

Here's the same PivotTable, explained:

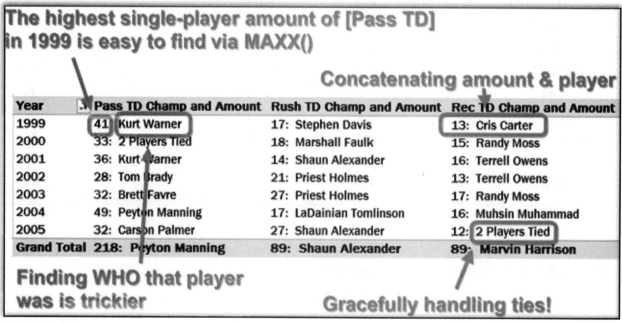

Figure 4.75

> **Note**
>
> For information on finding the top-selling date for a particular product, see http://ppvt.pro/TOPSELLING. You can use the technique described there to find the top-performing "thing," but this trick describes an even better method.

You need a simple measure that finds the largest single-player pass TD total:

```
[League Leading Pass TD Amount]=
MAXX(PlayersTable, [Pass TD])
```

This measure steps through each row of PlayersTable, evaluating the Pass TD measure at each step, and returns the single largest value it finds. This is what it yields:

Year	⊤ League Leading Pass TD
1999	41
2000	33
2001	36
2002	28
2003	32
2004	49
2005	32
Grand Total	**218**

Figure 4.76

Next, you need to find *who* had those 41 touchdown passes in 1999:

```
[Player with most Pass TD] =
CALCULATE (
        IF (
            HASONEVALUE (PlayersTable[FullName]),
            VALUES (PlayersTable[FullName]),
            COUNTROWS (VALUES (PlayersTable[FullName]))
                & " Players Tied"
            ),
        TOPN(1, PlayersTable, [Pass TD])
        )
```

The part of this formula that's boldfaced finds the single row from PlayersTable with the highest value of Pass TD. Because TOPN () is being used as a filter input to CALCULATE (), the IF () expression is "limited" to just that top row from PlayersTable.

But why is there an IF () for the measure expression input to CALCULATE () ? The thing is, if there are two players in PlayersTable who both have the top number of touchdowns, TOPN (1, …) will return both players! Therefore, the IF (HASONEVALUE (…)) test detects ties. If you have just one value, then there are not any ties, so you just get the name of the player via VALUES (PlayersTable [FullName]). If you have more than one value, the second branch of the IF () is triggered, and you get the number of ties via COUNTROWS (VALUES ()) and concatenate that number with the static text " Players Tied" (note the leading space).

Here's what the results look like:

Year	⊤ League Leading Pass TD	Player with Most Pass TD
1999	41	Kurt Warner
2000	33	2 Players Tied
2001	36	Kurt Warner
2002	28	Tom Brady
2003	32	Brett Favre
2004	49	Peyton Manning
2005	32	Carson Palmer
Grand Total	**218**	**Peyton Manning**

Figure 4.77

Then, if you want, you can write another measure that combines the other two into one, for compactness:

```
[Pass TD Champ and Amount] =
[League Leading Pass TD] & ": " & [Player with Most Pass TD]
```

Then you remove the other measures from the Pivot and get this:

Year	Pass TD Champ and Amount
1999	41: Kurt Warner
2000	33: 2 Players Tied
2001	36: Kurt Warner
2002	28: Tom Brady
2003	32: Brett Favre
2004	49: Peyton Manning
2005	32: Carson Palmer
Grand Total	218: Peyton Manning

Figure 4.78

Repeating that three-measure process for the other base measures, Rush TD and Rec TD, yields:

Year	Pass TD Champ and Amount	Rush TD Champ and Amount	Rec TD Champ and Amount
1999	41: Kurt Warner	17: Stephen Davis	13: Cris Carter
2000	33: 2 Players Tied	18: Marshall Faulk	15: Randy Moss
2001	36: Kurt Warner	14: Shaun Alexander	16: Terrell Owens
2002	28: Tom Brady	21: Priest Holmes	13: Terrell Owens
2003	32: Brett Favre	27: Priest Holmes	17: Randy Moss
2004	49: Peyton Manning	17: LaDainian Tomlinson	16: Muhsin Muhammad
2005	32: Carson Palmer	27: Shaun Alexander	12: 2 Players Tied
Grand Total	218: Peyton Manning	89: Shaun Alexander	89: Marvin Harrison

Figure 4.79

Why is this better than the older technique? There are three reasons:

- The formula is slightly simpler.

- The formula runs faster than the older method.

- This method handles ties.

> **Note**
>
> In the comments at http://ppvt.pro/TOPSELLING, Gerhard Brueckl suggests using SUMMARIZE(). That technique is also a *lot* faster than the FILTER() method. We don't know if this TOPN() approach is just as fast as SUMMARIZE().

Weighted Averages: Another Use of SUMX()

Let's say you have some data about zip (postal) codes in the United States:

ZIP Code	Jan Avg Low Temp	July Avg High Temp	Med Age	TTL Pop	IDX Pop Growth Range
23298	25.94000053	85.41000366	21.28000069	427	A: Very Rapid Growth
39710	26.92000008	91.15000153	22.73999977	277	A: Very Rapid Growth
33199	38.88999939	90.52999878	20.09000015	1464	F: Flat
30303	32.47999954	90.91999817	31.13999939	2535	D: Avg Growth
8102	20.27000046	84.45999908	28.12999916	9866	E: Slow Growth
30308	32.65999985	90.76000214	31.89999962	12046	A: Very Rapid Growth
51510	10.81999969	86.61000061	36.15999985	3248	E: Slow Growth
58204	-7.5	81.11000061	20.88999939	1384	F: Flat
8103	20.54999924	84.83000183	28.82999992	15528	F: Flat
32801	38.59000015	90.16000366	41.65999985	8212	A: Very Rapid Growth
63113	19.12999916	88.41999817	35.15999985	16840	F: Flat
63120	19.60000038	88.70999908	27.27000046	13282	G: Decrease
96853	65.90000153	86.93000031	21.57999992	1049	F: Flat
63112	18.87000084	88.66999817	31.47999954	23068	F: Flat
30312	32.56000137	91.05999756	31.02000069	21484	A: Very Rapid Growth

Figure 4.80

Now let's say you build a simple Pivot that shows total population and median age for each zip code, grouped by that last column, which is how fast the population of that zip code is growing:

Row Labels	Total Population	Average Median Age
⊟ A: Very Rapid Growth	107,245	32.5
30312	21,484	31.0
30305	20,669	36.7
30324	20,401	31.9
30309	18,456	32.6
30308	12,046	31.9
32801	8,212	41.7
64153	3,579	30.7
59648	885	45.6
63101	809	31.2
23298	427	21.3
39710	277	22.7
⊟ C: Rapid Growth	63,645	37.8
30310	34,032	31.2
30314	26,776	28.2
78597	2,837	54.0
⊟ D: Avg Growth	50,224	34.7
30306	21,219	33.1
32803	19,109	37.1

Figure 4.81

Here you use a simple SUM() measure for population and a simple AVERAGE() for median age.

Here's the `Average Median Age` measure:

```
[AVERAGE MEDIAN AGE]=
    AVERAGE(Zips[Med Age])
```

It treats all zip codes as equal, even if they have wildly different populations:

Med Age	TTL Pop	IDX Pop Growth Range
31.03000069	21484	A: Very Rapid Growth
36.66999817	20669	A: Very Rapid Growth
31.85000038	20401	A: Very Rapid Growth
32.61000061	18456	A: Very Rapid Growth
31.89999962	12046	A: Very Rapid Growth
41.65999985	8212	A: Very Rapid Growth
30.65999985	3579	A: Very Rapid Growth
45.63999939	885	A: Very Rapid Growth
31.17000008	809	A: Very Rapid Growth
21.28000069	427	A: Very Rapid Growth
22.73999977	277	A: Very Rapid Growth

Figure 4.82

The problem here is that the median age of very low-population zip codes (like population=277) is counted equally to that of higher-pop zip codes (like population=21484).

Weighting Median Age by Population

To fix the problem you see above, you need to write a new measure:

```
[Average Med Age Weighted by Pop]=
SUMX(Zips, Zips[TTL Pop] * Zips[Med Age]) / [Total Population]
```

Here are the results:

Row Labels	Total Population	Average Median Age	Avg Med Age Weighted by Pop
A: Very Rapid Growth	107,245	32.5 Different	33.5
30312	21,484	31.0	31.0
30305	20,669	36.7	36.7
30324	20,401	31.9 Equal	31.9
30309	18,456	32.6	32.6
30308	12,046	31.9	31.9
32801	8,212	41.7	41.7
64153	3,579	30.7	30.7
59648	885	45.6	45.6
63101	809	31.2	31.2
23298	427	21.3	21.3
39710	277	22.7	22.7
C: Rapid Growth	63,645	37.8	30.9
30310	34,032	31.2	31.2
30314	26,776	28.2	28.2
78597	2,837	54.0	54.0
D: Avg Growth	50,224	34.7	36.9
30306	21,219	33.1	33.1

Figure 4.83

You can see the Power Pivot weighted average measure compared to the non-weighted average. This is what you'd expect: Since the smaller zip codes of population 277 and 427 both have very young median ages, they were "unfairly" skewing the subtotal younger. Overall, though, fast-growing zip codes have a lower median age when you weight them for population.

Even cooler: You can remove the zip code field (`ZIPCode`) from the Pivot, and the weighted-average measure still works:

Row Labels	Total Population	Average Median Age	Avg Med Age Weighted by Pop
A: Very Rapid Growth	107,245	32.5	33.5
C: Rapid Growth	63,645	37.8	30.9
D: Avg Growth	50,224	34.7	36.9
E: Slow Growth	62,821	30.5	33.1
F: Flat	169,446	30.8	32.6
G: Decrease	130,750	31.5	32.6
H: Rapid Decrease	36,899	35.4	33.2
Grand Total	**621,030**	**32.3**	**33.0**

Figure 4.84

> **Note**
>
> For more information on `SUMX()`, see
> http://ppvt.pro/SUMX5PT

Moving Averages, Sums, etc.

In the following chart, the thicker line smooths out random fluctuations and shows a less "overreactive" trend than the thinner, more jagged line:

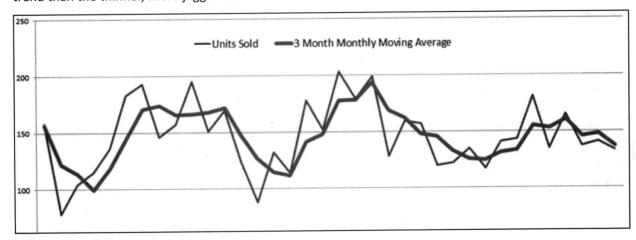

Figure 4.85

So how do you determine moving averages and moving sums using Power Pivot?

To see what you can do with state-of-the-art Power Pivot formulas, start with this simple model:

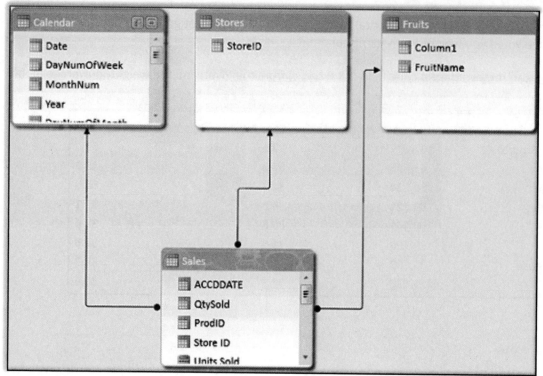

Figure 4.86

And a simple Pivot:

Year-Month ▼	Units Sold
2001-01	78
2001-02	55
2001-03	114
2001-04	129
2001-05	116
2001-06	175
2001-07	157
2001-08	210
2001-09	190
2001-10	134
2001-11	190
2001-12	193

Figure 4.87

The `Units Sold` measure is the jagged thinner line in the chart in Figure 4.85, and its formula is very simple:

```
[Units Sold] = SUM(Sales[QtySold])
```

Here you'll see how to make a version of `Units Sold` that is "smoothed" over a three-month period (the thicker line in Figure 4.85).

Moving Sum

Here's a formula that sums the most recent three months (including the current one):

```
[3 Month Moving Sum Units Sold] =
CALCULATE([Units Sold],
          DATESINPERIOD(Calendar[Date],
                        LASTDATE(Calendar[Date]),-3, Month
                       )
         )
```

And here's what it gives you:

Year-Month ▼	Units Sold	3 Month Moving Sum Units Sold
2001-01	78	78
2001-02	55	133
2001-03	114	247
2001-04	129	298
2001-05	116	359
2001-06	175	420
2001-07	157	448
2001-08	210	542
2001-09	190	557
2001-10	134	534
2001-11	190	514

Figure 4.88

Moving Average: First Attempt

The number in Figure 4.88 is bigger than a single month and doesn't match the scale of a real-world business, so you wouldn't want to chart that. Instead, you want the average version of that. It's a three-month moving sum, so to get the average, you *could* just divide by 3:

```
[3 Month Avg Divide 3] =
[3 Month Moving Sum Units Sold] / 3
```

Which gives you this:

Year-Month ▼	Units Sold	3 Month Moving Sum Units Sold	3 Month Avg Divide 3
2001-01	86	86	28.7
2001-02	57	143	47.7
2001-03	101	244	81.3
2001-04	127	285	95.0
2001-05	117	345	115.0
2001-06	148	392	130.7

Figure 4.89

You can see the drawback here: Those first two months, since they are the first two months in the calendar, are summing up less than three months' worth of sales but still dividing by 3. This "unfairly" drives down the average of those two months.

Moving Average: Corrected

You can account for the drawback just uncovered by changing the denominator so it uses logic similar to that in the numerator:

```
[3 Month Moving Avg Corrected]=
[3 Month Moving Sum Units Sold] /
CALCULATE(DISTINCTCOUNT(Calendar[Year Month]),
        DATESINPERIOD(Calendar[Date],
              LASTDATE(Calendar[Date]),-3,Month
              )
        )
```

In English, this formula means "take the three-month sum measure you already have and divide it by the number of distinct (unique) months you have over that same three-month period." Here's the result:

Year-Month ▼	Units Sold	3 Month Moving Avg Corrected
2001-01	86	86.0
2001-02	57	71.5
2001-03	101	81.3
2001-04	127	95.0
2001-05	117	115.0
2001-06	148	130.7
2001-07	151	138.7
2001-08	199	166.0

Figure 4.90

This calculation is more "fair" to the months at the beginning of the period.

Variations on This Approach

You can implement a number of variations on this approach—daily/weekly/quarterly versions, correcting for calendars that extend beyond the range of dates where you have sales, or adapting it to custom calendars via the greatest formula in the world (see http://ppvt.pro/GFITW1).

Moving Averages Controlled by a Slicer

In the figure below, you can see that a two-month moving average is pretty smooth, but a six-month moving average is smooooooother. (Imagine Barry White saying that: "Ohhh, yeaahhh...a six-month moooving average. Smoooooth...")

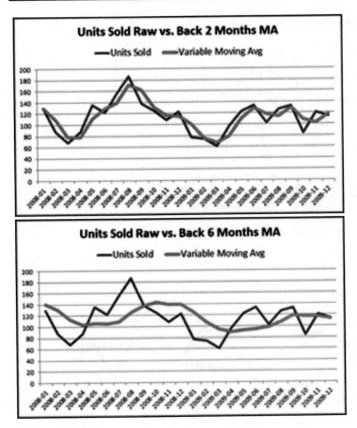

Figure 4.91

You just learned a trick for calculating simple moving averages in Power Pivot. Now, how do you control the length of a moving average dynamically? To figure it out, let's work backward from this result:

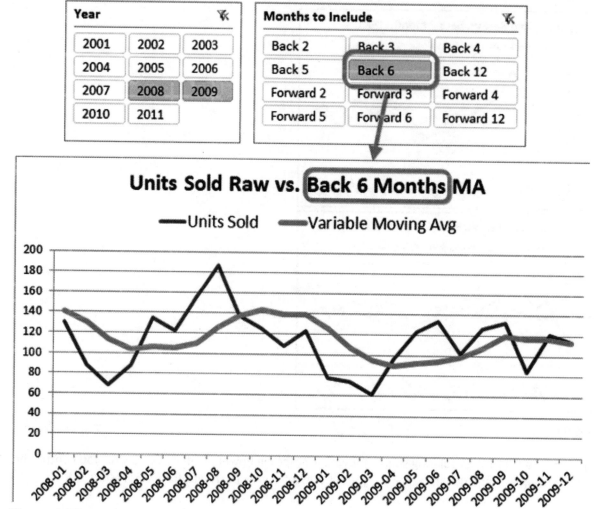

Figure 4.92

This slicer controls the length of the moving average (MA) period and the chart title. Now that's smoooooth!

This technique involves another disconnected slicer. First, you create a table in Excel and copy it to the Clipboard:

Months to Include	Number of Months
Back 2	-2
Back 3	-3
Back 4	-4
Back 5	-5
Back 6	-6
Back 12	-12
Forward 2	2
Forward 3	3
Forward 4	4
Forward 5	5
Forward 6	6
Forward 12	12

Figure 4.93

Then paste it into Power Pivot:

Figure 4.94

The result is this table:

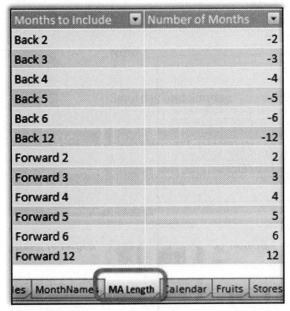

Months to Include	Number of Months
Back 2	-2
Back 3	-3
Back 4	-4
Back 5	-5
Back 6	-6
Back 12	-12
Forward 2	2
Forward 3	3
Forward 4	4
Forward 5	5
Forward 6	6
Forward 12	12

Figure 4.95

To cause the slicer tiles from the Months to Include column to sort sensibly, add a calculated column:

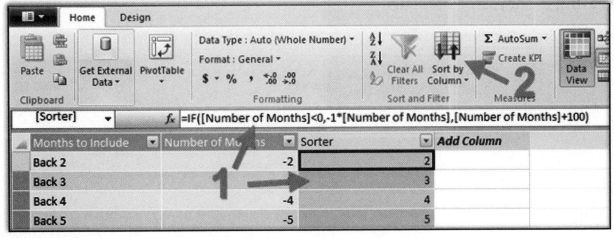

Figure 4.96

Now use that column as your SortBy column for the Months to Include column:

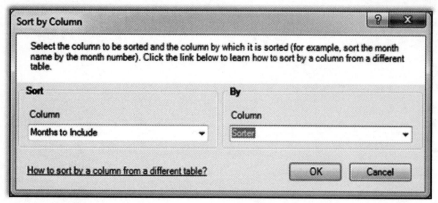

Figure 4.97

Then put the slicer on a Pivot, and it sorts in your desired order:

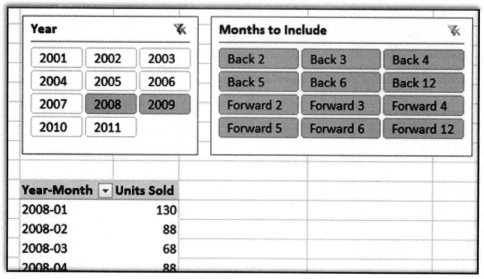

Figure 4.98

Creating a Harvester Measure

Next, you create a "harvester" measure:

```
[Selected MA Length] =
    MAX('MA Length'[Number of Months])
```

It yields something like this:

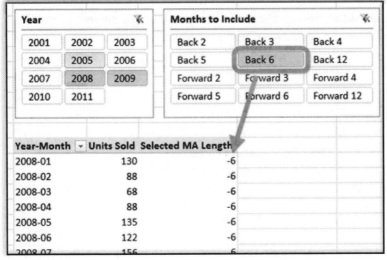

Figure 4.99

Creating Variable Moving Sum and Moving Average Measures

Now it's time to do something with the harvester measure. First you use it with the `Variable Moving Sum` measure:

```
[Variable Moving Sum] =
    CALCULATE([Units Sold],
            DATESINPERIOD(Calendar[Date],
                    LASTDATE(Calendar[Date]),
                    [Selected MA Length],
                    Month
                    )
            )
```

The boldfaced section is the only difference between this measure and the moving sum you saw earlier in this chapter. Previously, that part was "hardwired" to −3, to get a three-month moving average.

Then you use the harvester with the `Variable Moving Average` measure:

```
[Variable Moving Average] =
    [Variable Moving Sum] /
    CALCULATE(DISTINCTCOUNT(Calendar[Year Month]),
            DATESINPERIOD(Calendar[Date],
                    LASTDATE(Calendar[Date]),
                    [Selected MA Length],
                    Month
                    )
            )
```

Again, the boldfaced portions are the only differences between this measure and the fixed three-month moving average measure.

Handling a Bug

If the user of this report/dashboard picks one of the "forward" options on the slicer, the current month is *not* going to be counted, whereas it *is* counted in the "backward" options. Why?

Here's the moving sum formula again, with the offending section boldfaced:

```
[Variable Moving Sum] =
    CALCULATE([Units Sold],
            DATESINPERIOD(Calendar[Date],
                    LASTDATE(Calendar[Date]),
                    [Selected MA Length],
                    Month
                )

        )
```

When you go backward from `LASTDATE` of the current month, the current month is included. But when you go forward, well, the current month is not included.

So you need an `IF` that checks whether `Selected MA Length` is positive, and if it is, that switches `LASTDATE` to `FIRSTDATE`.

The Chart Readout

One last thing you might want to do here is make a dynamic chart title by selecting the chart title, typing = in the formula bar, and picking a cell (G6 in this case):

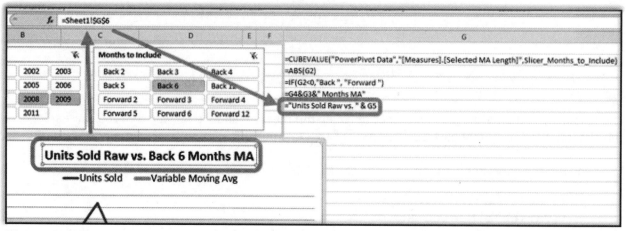

Figure 4.100

The formulas above G6 are used to construct G6 itself.

Counting Things That Didn't Happen

I (Rob) got an interesting question the other day: "I know how to report on the *presence* of a certain data element, but can I also report on its *absence*? We're working with healthcare data and have a list of patients who have had certain diagnostic tests. From this data, it's easy to find patients who have had a procedure (i.e., a mammogram), but can we use the same data to find patients who *haven't* had one?"

I love it. Let's dig in, using a simple sales data example:

Product	Qty Sold
All-Purpose Bike Stand	249
AWC Logo Cap	2190
Bike Wash - Dissolver	908
Classic Vest, L	195
Classic Vest, M	199
Classic Vest, S	168
Fender Set - Mountain	2121
Half-Finger Gloves, L	443
Half-Finger Gloves, M	499
Half-Finger Gloves, S	488
Hitch Rack - 4-Bike	328
HL Mountain Tire	1396
HL Road Tire	858

Figure 4.101

`Qty Sold` is a simple explicit measure:

```
[Qty Sold] = SUM(Sales[OrderQuantity]
```

`ProductName` comes from a separate Products table:

Figure 4.102

You need to write a new measure named `Did Not Sell`:

```
[Did Not Sell] = IF(ISBLANK([Qty Sold]),1,BLANK())
```

This yields:

ProductName ▼	Qty Sold	Did Not Sell
All-Purpose Bike Stand	249	
AWC Logo Cap	2190	
Bike Wash - Dissolver	908	
Cable Lock		1
Chain		1
Classic Vest, L	195	
Classic Vest, M	199	
Classic Vest, S	168	
Fender Set - Mountain	2121	
Front Brakes		1

Figure 4.103

Here you can see that cable lock, chain, and front brakes did not sell.

Then you can remove the `Qty Sold` measure from the Pivot so you just see things that didn't sell:

ProductName ▼	Did Not Sell
Cable Lock	1
Chain	1
Front Brakes	1
Front Derailleur	1
Full-Finger Gloves, L	1
Full-Finger Gloves, M	1
Full-Finger Gloves, S	1
Headlights - Dual-Beam	1
Headlights - Weatherproof	1

Figure 4.104

Where This Fails

The simple `IF ISBLANK()` formula might seem too simple, and it is. Check out the grand total at the bottom of the Pivot:

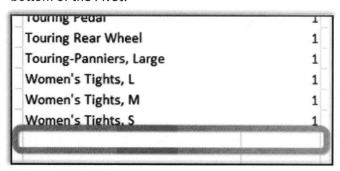

Touring Pedal	1
Touring Rear Wheel	1
Touring-Panniers, Large	1
Women's Tights, L	1
Women's Tights, M	1
Women's Tights, S	1

Figure 4.105

The grand total row for this Pivot is blank. Given the `IF ISBLANK()` formula, this actually makes sense. `Qty Sold` is *not* blank for that cell, so the `IF()` evaluates to `false`, and the `Did Not Sell` measure returns `BLANK()`.

You can instead sum up the blanks:

```
[Products that Did Not Sell] =
SUMX(Products, [Did Not Sell])
```

This formula iterates over each row in the Products table, summing up the `Did Not Sell` values it gets from each step.

In the case of a single-product row of the Pivot, the formula has only one product to evaluate, so you get the same result as with `Did Not Sell`:

Touring Pedal	1	1
Touring Rear Wheel	1	1
Touring-Panniers, Large	1	1
Women's Tights, L	1	1
Women's Tights, M	1	1
Women's Tights, S	1	1
Grand Total		239

Figure 4.106

For each single-product row, `SUMX()` returns the same answer. But for totals, it adds them all up.

Are you finished now? Maybe. Consider the following notes.

Note 1: Be Careful About Labels Versus Rows!

At the top of the Pivot you see something disturbing:

ProductName	Did Not Sell	Products that Did Not Sell
AWC Logo Cap		2
Cable Lock	1	1
Chain	1	1
Front Brakes	1	1
Front Derailleur	1	1
Full-Finger Gloves, L	1	1

Figure 4.107

AWC Logo Cap apparently *did* sell but also *didn't*? Didn't it actually sell *twice*? The answer lies in the Products table:

ProductKey	ProductName	StandardCost
223	AWC Logo Cap	5.7052
224	AWC Logo Cap	5.2297
225	AWC Logo Cap	6.9223

Figure 4.108

There are three rows in the Products table with that name. One of these products sold a lot of units, and two sold none.

What you do about this really depends on the needs of the business. Maybe you leave everything alone because you *want* to be told that there are two product IDs with the name AWC Logo Cap that have never sold. Or maybe you change the formula to explicitly only return names of products that have never sold:

```
[Product Names that Did Not Sell] =
SUMX(VALUES(Products[ProductName]), [Did Not Sell])
```

In this version of the measure, AWC Logo Cap is *not* counted as unsold:

ProductName	Did Not Sell	Products that Did Not Sell	Product Names that Did Not Sell
AWC Logo Cap		2	
Cable Lock	1	1	1
Chain	1	1	1
Front Brakes	1	1	1
Front Derailleur	1	1	1
Full-Finger Gloves, L	1	1	1

Figure 4.109

> **Note**
>
> For more on SUMX(), see http://ppvt.pro/SUMX5PT.

Note 2: This Example Is Specific to Products

Since the first input to SUMX() in both examples above is aimed at the Products table, it will only be useful for counting products. If you wanted to count, say, customers who didn't buy anything, you would need new versions of these measures, aimed at customers columns or tables.

Chapter 5: Power Query

Excel is incredibly powerful in the right hands. Experienced analysts have many tricks and techniques for massaging malformed data into useful data. As an experienced analyst, I (Bill) relish the fact that I can apply 13 crazy steps to make data useful. I love knowing that I can do something that most people using Excel could never do.

The team that developed Power Query wanted to level that field. Power Query is incredibly exciting. It is Microsoft's downloadable data-shaping engine and add-in for Excel 2010 and 2013. And it is aimed at the Power Pivot "generation." Power Query takes a whole class of "ugly Excel data" problems and gives people an intuitive interface for easily dealing with those problems.

Power Query was not developed by experienced analysts. If you had asked experienced analysts to build Power Query, they would have scoffed and said, "But we already can do all that stuff in Excel" and then rattled off the 13 arcane steps. Experienced analysts never would have given the world Power Query because we enjoy being able to do the impossible in Excel.

However, with Power Pivot, a whole bunch of SQL Server and SharePoint people started using Excel. They needed ways to deal with ugly data. And thus, Power Query was born.

As an experienced analyst, what is my reaction to Power Query? I love it. It turns out that I never really enjoyed doing the 13 arcane steps. I love that I can now replace those 13 steps with a few clicks.

Combining Multiple Worksheets or Workbooks into a Single Power Pivot Table

This trick doesn't actually use Power Query, but it's a really neat trick, and the next trick—which does use Power Query—builds on this one. Let's say you have multiple worksheets (or workbooks) that all contain the same sort of data:

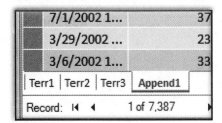

Figure 5.1

These worksheets all come to you separately, but you really want them to appear as one big table. So you need to combine all of them into a single Power Pivot table.

Naturally, if you're working with a small number of sheets, and the sheets aren't massive, you can just copy and paste them all into one table in Excel and then copy and paste them into Power Pivot, or you can link the table into Power Pivot or export it as a CSV file so you can import it elsewhere. One other technique would be to use Paste Append to directly paste into Power Pivot.

If the combined data set exceeds 1 million rows, you won't be able to combine the sheets into one because you will exceed the worksheet row limit. And you can't use Paste Append to paste a data set of that size into Power Pivot; pasting large data sets into Power Pivot takes forever, if it completes at all.

Here you'll see how to tackle this problem.

Removing the Header Row

First, you need to delete the header row because you don't want the header duplicated multiple times in the combined data set:

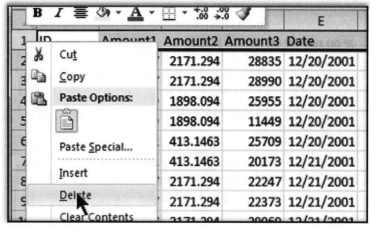

Figure 5.2

It's also important to ensure that the data starts in cell A1:

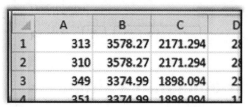

Figure 5.3

Saving Each Sheet as a CSV File

When you save as CSV, Excel saves only the active sheet, so you have to repeat this for each sheet (or each workbook). This yields, for instance:

Figure 5.4

Now you have a bunch of individual CSV files.

Opening a Command Prompt

Next, you need to open a command prompt by selecting Start, All Programs, Accessories, Command Prompt:

Figure 5.5

A command prompt window appears:

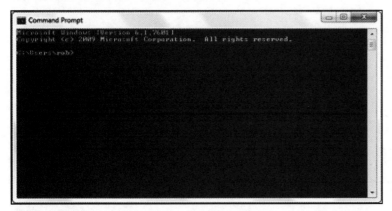

Figure 5.6

Changing Directory to the Folder Containing Your CSV Files

Use these commands to change directory to the folder holding your CSV files:

```
Command Prompt

Microsoft Windows [Version 6.1.7601
Copyright (c) 2009 Microsoft Corpor

C:\Users\rob>cd desktop

C:\Users\rob\Desktop>cd csvfiles

C:\Users\rob\Desktop\CSVFiles>
```

Figure 5.7

Copying Them All into One File

Here's the only real "trick" in this whole process. You enter `copy *.csv combined.csv` at the command prompt:

```
C:\Users\rob\Desktop\CSVFiles>copy *.csv combined.csv
File1.csv
File2.csv
File3.csv
File4.csv
        1 file(s) copied.
```

Figure 5.8

This command merges all your CSV files into a single one. This is what you then see in Windows Explorer, in the folder that contains your CSV files:

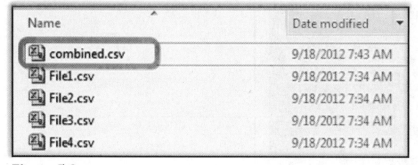

Name	Date modified
combined.csv	9/18/2012 7:43 AM
File1.csv	9/18/2012 7:34 AM
File2.csv	9/18/2012 7:34 AM
File3.csv	9/18/2012 7:34 AM
File4.csv	9/18/2012 7:34 AM

Figure 5.9

Importing the Combined CSV File into Power Pivot

Finally, you important the new combined CSV file into Power Pivot by opening Power Pivot and selecting Home, From Text:

Figure 5.10

Bonus: A Macro to Save All Workbooks in a Folder as CSV

If you have a bunch of workbooks in a folder and you need to save them all as CSV files, here's a macro that will do it all for you:

```
Sub ProcessWorkbooksInFolder()
Dim sPath As String
Dim sFile As String
Dim sDir As String
Dim oWB As Workbook
Dim sNewPath As String
'***Set this to your folder of workbooks***
sPath = "C:\Users\rob\desktop\csvfiles"
If Right$(sPath, 1) <> Application.PathSeparator Then
    sPath = sPath & Application.PathSeparator
End If
sDir = Dir$(sPath & "*.xlsx", vbNormal)
Do Until LenB(sDir) = 0
    Set oWB = Workbooks.Open(sPath & sDir)
    sNewPath = ActiveWorkbook.FullPath
    sNewPath = Left(sNewPath, Len(sNewPath) - 4) & "csv"
    ActiveWorkbook.SaveAs sNewPath, xlCSV
    oWB.Close False
    sDir = Dir$
Loop
End Sub
```

> **Note**
>
> If your goal is to combine several worksheets into a regular Pivot-cache PivotTable, check out Fazza's amazing macro, available at http://ppvt.pro/PIVOTMACRO2.

Using Power Query to Merge CSV Files

To illustrate how exciting Power Query is, this trick shows you how to merge CSV files into one table by using Power Query rather than manually saving and merging files with the command prompt (as discussed earlier in this chapter). Just to make things a bit more difficult, let's start out with three CSV files, with identical structures, that are stored on a website:

Terr3 CSV

CallDate	ProductID	CustomerID	Minutes	Resolution
2/4/2003	560	24045	34	Positive
10/4/2001	536	13291	17	Negative
5/25/2003	344	28139	43	Positive
4/25/2002	589	14318	39	Negative

Terr2 CSV

CallDate	ProductID	CustomerID	Minutes	Resolution
9/23/2002	605	29006	1	Negative
9/26/2003	482	23216	43	Positive
4/21/2002	335	18960	2	Negative
2/10/2003	591	27468	60	Positive

Terr1 CSV

CallDate	ProductID	CustomerID	Minutes	Resolution
8/10/2002	463	19623	16	Neutral
11/3/2002	342	27742	98	Positive
2/14/2002	374	19675	23	Negative
9/9/2002	328	20293	1	Positive

Figure 5.11

You don't need to download the CSV files to your computer! You can leave the files where they are and build a completely automatic system—one that requires *zero* manual intervention on an ongoing basis.

Connecting to One of the CSV Files

Once Power Query is downloaded and installed, you get a Power Query ribbon tab, which has a From Web button on it (the Excel 2013 version is pictured here):

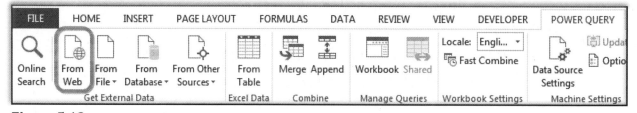

Figure 5.12

After you click this From Web button on the Power Query ribbon tab, enter the URL for one of the CSV files:

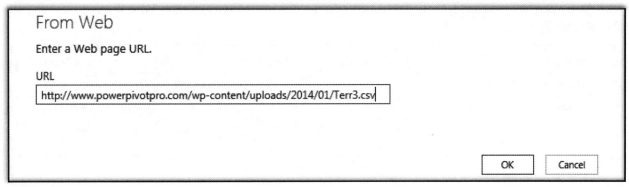

Figure 5.13

You now get a pop-up query window with its own ribbon:

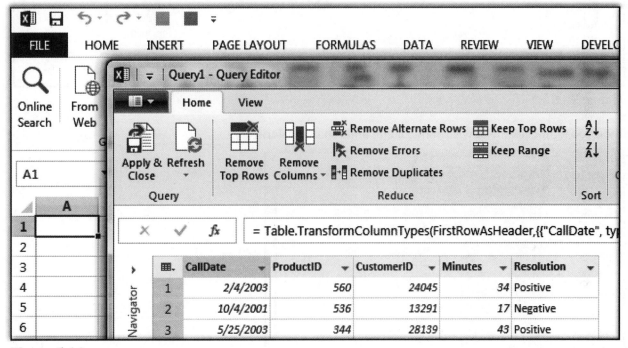

Figure 5.14

Adding a Custom Column to "Tag" This File

Next, you need to insert a custom column and enter a static formula (=1) to "tag" this file as containing the data for Territory 1:

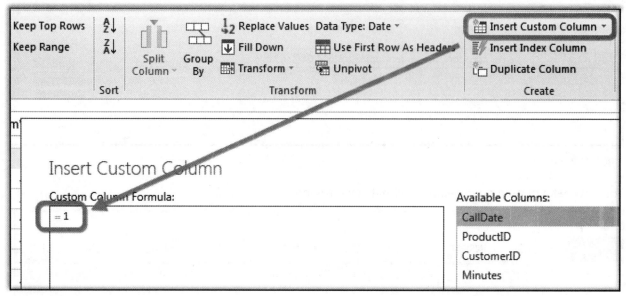

Figure 5.15

Then you right-click the new custom column and rename it Territory:

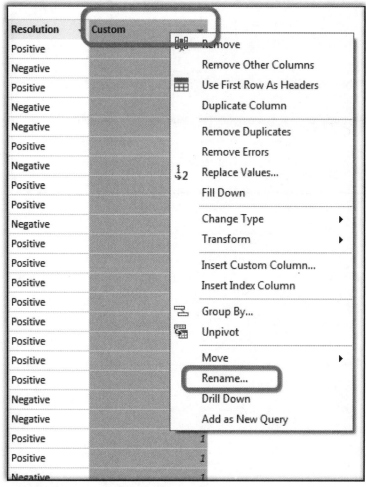

Figure 5.16

Then you rename this query Terr1 and click Apply & Close:

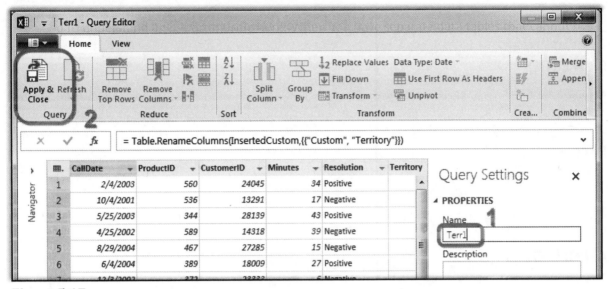

Figure 5.17

Excel now shows the data like this:

	A	B	C	D	E	F	G
1	CallDate	ProductID	CustomerID	Minutes	Resolution	Territory	
2	2/4/2003	560	24045	34	Positive	1	
3	10/4/2001	536	13291	17	Negative	1	
4	5/25/2003	344	28139	43	Positive	1	
5	4/25/2002	589	14318	39	Negative	1	
6	8/29/2004	467	27285	15	Negative	1	
7	6/4/2004	389	18009	27	Positive	1	
8	12/3/2002	372	23333	6	Negative	1	

Figure 5.18

This is not *quite* what you want. You want the data in Power Pivot, aka the data model. No sweat. Just edit the query you just wrote:

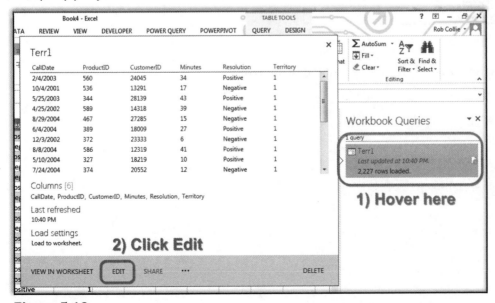

Figure 5.19

Next, you uncheck Load to Worksheet and check Load to Data Model, and then you click Apply & Close:

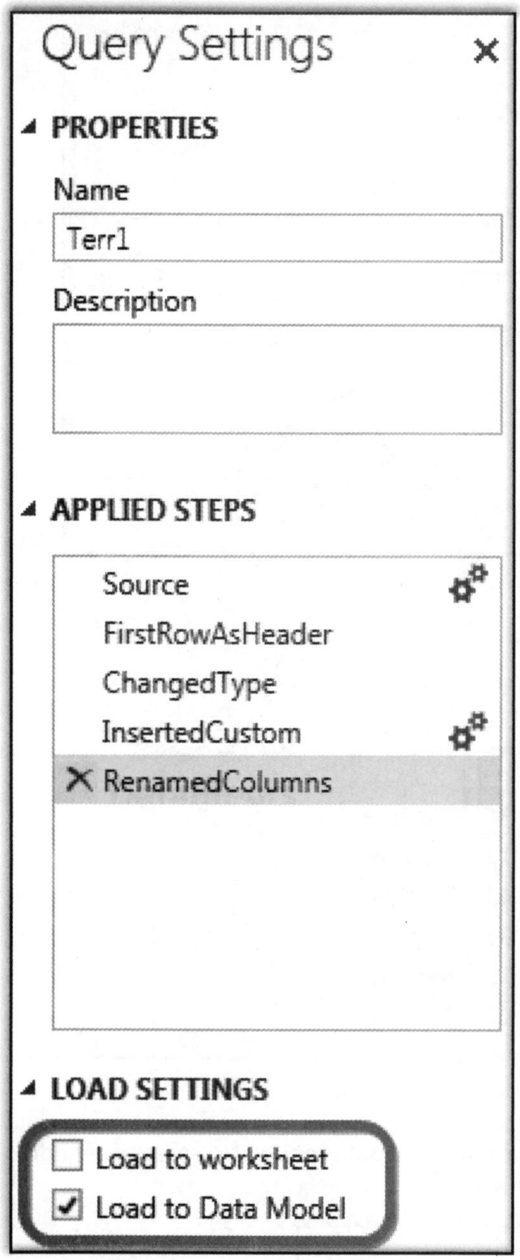

Figure 5.20

Now you see the data in the Power Pivot window instead of in Excel:

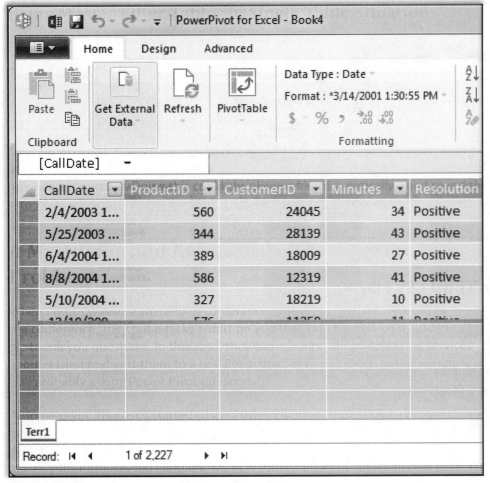

Figure 5.21

Connecting to the Second CSV File

To connect to the second CSV file, you use the same steps as for the first one, but with a different URL:

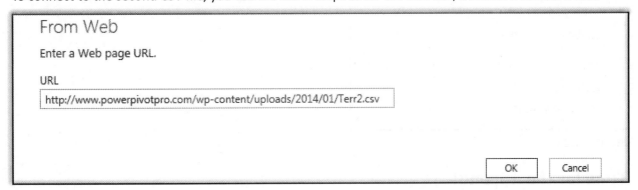

Figure 5.22

You also assign the custom column (Territory) a static value of 2 rather than 1:

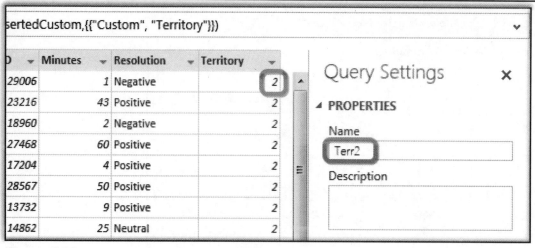

Figure 5.23

Connecting to the Third CSV File

As you might guess, connecting to the third CSV file is just like connecting to the first two, but with 3 instead of 2 or 1 in the custom column and query name.

After you connect to the third file, you have three queries defined in the workbook. The Workbook Queries pane now shows all three CSV queries:

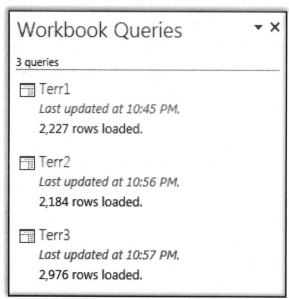

Figure 5.24

Time for the Append!

Now, back on the Power Query ribbon, you click Append:

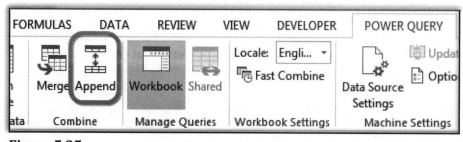

Figure 5.25

In the Append dialog, you specify Terr1 and Terr2:

Append

Select the primary table to which you want to append more data.

Terr1 ▼

Select the table to append with the primary table.

Terr2 ▼

OK   Cancel

Figure 5.26

The Append dialog lets you choose only two tables/queries, but that's okay for now.

Next, Power Query asks you about privacy. Since these CSV files are on a 100% public website, you can select Public:

Privacy levels

The privacy level is used to ensure that data is combined securely.

⊕ http://www.powerpivotpro.com/wp-content/uploads/2014/01/Terr3.csv   Public ▼

⊕ http://www.powerpivotpro.com/wp-content/uploads/2014/01/Terr2.csv   Public ▼

Figure 5.27

Append1 is a fine name for the new query:

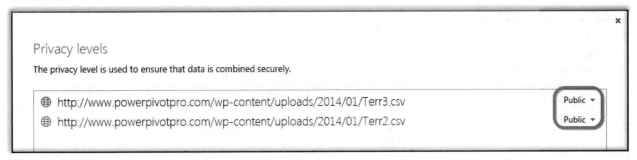

= Table.Combine({Terr1,Terr2})					

	ProductID	CustomerID	Minutes	Resolution	Territory
4/2003	560	24045	34	Positive	
4/2001	536	13291	17	Negative	
5/2003	344	28139	43	Positive	
5/2002	589	14318	39	Negative	
9/2004	467	27285	15	Negative	
4/2004	389	18009	27	Positive	
3/2002	372	23333	6	Negative	
8/2004	586	12319	41	Positive	

Query Settings

▲ PROPERTIES

Name

Append1

Description

Figure 5.28

But check out the formula bar. Can you modify that directly and add Terr3?

Yes, you absolutely can edit the formula yourself and create a three-table append—all in one step:

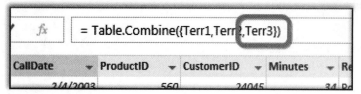

Figure 5.29

"Keeping" Only the Appended Query

You now have four tables in the Power Pivot window: the three original CSV queries, plus the Append result:

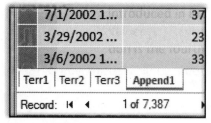

Figure 5.30

Although you have four tables, you really only need the one combined/appended table. Fixing the needless duplication is no problem. Just revisit the three original queries and uncheck *both* check boxes:

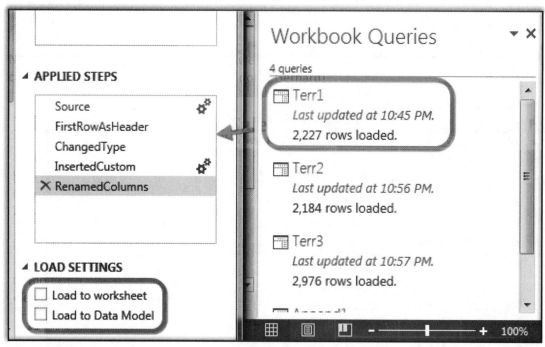

Figure 5.31

After you uncheck both boxes for all three original queries, click Apply & Close. Now you get just one table in Power Pivot—and, *yes*, it does contain all three tables combined:

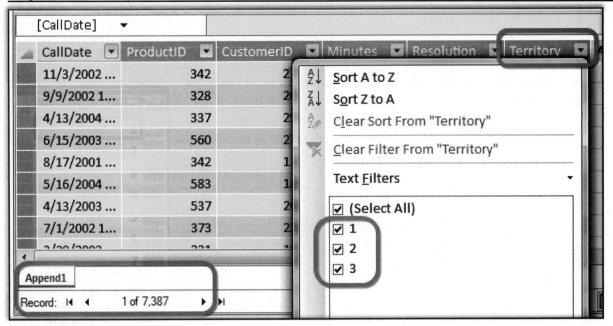

Figure 5.32

Notice that there is now only one tab in Power Pivot. It has 7,387 rows, which is all three CSV files combined. And the Territories column, which did *not* exist in any of the CSV files, is present in the result, with all three different values for Territory.

Testing Refreshing

With only the final result table "landing" in Power Pivot, will Refresh know what to do? Test it to find out:

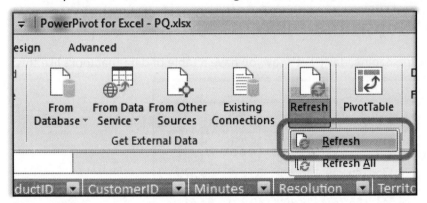

Figure 5.33

After you click Refresh (not even Refresh All), Power Query successfully reruns the three "child" queries, fetching all three CSV files and then appending them together:

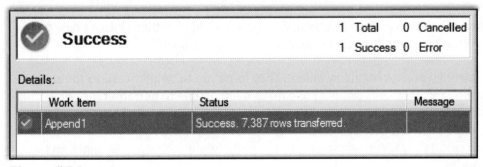

Figure 5.34

Why Is This So Amazing?

This trick in Power Query makes for some very happy Excel pros for a few reasons:

- You don't have to import the CSV files as three different tables, write duplicate measures against each one (like `Support Calls Territory 1`, `Support Calls Territory 2`, etc.), and then add them all together to form something like `Total Support Calls`. Writing four times the formulas is never fun, convenient, or maintainable.

- You don't have to perform manual steps every time you want to refresh.

> **Note**
>
> The command prompt solution from the beginning of this chapter avoids the multiple-formulas problem but introduces a manual refresh step, which may arguably be even worse.

- Despite both of those advantages, you can still do this 100% on your own, in Excel, without having to recruit the help of a database to get it done. Until now, if you wanted to write few formulas *and* have autorefresh, you needed a database "intermediary" standing between your workbook and the data sources (the CSV files). And that usually meant both a hardware investment (a database server that is always on) *and* a human investment (a database pro to set it all up). And this is often neither practical nor possible. Now you can avoid all that.

- This trick is *not* limited to CSV files. Any of the many sources that Power Query supports can be appended like this. If the files on your website were XML or Excel, or even a mixture of types, or if some of the files were on the web and some on a network drive, this would all still work.

Using Power Query to "Unpivot" a Table

Unpivoting a table is a very common "reshaping" task. Let's say you have a table of data that looks like this:

	A	B	C	Jan	Feb	Mar	Apr	May	
1	MODEL	Region	Market	Jan	Feb	Mar	Apr	May	
2	6000B	East	New York	116,176	110,240	57,874	35,456	6,395	
3	3500C	South	Dallas	119,919	47,503	30,906	38,220	6,287	3
4	3500C	Central	Milwaukee	132,794	93,632	114,358	32,779	23,561	
5	3500C	East	New York	126,176	126,209	118,290	33,522	29,579	
6	2500C	West	Seattle	140,135	88,710	79,771	68,225	38,043	1
7	6000B	Central	Milwaukee	129,644	96,757	138,893	49,891	54,516	3
8	2500C	West	San Francisco	67,295	53,376	37,238	30,613	15,585	
9	4500C	South	Houston	129,861	46,381	38,456	81,549	35,847	2
10	6000B	Central	Cleveland	76,204	53,190	33,103	46,613	24,511	1

Figure 5.35

When you have date-related columns in your source data, you *really* should turn those into a single date column. By doing so, you turn a wide and short table into a narrow and tall table.

Date columns like this in Power Pivot are very inconvenient. They force you to write measures for each month (for instance, `Jan Sales`, `Feb Sales`, etc.) *and* make it impossible to perform time-series analysis using things like `DATEADD()`, `DATESYTD()`, and the greatest formula in the world (all of which are covered in *DAX Formulas for Power Pivot*; also see http://www.powerpivotpro.com/2011/12/the-greatest-formula-in-the-world-part-one/ for more on the greatest formula in the world).

So how do you reshape this table into something that is much more Power Pivot friendly? Again, Power Query to the rescue:

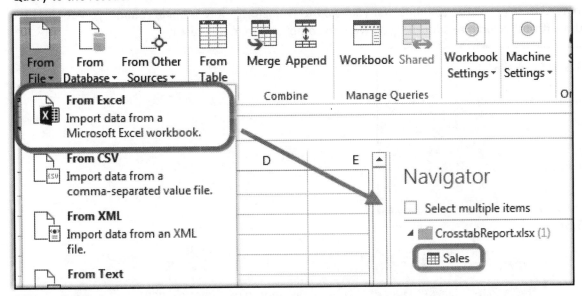

Figure 5.36

This time, the source data lives in an XLSX file. No problem. Once you have browsed to the source XLSX, you are presented with a list of all the tables available in that workbook (in this case, it's just the Sales worksheet).

Handling the Header Row

Select the Sales table in the navigator, click Edit, and you get this:

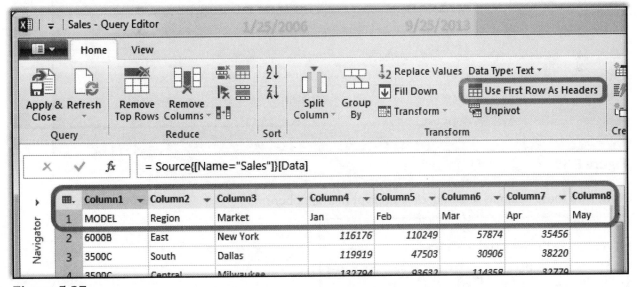

Figure 5.37

Initially, Power Query treats the first row of the table as data rather than as a header row. No problem: Just click the Use First Row as Headers button to take care of the header row issue once and for all.

Unpivoting

Next, you need to select all the columns that you want to "transform" into a single column. You do this by clicking the leftmost column header that you want to combine (Jan in this case):

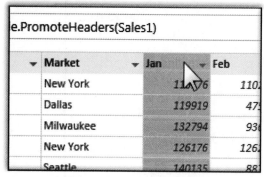

Figure 5.38

> **Note**
>
> Note that the Power Query team is rapidly improving their product, and they release new versions all the time. By the time you read this, it is VERY likely that the Power Query UI will have changed significantly, so the images here may no longer precisely match the product. The "heart" of the techniques, however, remains the same.

Then scroll to the rightmost column that you want to combine and Shift+click it:

Jun	Jul	Aug	Sep	Oct	Nov	Dec
6305	23148.5	52602	82055.5	111509	140962.5	170416	19! 9.5
286.5	32455.9	58625.3	84794.7	110964.1	137133.5	163302.9	189472.3
23561	4370.9	32302.8	60234.7	88166.6	116098.5	144030.4	171962.3
29579	990.9	27597.2	56185.3	84773.4	113361.5	141949.6	170537.7
38043	15576.1	6890.8	29357.7	51824.6	74291.5	96758.4	119225.3

Figure 5.39

Now, with those columns selected, click Unpivot on the ribbon:

Figure 5.40

This gives you *almost* what you want:

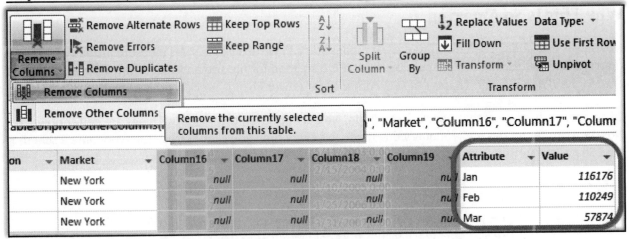

Figure 5.41

You now have an Attribute column that is the desired month column, but you also still have some blank columns, which you need to remove. (You also could have removed them prior to unpivoting.)

After you delete those needless columns and right-click and rename the Attribute column Month, you see this:

	MODEL	Region	Market	Month	Value
1	6000B	East	New York	Jan	116176
2	6000B	East	New York	Feb	110249
3	6000B	East	New York	Mar	57874
4	6000B	East	New York	Apr	35456
5	6000B	East	New York	May	6305
6	6000B	East	New York	Jun	23148.5

Figure 5.42

Bingo. Next, you check Load to Data Model and click Apply & Filter to get this:

MODEL	Region	Market	Month	Value
4500C	South	Houston	Jan	129861
4500C	South	Houston	Feb	46381
4500C	South	Houston	Mar	38456
4500C	South	Houston	Apr	81549
4500C	South	Houston	May	35846.5
4500C	South	Houston	Jun	20560.4
4500C	South	Houston	Jul	5274.3
4500C	South	Houston	Aug	0011.8
4500C	South	Houston	Sep	25297.9

Append: Sales

Record: 1 of 576

Figure 5.43

You now have the right shape, with the right column, and 576 rows. (The original wide data set had only 48 rows but far more columns.) When you click Refresh, it all just works.

Why This Is So Amazing

Not only is unpivoting good for formulas—it means you can write a single sales measure instead of 12, and time intelligence calculations are possible—but it is *also* good for file size and speed. One of the topics covered in the "Performance" chapter of *DAX Formulas for Power Pivot* is precisely this unpivot operation.

Of course, at the time of that book's first edition, we did not have Power Query. Things are better now. Now you can set up this unpivot query one time, and every time you click Refresh (or every time a scheduled SharePoint refresh runs), the right thing just happens.

> **Note**
>
> It's kinda funny, isn't it? In a world of Pivots, one of the most useful tools is Unpivot. And you use it to feed data into Power Pivot.

Using Power Query to Create a Lookup Table from a Data Table

DAX Formulas for Power Pivot covers the many benefits of using separate data and lookup tables. Performance, file size, and the ability to analyze multiple data tables in the same Pivot (such as Budget and Actuals) all are greatly improved by separating your lookup and data tables.

If lookup tables are a good thing, what do you do when you don't actually *have* a lookup table, and all you have is a data table? For example, is this Bookings table a data table, or is it a data table with a lookup table hiding inside it?

Date	CustomerKey	FullName	Phone	AddressLine1	Amount
7/22/2001	11000	Jon Yang	1 (11) 500 555-0162	3761 N. 14th St	$3,400
7/22/2003	11000	Jon Yang	1 (11) 500 555-0162	3761 N. 14th St	$2,342
11/4/2003	11000	Jon Yang	1 (11) 500 555-0162	3761 N. 14th St	$2,507
7/18/2001	11001	Eugene Huang	1 (11) 500 555-0110	2243 W St.	$3,375
7/20/2003	11001	Eugene Huang	1 (11) 500 555-0110	2243 W St.	$2,420
6/12/2004	11001	Eugene Huang	1 (11) 500 555-0110	2243 W St.	$589
7/19/2001	11002	Ruben Torres	1 (11) 500 555-0184	5844 Linden Land	$2,400

Figure 5.44

Each row in this table captures three essential pieces of information: who, when, and how much. A single column (CustomerKey, Date, and Amount, respectively) is responsible for capturing each piece of information. This is the kind of information that data tables are meant to capture. So far, so good.

But the table *also* contains additional information about each customer: full name, phone, and address. This is overkill; there is no need for each of the first three rows, for instance, to tell us that customer 11000 lives at 3761 N. 14th St. If we know it's customer 11000, we could *look up* that customer's address in a separate table! This sort of information is better captured in lookup tables, and ideally, you would "outsource" such columns (FullName, Phone, and Address) to a lookup table.

Ways to Create Lookup Tables

There are several ways to build a lookup table. You *could* use a flat Pivot to create a four-column (Pivot) table in Excel with just CustomerKey plus the three columns in question, and then you could copy/paste or link (or save as CSV) that table back into Power Pivot to create a new Customers (lookup) table. But that would require manual effort each time you wanted to refresh and import the latest Bookings table data. New customers are likely to be appearing in the data all the time, and with this method, the manually created Lookup table will constantly fall out of date.

You could instead build a lookup table in the original source database (or ask nicely for someone else to do that for you). This is a fabulous solution—when it's actually an option. But you don't always have access to a database (and/or the skills to operate one).

You now have a really good third solution to this problem. As you can probably guess, you can use Power Query to create a lookup table. Because the Bookings table lives in Access, that's the Power Query button you need to click:

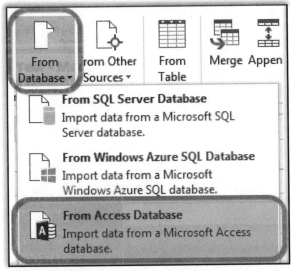

Figure 5.45

Then you remove the columns that you do not want in the new Customers table. Date and Amount are not relevant in a table that describes each customer, so you Ctrl+click those two columns to select them and then right-click and choose Remove Columns:

fx	= Source{[Schema="",Item="Bookings"]}[Data]					

⊞	Date	CustomerKey	FullName	Phone	AddressLine1	Amount	
1	7/1/2001 12:00:00 AM	11003	Christy Zhu	1 (11) 500 555-0162	1825 Village Pl.	$3,400	Remove Columns
2	7/1/2001 12:00:00 AM	14501	Ruben Prasad	175-555-0159	249 Alexander Pl.	$699	Remove Other Columns
3	7/1/2001 12:00:00 AM	21768	Cole Watson	110-555-0129	601 Asilomar Dr.	$3,578	Remove Duplicates

Figure 5.46

Now, to get a single row for each customer key, you just select the CustomerKey column and click Remove Duplicates:

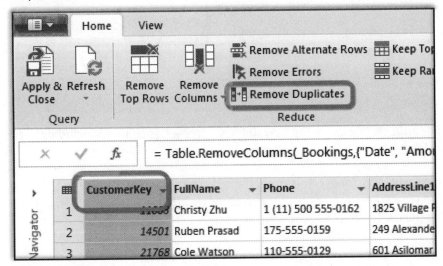

Figure 5.47

Finally, you rename this query Customers and select Load to Data Model:

Figure 5.48

Working with the Results

Here's the freshly minted Customers table in Power Pivot:

Figure 5.49

It's sorted by CustomerKey. Each key appears just once, but you still have properties columns including FullName, Address, and Phone. Perfect!

Now you can import the original data table (Bookings). This time, the only change you will make to the "raw" Bookings table is to remove the excess customer property columns (FullName, Phone, and Address) by right-clicking them and selecting Delete Column:

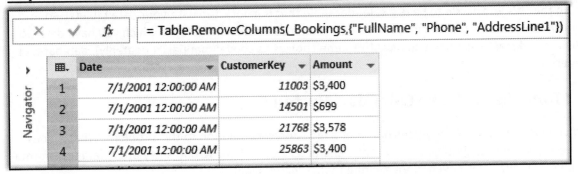

Figure 5.50

You then load the Bookings table into Power Pivot and relate it to Customers via CustomerKey:

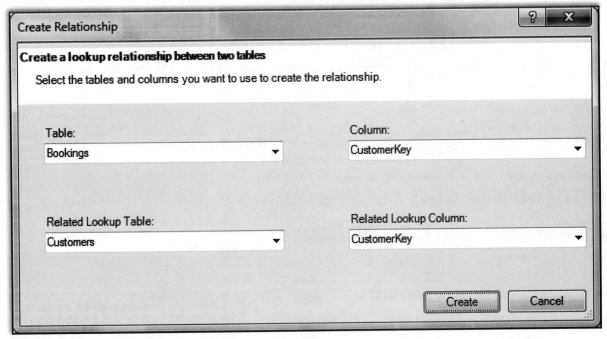

Figure 5.51

With just a few simple steps, you have a refreshable, self-maintaining lookup/data table pair. You could even call this an elegant solution to a very common problem.

Creating a Calendar Table: Advanced Usage of Power Query

Power Pivot needs a calendar table like I (Rob) need coffee: When deprived of this essential ingredient, both of us are still useful to an extent but fall short of our potential...and sometimes return incorrect or confusing answers.

<Pause for a sip of coffee.>

Of course, creating a calendar table involves all the same problems as creating a lookup table; after all, a calendar table is merely a special *kind* of lookup table! If you manually create a calendar table, you have to update it frequently to include more recent dates (and sometimes drop older dates from the past) or you have to be okay with a calendar table that extends "into the future"—which can pollute your slicers and Pivots with needless date values and make some of your calculations do funny things in the most recent (incomplete) month.

Trust me on this: It's less hassle to have a calendar table that is in lockstep with your data table(s)—one that starts on the first date for which you have data and ends on the last date for which you have data. To create such a "lockstep" calendar, you have the same choices as above: manual (repeatedly), database, or Power Query.

"Wait, I Don't See a 'Make Calendar' Button!"

Yes, as of version 2.9, Power Query does *not* offer a nice one-click solution to this problem. What it *does* have, however, is something called *M*. M is not a character from a James Bond story but a data transformation formula language. So it's even more exciting than a secret agent.

The bad news: M is brand new and uses different syntax than Excel and DAX. The good news: If you've been following the Power Query examples above, you've already been writing M:

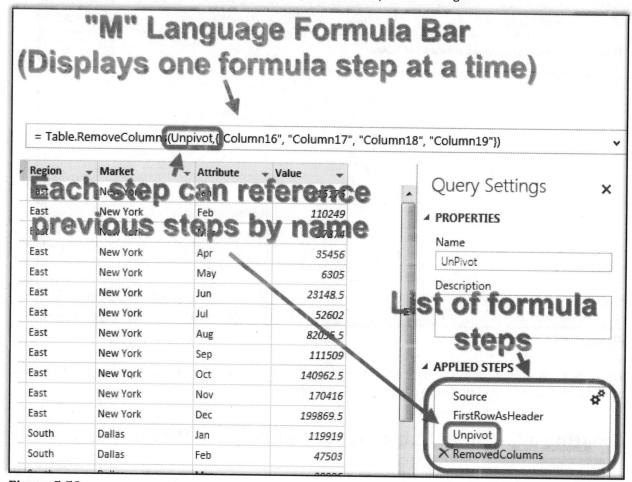

Figure 5.52

Consider the earlier unpivot example: The language you see in the formula bar is M, and it was generated by via ribbon button clicks. A query can contain multiple formula steps, and each step can reference previous steps by name.

So the ribbon buttons on the Power Query ribbon tab are similar to the Macro Recorder for VBA macros: They help you write M without *knowing* M, but then you can edit the M by hand if you want.

> **Note**
>
> We won't lie to you. We did *not* know how to write the M formulas
> to generate a lockstep calendar table. But we did know who to ask at
> Microsoft, and they happily sent us the M we needed.

Keeping It Brief

We'd consume about 10 pages here if we shared every screenshot involved in using M, but that would just make this look harder than it is. And you can always grab the workbook and inspect it yourself. So instead, we'll just show you what it looks like when it's done:

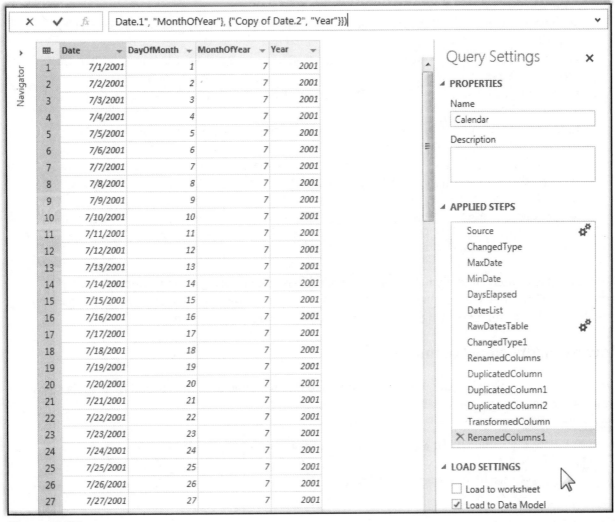

Figure 5.53

This lockstep calendar table is generated from the Bookings data table, using a multistep query in Power Query. Here are the M formulas for each of those steps:

```
ChangedType = Table.TransformColumnTypes(_Bookings,{{"Date", type
date}}),
MaxDate = Record.Field(Table.Max(ChangedType, "Date"),"Date"),
MinDate = Record.Field(Table.Min(ChangedType, "Date"),"Date"),
DaysElapsed = Number.From(MaxDate-MinDate),
DatesList = List.Dates(MinDate, DaysElapsed+1,Duration.From(1)),
RawDatesTable = Table.FromList(DatesList, Splitter.SplitByNothing(),
null, null, ExtraValues.Error),
ChangedType1 = Table.TransformColumnTypes(RawDatesTable,{{"Column1",
type date}}),
RenamedColumns = Table.RenameColumns(ChangedType1,{{"Column1",
"Date"}}),
DuplicatedColumn = Table.DuplicateColumn(RenamedColumns, "Date",
"Copy of Date"),
DuplicatedColumn1 = Table.DuplicateColumn(DuplicatedColumn, "Date",
"Copy of Date.1"),
DuplicatedColumn2 = Table.DuplicateColumn(DuplicatedColumn1,
"Date", "Copy of Date.2"),
TransformedColumn = Table.TransformColumns(DuplicatedColumn2,{{"Copy
of Date", Date.Day}, {"Copy of Date.1", Date.Month}, {"Copy of
Date.2", Date.Year}}),
RenamedColumns1 = Table.RenameColumns(TransformedColumn,{{"Copy of
Date", "DayOfMonth"}, {"Copy of Date.1", "MonthOfYear"}, {"Copy of
Date.2", "Year"}})
```

These formulas all assume that you have an original table named Bookings, and it contains a column named Date. (The three places where these names appear are formatted in italics in the formulas above, so that you can see where to change them in order to match your own data set.)

How to Insert New Formulas

If you're not using ribbon buttons, it's a little difficult to discover how to manually add M formula steps. But it's a simple matter of clicking the fx button:

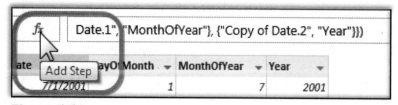

Figure 5.54

There's also another method. The intrepid among you may decide to use the Advanced Editor:

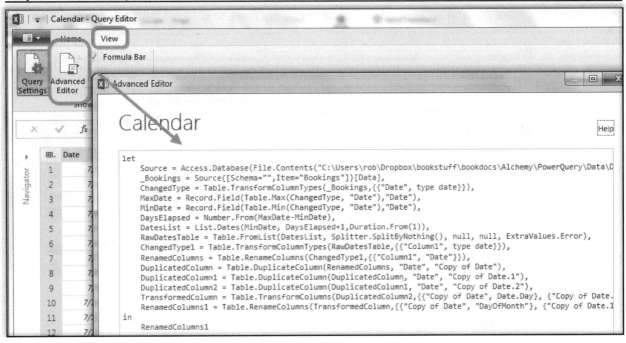

Figure 5.55

This method can be easier for bulk copying and pasting of formula steps.

The Results

The "punchline" of all this is that you get a calendar table, in Power Pivot, that starts on the oldest date from the data table and continues up to (and including) the most recent date in the data table. Each date appears only once, and *no* dates are skipped. These are all important qualities of a calendar table. And, of course, everything updates automatically and properly every time you click Refresh (or every time a scheduled refresh runs on SharePoint).

Here you can see that Power Query used the original Bookings table (27,617 rows) to produce a calendar table (1,127 rows) with one instance of each date and no gaps:

Date	DayOfMonth	MonthOfYear	Year
1/1/2002 ...	1	1	2002
1/2/2002 ...	2	1	2002
1/3/2002 ...	3	1	2002
1/4/2002 ...	4	1	2002
1/5/2002 ...	5	1	2002
1/6/2002 ...	6	1	2002
1/7/2002 ...	7	1	2002
1/8/2002 ...	8	1	2002
1/9/2002 ...	9	1	2002
1/10/200...	10	1	2002
1/11/200...	11	1	2002
1/12/200...	12	1	2002
1/13/200...	13	1	2002
1/14/200...	14	1	2002

Append1 | Sales | Customers | Bookings | Calendar | UnPivot

Record: ◄ ◄   8 o 1,127   ► ►|

Figure 5.56

You also use Duplicate Column and some transforms in Power Query to create a few of the other columns:

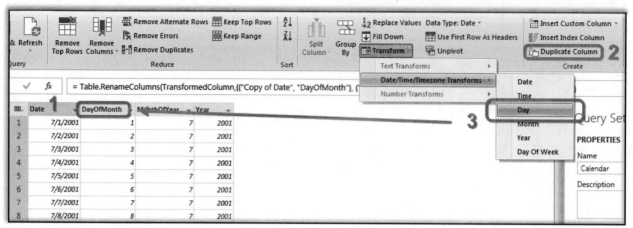

Figure 5.57

This figure shows how you add the DayOfMonth column in Power Query:

1. Select the Date column.

2. Click Duplicate Column.

3. Select the new (duplicated) Date column and click the Day transform.

Then, although it's not shown in the figure, you rename the duplicated-then-transformed column to DayOfMonth.

Removing Duplicates

In this trick, could you use Remove Duplicates instead? Maybe, but doing so would be risky. Remember that calendar tables need to be "unbroken"—that is, no gaps (missing dates). Even if your business is never open on weekends, you still need the weekend dates in there. If you use Remove Duplicates on the Date column in your data table, and there are some dates missing, you will get a poorly formed calendar table as a result.

Maybe you *know* that you *never* have such gaps in your Data table, and as a result, you are comfortable using Remove Duplicates. This is absolutely fine. We just wanted to make sure you understand the risks and provide a safer alternative.

Chapter 6: Power View

Power View is a relatively new Microsoft tool for creating great-looking interactive dashboards. The Power View dashboard worksheet is a special type of worksheet in Excel 2013 that uses data from the Power Pivot model.

For all its apparent simplicity, Power View has a lot of features that you will be hard-pressed to figure out without someone giving you a hand. A lot of things about Power View are hard to figure out, but this chapter will help you cut through the confusion quickly.

How to Use Power View

Here's the basic process for using Power View: Load tables into the Power Pivot model, add relationships, and add elements to the Power View canvas. When you're working in Power View, you need to take one extra step that is not required in Power Pivot: Make selections from the Data Category drop-down. In the Power Pivot window, go to the Advanced tab and click the Data Category drop-down. This drop-down lets you specify that a selected column represents a specific geography or other data type. Look through the columns in your model and select from the Data Category drop-down every category that fits one of your columns:

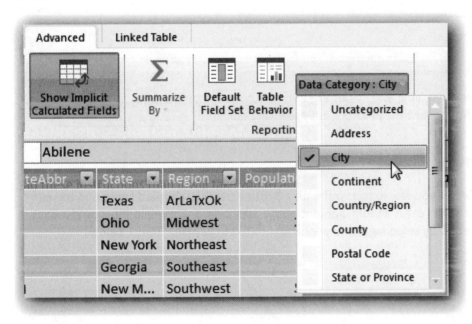

Figure 6.1

These are some commonly used categories:

- City
- State or Province
- Postal Code (for zip code fields)

You may find that other categories are worthwhile. If you have a product name field, select More Categories, Product, Product. For a company name, select More Categories, Organization, Company.

Two interesting categories are Image URL and Web URL. Image URL is for an image stored on your local hard drive or a network drive. Web URL is for images located on a website. Obviously, Web URL is far more portable and generally superior. These two types both let you show pictures in a dashboard.

> **Note**
>
> When you open a Power View dashboard that uses Web URL, Microsoft warns users that they are about to see external pictures. Maybe Microsoft is afraid you are going to slip porn in there instead of product pictures, but a person opening the workbook will have to choose to enable the external pictures before he or she can see your pictures.

Once you are done marking the data types for as many columns as you can, you close the Power Pivot window and return to Excel.

Inserting a Power View Report

Once your data is in the Power Pivot model, go to the Insert tab in the Excel 2013 ribbon and choose Power View. It is about halfway over, just between Chart Types and Sparklines:

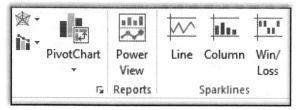

Figure 6.2

> **Note**
>
> It seems like PivotTable and Power View should be found on the Data tab of the ribbon, but they're here, on the Insert tab.

The Default First Power View Table

In earlier versions of Power View, you would start out with a pristine blank dashboard canvas. In the current version, Microsoft arbitrarily creates a table element on the dashboard. This element is rarely what you want, so feel free to delete it by selecting it and pressing the Delete key (see item 1 below):

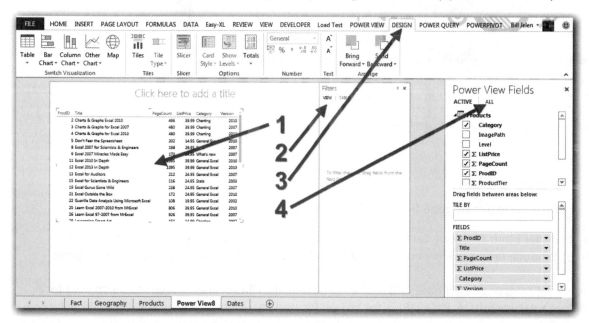

Figure 6.3

You now have a big empty white canvas and Filters pane, as well as the Pivot Table field list on the right side.

The figure above points out a few confusing points about Power View:

• As shown at number 2, the blank Filters pane defaults to being open and taking up space. Because every element on a Power View dashboard is a filter for every other element, you may never have to use the Filters pane. Click the < icon at the top right of the Filters pane to collapse it.

• As shown at number 3, a variety of contextual ribbon tabs come and go while you are working with Power View. In a regular Excel feature, you would expect these ribbon tabs to be labeled Power View Tools, Design. But in Power View, you see just Design. Find the Power View ribbon tab. From there, scan right until you find either Power Query or Power Pivot. Anything between Power View and one of those two tabs is related to Power View. And, yes, the number and name of these tabs will change frequently, depending on what you are doing.

• As shown at number 4, The Power View field list starts out showing only one table. You need to click All to see the other tables.

Creating a New Dashboard Element

With your blank Power View canvas showing, follow these steps:

1. In the Power View field list, click All to see all tables.

2. Expand the Product table and choose Title.

3. Expand the Fact table and choose Revenue.

You now have a table element on the dashboard, showing title and total revenue per title:

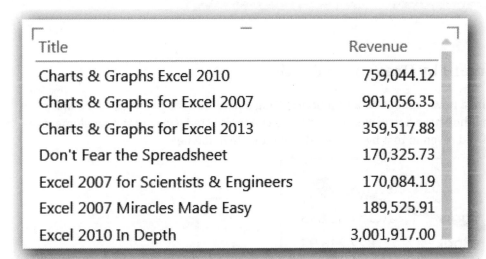

Title	Revenue
Charts & Graphs Excel 2010	759,044.12
Charts & Graphs for Excel 2007	901,056.35
Charts & Graphs for Excel 2013	359,517.88
Don't Fear the Spreadsheet	170,325.73
Excel 2007 for Scientists & Engineers	170,084.19
Excel 2007 Miracles Made Easy	189,525.91
Excel 2010 In Depth	3,001,917.00

Figure 6.4

You are free to change this table into a chart or some other type of element. Just remember that every new element starts as a table.

Finding the Hidden Controls on an Element

In Figure 6.4, it seems like there are not a lot of controls. There actually are controls, but they are hidden. When you hover your mouse over the table, controls appear at the top. In the next figure, you can see a control for applying a filter and another control, called Pop Out, for making a small element appear full screen:

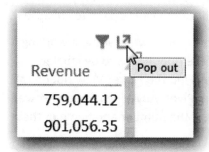

Figure 6.5

In addition, some controls that are visible all the time don't look like controls. For example, you can click on any heading to sort the table based on that column. For example, click once on the Revenue heading to sort smallest to largest and click again to sort in descending order:

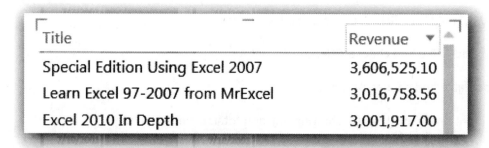

Figure 6.6

Adding a New Element by Dragging a Field

Say that you want to create a new element on a dashboard. Drag a field, such as Channel, to a blank section of the dashboard. You then have a new element with the channels listed. Once that new element exists and is active, you can add revenue to it by simply selecting the Revenue field:

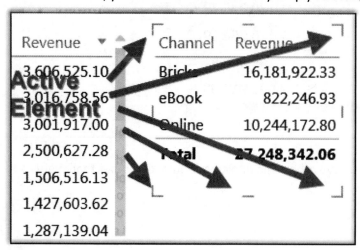

Figure 6.7

Understanding the Field List

Even when you have two elements on a dashboard, you see only one Power View field list, and it refers to the currently active element. You can tell which element is active by looking for the eight resizing handles around the element. Spotting those handles can be tricky.

To move an element, hover your cursor over the edge of the active element, and the cursor changes to a hand. Drag the element to a new location.

> **Note**
>
> The drop zones in the Power View field list change, depending on the type of active element. For example, the field list for a column chart is different from the list for a card view or a map.

Changing a Table to a Chart

As mentioned earlier, every new element in a dashboard starts as a table, but it does not have to stay a table. The Design tab includes Table, Bar Chart, Column Chart, Other Chart, and Map drop-downs that offer choices for variations:

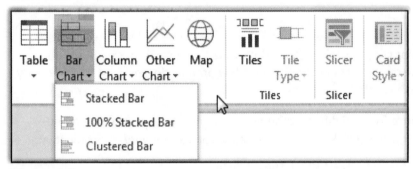

Figure 6.8

Ahhh, but there is a problem here: When you change a small table to a chart, Microsoft tries to jam the chart into the small space formerly occupied by the table. This rarely looks good:

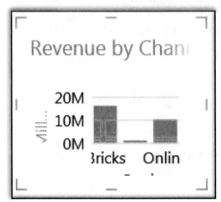

Figure 6.9

Plan on cursing in the direction of Redmond and then making the element large enough to actually hold the chart. After you resize it, the chart looks better:

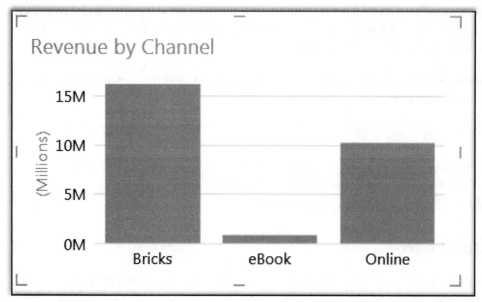

Figure 6.10

Formatting Options

As an Excel pro, you will want to format charts. You'll look for things like the Format task pane and the Excel 2013 Paint Brush icon. But these don't exist in Power View. A few options do exist, but they are fairly boring compared to what you can do in Excel:

- **Power View, Themes:** Choose from 46 different themes. A theme changes from one mono-chrome chart color to another monochrome chart color. Sadly, you cannot vary colors by point.

- **Power View, Font:** Change the font style used in the element.

- **Power View, Text Size:** Choose 75%, 100%, 125%, and so on.

- **Power View, Background:** Change the background for the Power View canvas. These are ugly backgrounds that you might recognize as being borrowed from PowerPoint.

- **Power View, Set Image:** Replace an ugly PowerPoint background with a picture. You can then use adjacent icons to change the position and transparency.

- **Power View, Set Image, Remove Image:** Takes your canvas back to white.

- **Layout, Title:** Choose None or Above Chart. You cannot actually edit the title.

- **Layout, Legend:** Set the legend position.

- **Layout, Data Labels:** Choose None or Show. It seems like you'd be able to change the number format here, but you can't.

Understanding Hierarchy

Hierarchy is a really cool feature in Power View. To see how it works, consider this chart, which shows revenue by region:

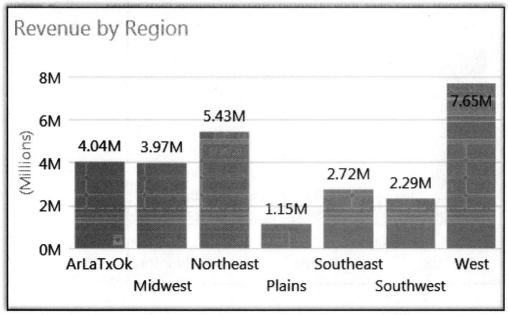

Figure 6.11

In the Power View field list, add the State and City fields to the Axis drop zone:

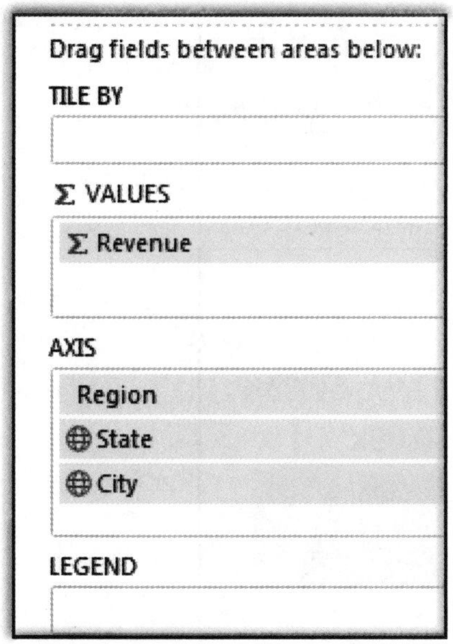

Figure 6.12

Now look at the chart. It appears that nothing has changed from Figure 6.11. However, you have created a powerful hierarchy. Double-click the West column in the chart, and the chart instantly updates to show the states in the West region:

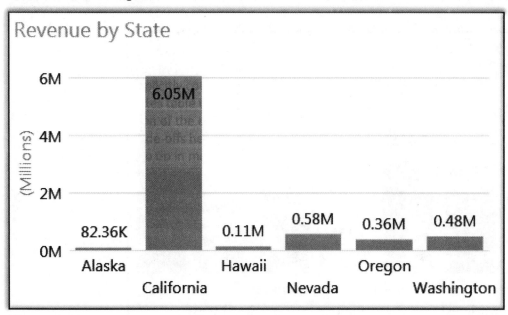

Figure 6.13

Double-click Nevada. The chart drills down to show the cities in Nevada. Now, this is cool! When you hover over the chart, a Drill Up icon appears in the top right:

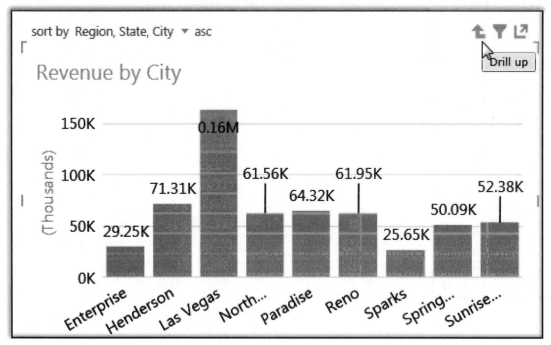

Figure 6.14

Click the Drill Up icon to return to the State level and then click it again to return to Region.

Thanks to this Power View tool, hierarchies are very easy to set up—and they work well.

Alien Explicit Slicers and Implicit Slicers

Slicers debuted at Microsoft in Excel 2010. The Power View team has invented different-looking slicers, but they can still be either explicit or implicit.

Setting Up an Explicit Slicer

Every new element—including a slicer—starts as a table in Power View. To create a slicer by level, drag Level to a blank area of the canvas, and you get a table that lists the levels. Then go to the Design tab and choose Slicer to convert the table to an explicit slicer:

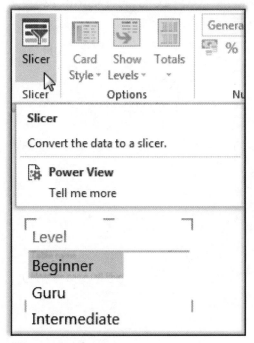

Figure 6.15

Here you can see that two of the three levels are selected:

Figure 6.16

When you hover your mouse over the slicer, you see the Clear Filter icon, which is an eraser icon instead of an X funnel icon. To choose a single item in the slicer, simply click it. To choose two items, you cannot click-and-drag as you can with normal Excel slicers. Instead, you click the first item and then Ctrl+click the other items.

Setting Up an Implicit Slicer

It turns out that you may not need explicit slicers at all. In Power View, every chart is a slicer for every other element. Here is a column chart that shows revenue by version:

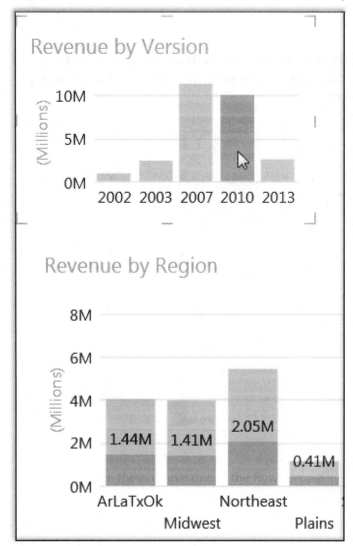

Figure 6.17

When you click the 2010 column in the top chart, the other chart updates to show the revenue associated with the selected item. If you click 2007 instead of 2010, the lower chart updates to show the revenue associated with sales of Excel 2007.

To clear a filter, you click the selected column again, and the implicit slicer is cleared.

Comparing Explicit and Implicit Slicers

When you use an explicit slicer to filter this chart to only history books, the only version that appears is Excel 2003:

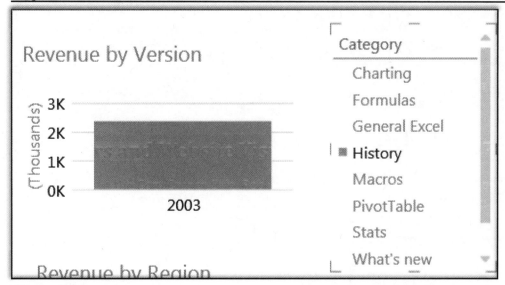

Figure 6.18

In contrast, when you choose History from an implicit slicer, the other chart continues to show a faint column with total revenue for Excel 2002, Excel 2003, Excel 2007, Excel 2010, and Excel 2013:

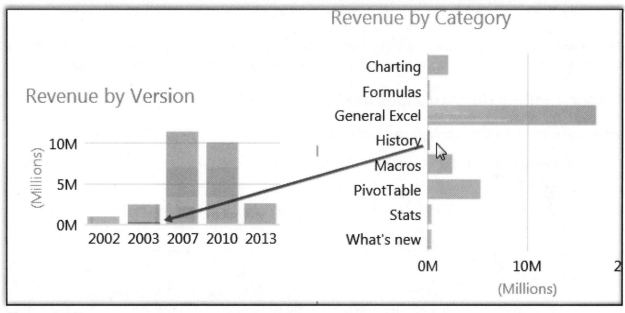

Figure 6.19

The bright section of the Excel 2003 column represents the one history title—a history book called *The Spreadsheet at 25* that I (Bill) wrote a long time ago. It was a fun little book, in color, with a pop-up page. But of course you don't see many history books about spreadsheets.

Before moving on, it's important for you to be aware of two cautions related to the previous example. First, the values for the Level field are all numeric: 2002, 2003, 2007, 2010, and 2013. When you add this field containing numeric values to an element, Power View automatically chooses to sum the level, which is meaningless. To prevent this, in the Power View field list, open the drop-down next to Sum of Level and choose Do Not Summarize:

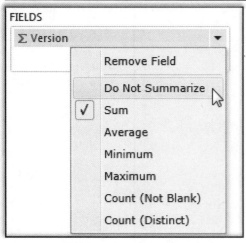

Figure 6.20

> **Note**
>
> Check out Count (Distinct) in the image above. Coming up with a distinct count is hard to do in a regular PivotTable but easy in Power Pivot and Power View.

The second caution is that while it is easy to convert a table to a slicer, you cannot convert a slicer back to a table or a chart. If a table or chart is your goal, you have to delete the slicer and add a new element.

Understanding the Two Kinds of Filters

When you expand the filter pane, you see two kinds of filters:

- **View filters:** This type of filter goes back to the original data set and applies a filter to the individual detail records.

- **Chart (or table) filters:** This type of filter applies to the summarized values that appear in the active chart or table.

> **Note**
>
> Bookmark this page so you can come back here to recall how this works. You're going to need this information later.

What's really the difference between these filters? Consider this unfiltered chart, which shows revenue by title:

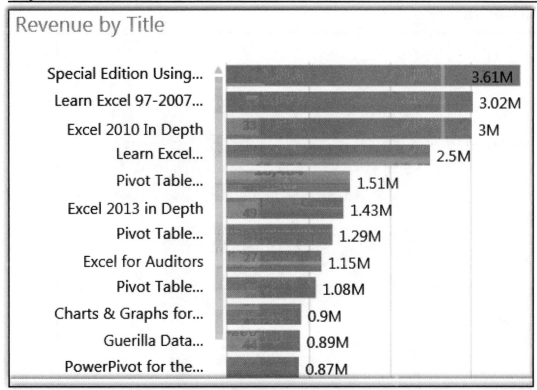

Figure 6.21

If you open the Filters pane, choose Chart, and drag the slider to select approximately $2 million, you see only the titles where the total revenue is greater than $2 million in aggregate:

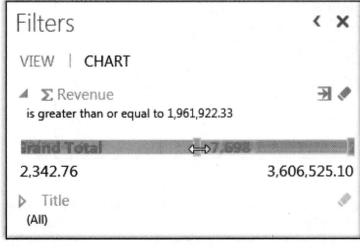

Figure 6.22

Then you see four titles in the chart:

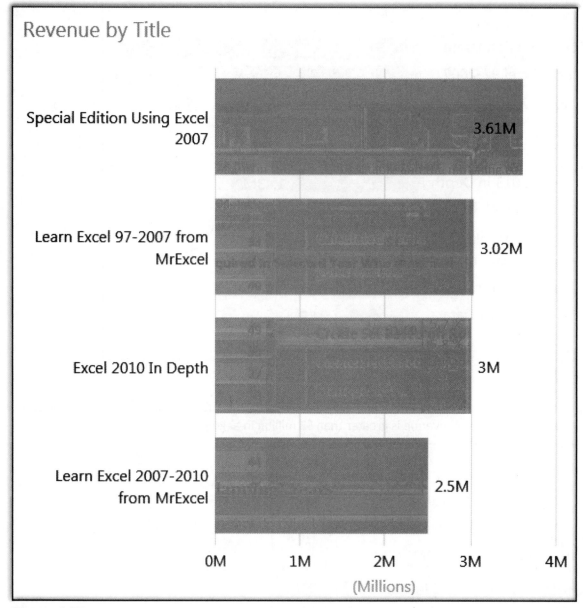

Figure 6.23

Now clear the chart filter and select View. Drag Revenue from the field list to the view filter. The slider now runs from $3.79 to $16,219. Choose a value close to $10,000. Power View now goes back to the original 400,000-row data set and looks for single transactions of more than $10,000 each:

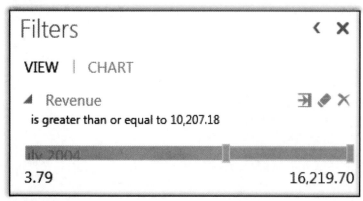

Figure 6.24

Let's face it: It is rare to sell more than $10,000 of books in a single transaction. So you could use this filter only for things like seeing the book sales made through really large seminars. Note that the total sales in the figure above are much smaller than the results shown here:

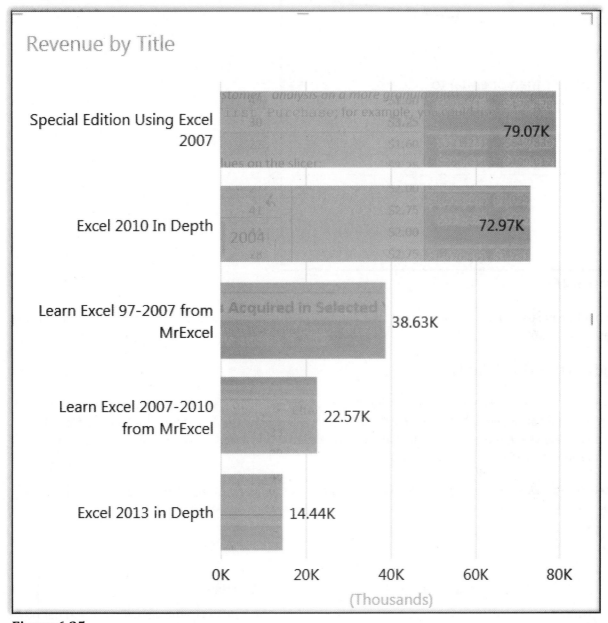

Figure 6.25

Setting Precise Filter Numbers

The last few examples say to drag the slider to *approximately* $2 million or *approximately* $10,000. It is impossible to have the slider land right on a particular number. Nudge the slider 1 pixel, and you will jump from 9978.79 to 10035.88.

If you need to get exactly to $10,000, click this icon until Power View shows the advanced filter:

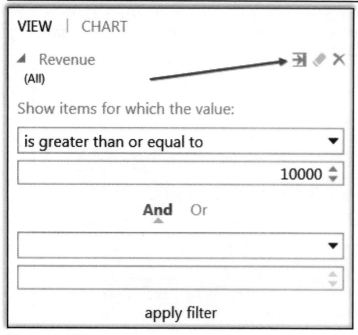

Figure 6.26

You might have to click twice: once to get to the not-so-useful list filter and then again to get to advanced filter.

Understanding Tile By

Doesn't the name Tile By make you think that Power View is going to give you multiple versions of your chart, in a tiled arrangement? Unfortunately, it doesn't. Tile By creates a tab strip that lets you filter the one chart. (However, the good news is that a feature called Vertical Multiples, described in the next section, creates many tiles of the same chart.)

To see Tile By, consider this chart, which has Year as the Axis field and Channel as the Legend field:

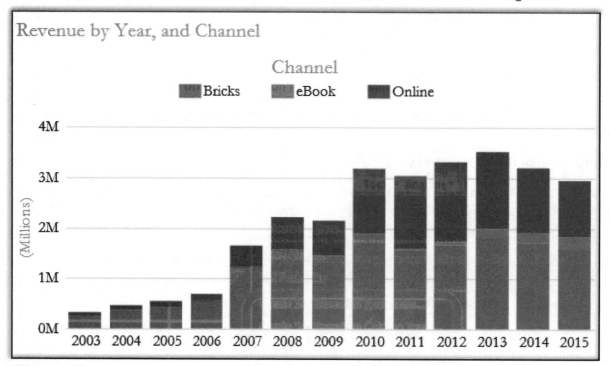

Figure 6.27

Drag the Region field to the Tile By drop zone in the Power View field list. A new tab strip appears above the chart. Select West from the tab strip, and the chart updates to show only the West region:

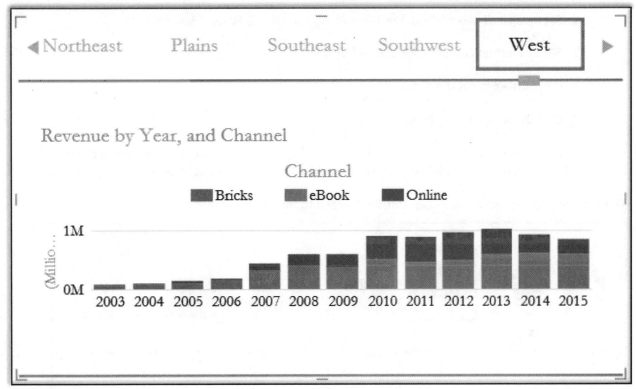

Figure 6.28

Try dragging the Web URL field to the Tile By drop zone. You can now choose pictures from the tab strip:

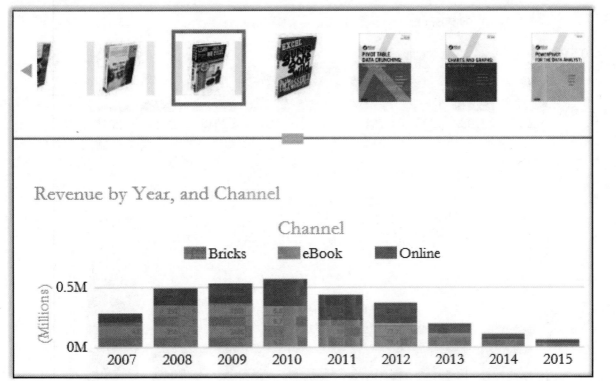

Figure 6.29

Tile By applies only to the chart between the horizontal lines. If you want a single Tile By to apply to two different elements, you need to follow these steps:

1. Set up a chart and add it to the Tile By drop zone in the Power View field list.

2. Set up another chart outside the Tile By lines.

3. Press Ctrl+X to cut the chart.

4. Click inside the Tile By lines.

5. Press Ctrl+V to paste the chart inside the Tile By area. You are now trying to squeeze two charts into a small area. You will have to resize both charts and/or the Tile By lines to make everything fit.

The following figure shows the PictureURL field added to the Tile By area:

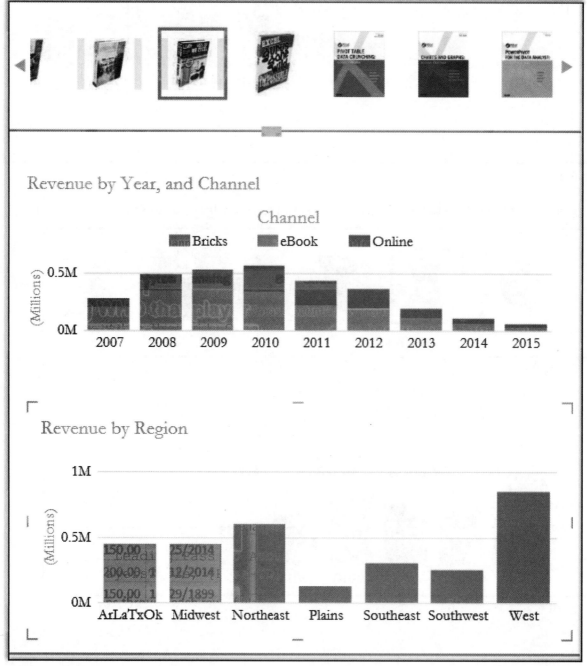

Figure 6.30

Using Vertical Multiples to Create Tiled Charts

After you create a single chart, you can make multiple copies of it by dragging a field to the Vertical Multiples drop zone. Note that Power View offers both Horizontal Multiples and Vertical Multiples tools. Horizontal Multiples shows the charts in a single row. Vertical Multiples fits the charts into a rectangular matrix. This figure shows Horizontal Multiples:

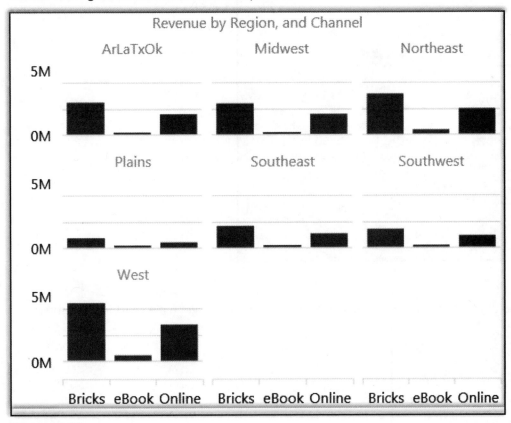

Figure 6.31

Creating Maps in Power View

To create a map, you have to have some fields that are categorized in the Power Pivot window as geographic fields. For example, you can start with a table of revenue by state and convert that table to a map. If you are connected to the Internet, Power View uses Bing to show the data points on a map:

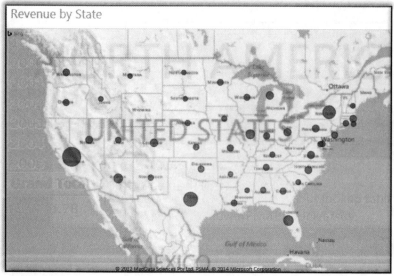

Figure 6.32

If you add Channel to the Color drop zone in the Power View field list, you get a pie chart in each state:

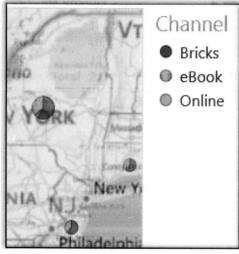

Figure 6.33

Even if your data is all in one country, you should consider adding a Country column to the original data set. Otherwise, sales in Paris, France, will show up in Paris, Kentucky. On the flip side, sales in Melbourne, Florida, will appear in Melbourne, Australia.

Creating Animated XY Charts

Follow these steps to create an animated XY chart:

1. Drag Revenue onto the canvas.

2. Set Table to Other Chart, Scatter.

3. Drag Title to the Details drop zone to ensure that each product gets a dot in the chart.

4. Drag List Price to the X Value drop zone. Use the drop-down to change from Sum to Average.

5. Drag Page Count to the Y Value drop zone.

6. Drag Version to the Color drop zone.

7. Drag Year to the Play Axis drop zone. (You might have to scroll the field list to see this drop zone.)

When you click the Play button, you see the chart animate over time. The chart conveys year, page count, list price, version, and total revenue—five different dimensions on a single chart:

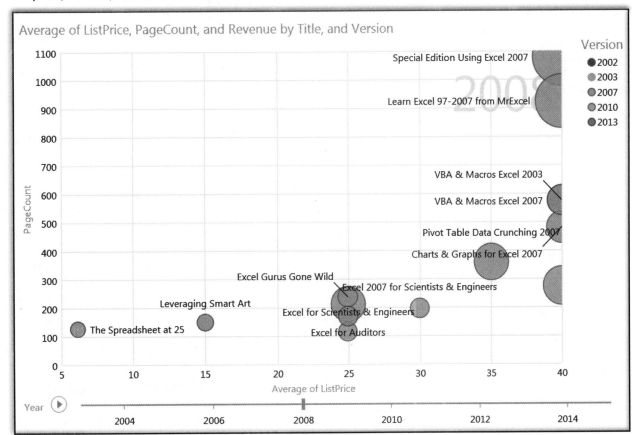

Figure 6.34

> **Note**
>
> Check out the TED talk with Hans Rosling for a great example of an animated XY scatter chart in Power View.

Chapter 7: Power Map

Power Map is a component of the Power BI suite for Office 2013 Pro Plus. Unlike Power View and Power Pivot, this component is not included with stand-alone Excel 2013. You must purchase either Office 2013 Pro Plus through volume licensing or rent Office 365 Pro Plus.

This chapter includes some tips to improve your Power Map experience.

> **Note**
>
> As with Power View, with Power Map, you should load your data to the Power Pivot model. If your data is in official tables, you can call Power Map directly from the Insert tab.

Geocoding

The first step in creating a map is to identify your geographic fields. Select them all and choose from the drop-down.

If you have a field such as 123 Main Street, assign it the data type Street instead of Address. If you have a field such as 123 Main Street, New York, NY 10123, choose the data type Address:

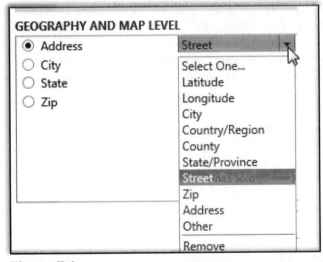

Figure 7.1

Importing Data That Is Already Geocoded

A lot of data sets on the web already include latitude and longitude information. You can import these sets into GeoFlow, provided that the coordinates are in decimal format instead of in degrees, minutes, and seconds (DMS).

> **Note**
>
> Before smartphones started providing navigation, many people owned dedicated GPS units for their cars. Many of these units could import custom point-of-interest (POI) files. Websites offered POI files that you could download—for everything from the location of every gas station to the location of every Chipotle restaurant. Search the Internet for GPS POI files. When you find a file, download it in CSV format, and you have a data set ready to be imported into Power Map.

When you were in geography class, you might have learned that Santa Monica, California, is at 34° north latitude and 118° west longitude. This can be shortened to 34° N, 118° W. However, while this will get you close on a real globe, if you used your GPS device to go to 34° N, 118° W, you would end up 33 miles east of Santa Monica. You need more specific coordinates. For example, for Santa Monica Pier, the exact coordinates are 34° 0′ 29.2026″ N and 118° 29′ 55.4094″ W. Inside each degree of latitude, there are 60 smaller units called *minutes* (notated with the ′ symbol). Inside each minute, there are 60 smaller units called *seconds* (notated with the ″ symbol). Thus, Santa Monica Pier is at 118° plus 29/60 + 55.4094/3600. In other words, it is located almost halfway between 118° and 119° west longitude.

When you are converting from DMS to decimal, remember that all west longitude values should be negative. Thus, all of the United States and North or South America should have a negative value for longitude. Latitude in the Northern Hemisphere is positive, and it's negative in the Southern Hemisphere.

If you are in the United States, your coordinate data should look like this:

Name	Latitude	Longitude
Santa Monica Pier	34.008112	-118.498725
Cocoa Beach Pier	28.367753	-80.601879

Figure 7.2

It would be great if you could use a VBA function to convert DMS to decimal, but there are not any standardized systems for presenting DMS. You might encounter DMS coordinates in any of these formats:

Valid Ways to Write DMS
40:26:46.302N 079:58:55.903W
40°26′46″N 079°58′56″W
40d 26′ 46″ N 079d 58′ 56″ W
40° 26.7717, -79° 58.93172
N40:26:46.302 W079:58:55.903
N40°26′46″ W079°58′56″
N40d 26′ 46″ W079d 58′ 56″
N40.446195 W79.982195

Figure 7.3

Depending on the format you're dealing with, some clever use of `MID()`, `LEFT()`, `RIGHT()`, `FIND()`, `LEN()`, and `SEARCH()` functions in Excel should do the conversion. This figure shows how to break out the latitude by using a series of formulas:

	A	B	C
1	Original	40°26'46"N 079°58'56"W	
2	Location of first °	3	=FIND("°",B1)
3	**Degrees portion of Latitude**	40	=LEFT(B1,B2-1)+0
4	Location of first '	6	=FIND("'",B1)
5	Location of first "	9	=FIND(""",B1)
6	Start position of Minutes	4	=B2+1
7	End position of Minutes	5	=B4-1
8	Length of Minutes	2	=B7-B6+1
9	**Minutes Latitude**	26	=MID(B1,B6,B8)+0
10	Start position of Seconds	7	=B4+1
11	End position of Seconds	8	=B5-1
12	Length of Seconds	2	=B11-B10+1
13	**Seconds Latitude**	46	=MID(B1,B10,B12)+0
14	Latitude Direction	N	=MID(B1,B5+1,1)
15	Direction multiplier	1	=IF(LOWER(B14)="s",-1,1)
16	**Latitude in Decimal**	40.44611111	=(B3+B9/60+B13/3600)*B15
17	Location of second °	15	=FIND("°",B1,B2+1)

Figure 7.4

You can keep combining the formulas into a single mega-formula to do the conversion:

	A	B	C
1	Original	Latitude	Longitude
2	40°26'46"N 079°58'56"W	**40.44611111**	**-79.98222222**
3		=((LEFT(A2,FIND("°",A2)-1)+0)+(MID(A2,(FIND("°",A2)+1),(FIND("'",A2)-1)-(FIND("°",A2)+1)+1)+0)/60+(MID(A2,(FIND("'",A2)+1),FIND(""",A2)-1-(FIND("'",A2)+1)+1)+0)/3600)*(IF(LOWER(MID(A2,FIND(""",A2)+1,1))="s",-1,1))	=(MID(A2,(FIND("'",A2)+3),(FIND("°",A2,FIND("°",A2)+1)-1)-(FIND("'",A2)+3)+1)+0+(MID(A2,FIND("°",A2,FIND("°",A2)+1)+1,FIND("'",A2,FIND("'",A2)+1)-1-(FIND("°",A2,FIND("°",A2)+1)+1)+1)+0)/60+(MID(A2,(FIND("'",A2,FIND("'",A2)+1)+1),FIND(""",A2,FIND(""",A2)+1)-1-(FIND("'",A2,FIND("'",A2)+1)+1)+1)+0)/3600)*IF(LOWER(RIGHT(A2,1))="w",-1,1)

Figure 7.5

Using Power Map for Tightly Clustered Local Data

You'll encounter a bit of an oddity if you use Power Map for tightly clustered data, such as to plot sale prices of individual houses in a neighborhood. By default, each column in Power Map takes up about one city block, and you cannot make out one house from another.

To address this problem, click the cog wheel icon and then Layer Options. You will find a pair of formatting sliders that control height and thickness. Change Thickness to about 10%:

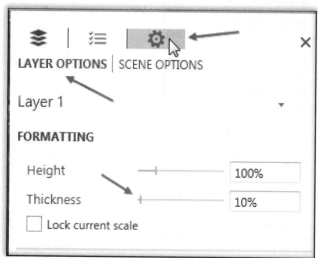

Figure 7.6

You can now make out each individual house on the street:

Figure 7.7

Power Map Navigation Tips

Flying through the map requires some unusual keyboard and mouse movements:

- Click and drag to re-center the map.
- Scroll the mouse wheel toward you to zoom in.

- Scroll the mouse wheel away from you to zoom out.

- Hold down Alt and drag the mouse side-to-side to rotate the image.

- Hold down Alt and drag the mouse down to tip the map so you are looking directly down on the map from above.

- Hold down Alt and drag the mouse up to look at the map from nearly ground level.

If you are using Power Map on a touchscreen, use these gestures:

- Double-tap to zoom to a location.

- Drag in any direction to pan the screen.

- Pinch closed to zoom in; pinch open to zoom out.

- Two-finger drag up or down to tilt the horizon.

- Two-finger drag left or right to rotate the map.

Showing Terrain and a Satellite Image

The Themes drop-down in the ribbon offers eight themes. Choose the second theme in the first row to see a hybrid map showing streets and satellite imagery.

Next to the Themes drop-down, choose Map Labels to add labels to streets or regions on the map. Note that the labels change as you zoom in and out.

Improving the Time Label on the Map

If you add a date to the play axis, you can animate the chart over time. A box appears on the chart, showing date and time format, even if your data is at the date level. Right-click the box containing the date and choose Edit to open the Edit Time Decorator dialog. The Time Format drop-down offers cleaner-looking date formats, such as June, 2010:

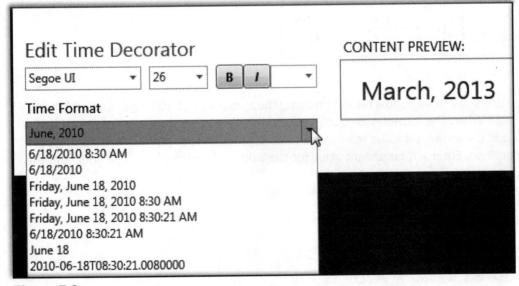

Figure 7.8

Three Ways to Show Time

When you add a date field to the Time drop zone, a tiny drop-down appears above the Time drop zone. In this menu, you can choose to have data appear for an instant and then disappear, have data accumulate over time, or have a data point stay on the map until it is replaced:

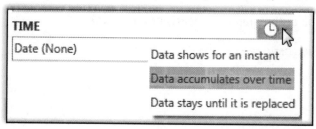

TIME	
Date (None)	
	Data shows for an instant
	Data accumulates over time
	Data stays until it is replaced

Figure 7.9

Drawing a Path Between Two Points

Power Map does not natively support drawing a path between two points. However, you can coerce a data set in Excel to show a line.

Say that you want to show a line from the Cocoa Beach Pier to the Santa Monica Pier. You could start by building a small table in Excel, showing the starting and ending latitudes and longitudes. Then you would enter starting and ending times, perhaps something over the course of a day. Next, you would decide on a number of points. If, for example, you want the animation to last for 3 seconds, at 29 frames per second, you need about 90 or 100 points to produce a smooth animation:

	f_x	=(I3-I2)/I4	
	G	H	I	J
		Time	Latitude	Longitude
Cocoa Beach		1/1/2015 0:01	28.367753	-80.601879
Santa Monica		1/1/2015 23:59	34.008112	-118.498725
# of Points		100	100	100
Delta		0.009986111	0.05640359	-0.37896846

Figure 7.10

If you plan on 100 points, you should build a table containing the numbers 1 to 101. Then you add the fields Date, Lat, Lon, and Value. The formulas for Date, Lat, and Lon should point to row 2 of the table. For each additional row, add the increment value from row 5 to slowly move the point from the starting position to the ending position. Enter any consistent value for the Value column, such as 10, throughout the data set:

C3			× ✓ f_x	=C2+I$5	
	A	B	C	D	E
1	Step	Date	Lat	Long	Value
2	1	1/1/15 12:01 AM	28.36775	-80.6019	10
3	2	1/1/15 12:15 AM	28.42416	-80.9808	10
4	3	1/1/15 12:29 AM	28.48056	-81.3598	10
5	4	1/1/15 12:44 AM	28.53696	-81.7388	10

Figure 7.11

To add your particular data to the Power Map, follow these customizations:

1. For Type, choose Bubble (for a single-color streak across the chart) or Heat Map (for a green/yellow/red blip across the map).

2. Set Size to Value (sum).

3. Set Time to Date (none).

4. Open the Time drop-down and choose Data For an Instant.

5. Click the Settings cog wheel at the top of the field list. Below the cog, choose Layer Options and choose 10% for Size. Open the Color drop-down and choose Red or any other color you want.

6. At the top of the field list, choose Scene Options.

7. Choose a scene duration of 2 to 3 seconds. Set Transition to 0 and Effect to Station.

Click the Play icon, and you see a streak of color move from the starting point to the ending point:

Figure 7.12

If you change the Time drop-down to Data Accumulates over Time, a line animates across the map and stays in place at the end of the scene.

When you use 100 points, you get a rather smooth line when the map is zoomed out to show the whole country. But if you zoom in, you see gaps between the points:

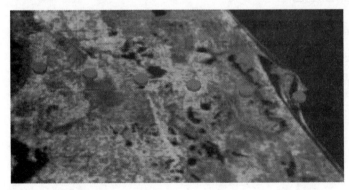

Figure 7.13

Tips for Building a Tour

Building a compelling video in Power Map involves telling a story. Rather than have the entire time line unfold in a single animation, you can show parts of the time line, pause to show a text box, and continue with another part of the time line.

Here is how you can build a tour of Merritt Island waterfront real estate:

1. Create an establishing shot. Zoom way out to show Florida. Using Scene Options, set both Start Date and End Date to the beginning of the time frame. Set Scene Duration to a few seconds, followed by a 2-second Push In transition. The scene name is not shown during the tour but is useful for helping you navigate the Tour Editor panel. Enter a scene name, such as Florida.

2. Click Add Scene. The current scene is copied and placed in the Tour Editor pane. You will want to make some changes to this scene. Use the mouse wheel to zoom in on Brevard County. Because the transition on the previous scene is 2 seconds, Power Map will take 2 seconds to transition from the view of Florida to this view of Brevard County. Name this scene Brevard and assign it a duration of a few seconds and a transition to follow of a few seconds.

3. Click Add Scene.

4. Zoom in to the view that will be used for most of the rest of the tour. Click the Text Box icon. Each Text Box is composed of a title and text, so enter some text to explain that it is 1961, and the development of the area is just beginning. You want the viewer to have time to read this text box, so give the scene a longer duration.

5. Click Add Scene. Delete the text box from the previous scene. This scene will be called The 60s. Leave Start Date at 1961. Change End Date to December 31, 1969. Set Scene Duration to 10 seconds. To preview how this will look, click the Play icon in the time line at the bottom of the screen.

6. Click Add Scene. This scene pauses and explains what just happened. Change Start Date to December 31, 1969. Set Scene Duration to 10 seconds. Add a text box that explains that development just started during the 1960s with the Apollo program.

7. Click Add Scene. This scene will have a starting date of January 1, 1970, and an ending date of December 31, 1979. Let the scene play for 10 seconds.

Continue building scenes by first showing a portion of the time line and then inserting a scene that freezes the time line and adds a text box.

Using the Calendar control to change start and end dates might seem a little tedious. Initially, the control lets you move only one month at a time:

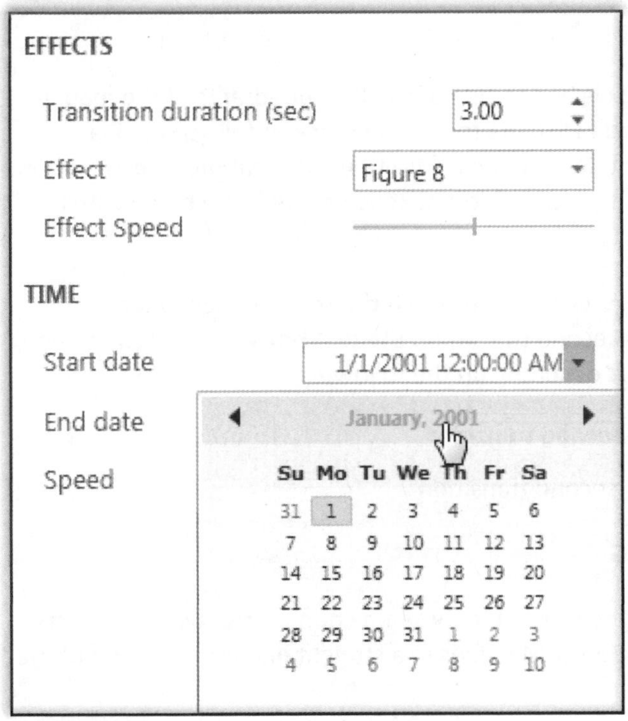

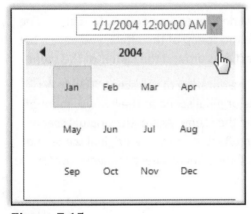

Figure 7.14

However, if you click the month name at the top of the control, you can move one year at a time:

Figure 7.15

Tip for Zooming In

Say that you have a view of an overall area and want to temporarily zoom in and then back out. Start with the initial scene. Click Add Scene two times. The first and third scenes will have an identical original view. Edit the second scene to zoom in. The tour will start from the first position, zoom in to the detail, and then return to the exact original position.

Tip for Text Boxes

An annotation is tied to a specific data point. A text box is tied to one of the four quadrants of the map. It is best to temporarily hide the Tour Editor pane and the task pane to see the scene at full screen. Place the text box in a location that is unlikely to cover important data but be aware that the location of the text box in the movie may be different from where you placed it. However, the text box should only move within the particular one-quarter of the screen.

Text boxes and annotations will appear throughout one scene and through the transition between two scenes. If you have a 6-second scene followed by a 20-second transition, the text box will be on the screen for 26 seconds. You might want to go to the extra effort of setting up the following:

- A 6-second scene with the text box and a 0-second transition

- A 1-second scene with no text box and a 20-second transition

Understanding Transitions and Effects

Effects happen to a scene throughout the duration of the scene. It may seem counterintuitive, but effects do not happen during transitions. During a transition, Power Map flies in a straight line from the end of the current scene to the beginning of the next scene.

Effects fall into three categories:

- **Station:** The scene does not move.

- **Circle & Figure 8:** The camera flies in an arc above the scene. Depending on how long the scene lasts, you may not get a full circle. However, if you increase the speed of the effect, you have a better chance of getting a full circle during the scene. The effect flies around the center of the scene.

- **Linear:** The camera moves in a straight line throughout the duration of the scene. The dolly moves the scene horizontally during the scene. You see the original scene at the halfway point of the scene. Fly Over has the camera fly in a straight line over the scene. Again, the original scene view is seen halfway through the scene. Finally, the Push In effect starts at the original scene and zooms in for the duration of the scene. Increasing the speed for a linear effect changes how far the camera travels.

Thank you to:

A Highly "Filtered" List :)

Daniel Dennehy	Jason Persinger	Gerald Strever
Serge Bouchard	James Crossett	Carlton Absher
Oliver Annells	Richard Silber	Stephen Parton
Adam Gilpatrick	Travis Lockhart	Andrew McClean
Carsten Bieker	Tim Stadelmann	David T Wetton
Jarmo Rajaniemi	Bernd Gellrich	Patrick Imbault
Paul Cunningham	Marcel Domingus	Hansjoerg Nitz
Roger Alexander	Andrew Bambic	Francisco Debs
Richard Peddie	James Mcalister	Quentin Brooke
David Vandenbos	Ray Willoughby	Austin Senseman
Kara Giangrasso	Rhys Mannering	Reuvain Krasner
Prasad Paranjpe	Tomislav Lulic	Lars Schreiber
Stephen Morfey	Stephen Jenkins	Ricky Sconberg
Laurent Sanchez	James Sorosiak	Leonard Murphy
Gordon Rowe III	Guan Ming Wong	Brent Alderton
Michael Miskell	Michael Griffin	Christian Hamel

Ryan Wade	Ken Puls	Joe Treanor
Edward Bunt	Amin Azizi	Jeff Lingen
Jay Lazzaro	Idan Cohen	Rick Cheslo
Jason Price	David Onder	Ken Jensen
Jan Hurt	Rob White	Mati Selg
Don Schulze	John Thomas	Andrew Todd
Amy Jarrow	Ps Lim	Ray Walker
Rick Wilson	Mark Baxter	Rob Adams
Jay Nickel	David Evans	Jim Fleming
Mark Polino	Ron Hill	John Lythe
John Vizard	Rafael Paim	James Byrd
Jeane Meade	Aden Zhao	Luke Smith
Tony Ghent	Sean Royle	Jimmy LaRue
Norah Fox	Anne Walsh	Earl Pearce
Ellen Su	Dan English	Lars Foss
Kevin Gould	Refa Abay	Eric Hutton
David Sharp	Rob Russell	Ken Melies
Paul Wyatt	Ryan Wilson	Randy Davis
Adam Lopuch	Rob Rak	Kyle Grice
Brian Grant	John Fox	John Hulme
Barry Weiss	Jack Miller	Steven Rutt
Owen Auger	Tim Rodman	

Mikhael Stotskiy	Jonathan Acampora
Nicholas Koivula	Bernadette Phillips
Frédéric Gilbert	Nicholas Hartshorn
Eduardo J. Belgrano	Christopher Hall
Mikhail Stotskiy	Bjarni Stefansson
Alexander Barbeau	Neal Waterstreet
Kenneth Rathkjen	Patrice Phillips
Michael Zajac Sr	Stanton Berlinsky
Thomas Sherrouse	Bruno Mariani Melo
Pasquale Massimo	Tommy Jørgensen
Ruth Pozuelo Martinez	Michael A. Dietterick
Stéphane-Robert Langer	Matthew Pawlowski
Guylaine Bélanger	Chung Chuan Huang
Christopher Ciancio	Melissa Williams
Juan Antonio Perez	William Patterson
Bartholomew Wistuk	Jeanyhwh Desulme
Micheal Reynolds	Elizabeth Pallone

Nigel Reardon	Ilya Fedorkov	Dale Rickard	Steffen Genz
Jeff Standen	Matt Pudduck	Lucas Wetzel	Dean Taunton
Jason Presley	Kevin Zandee	Yuming Huang	Art Jacobson
Shawn Horner	Gavin Turner	John Fairlie	Stephen Clark
Jeremy Bartz	James Rooney	Dennis Clark	Nathan Zelany
Jorge Blandon	Kai Hankinson	Rene Berends	Niraj Krishna
Troy Cochran	David Walton	Joanne Tudor	Katrin Hauser
Trevor Byrnes	Derek Rickard	Marc Russell	Eric Lundeen
Alex Barbeau	Sam Richards	Neil Tennyson	Andy Josolyne
Allen Beeson	Brian Johnson	Dale Cameron	Amanda Harley
Tan Kwang Hui	Alan O'Connor	Jeff Mckinnis	Dominik Petri
Stephen Reyes	Don Kollmann	Tanya Khmurov	Michael Drew
David Wetton	Colin Michael	Luke Antolini	Keith Barney
Bob Hazelton	Alain Winter	Austin Corley	George Gilmer
Jack L Miller	Aryeh Nielsen	Inge Lovasen	Donald Parish
Tommy Griffin	Andreas Zeil	Charles Brown	Stephen Matey
Henning Bree	Craig Tysall	Jim McAlister	Chris Finlan
Jacob Barnett	Erika Sturino	Nick Paavola	David Napoli
Søren Faurum	Jon Stielstra	Harlan Smith	Robert Cotton
Russell Chyz	David Duncan	Ryan D Peugh	Lori Eppright
Rüdiger Hein			

Index

X

Y

Notes:

DASHBOARDING AND REPORTING
Power Pivot and Excel
How to Design and Create a Financial Dashboard with Power Pivot - End to End

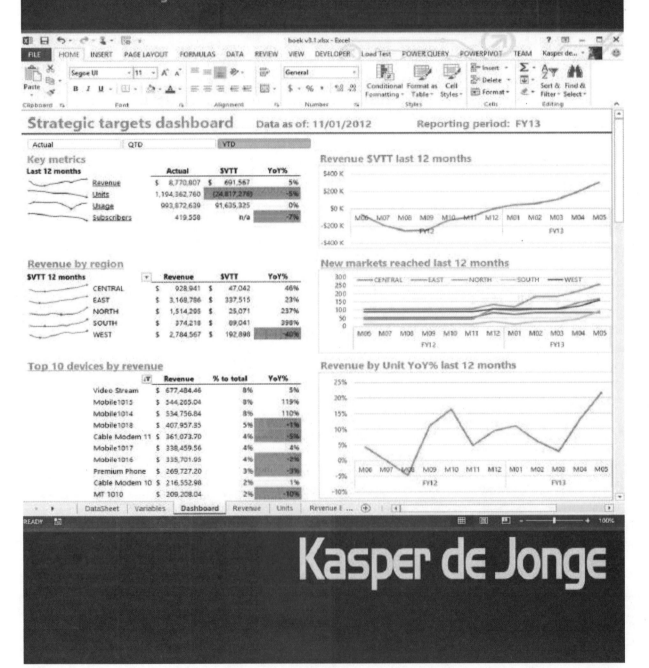

Kasper de Jonge

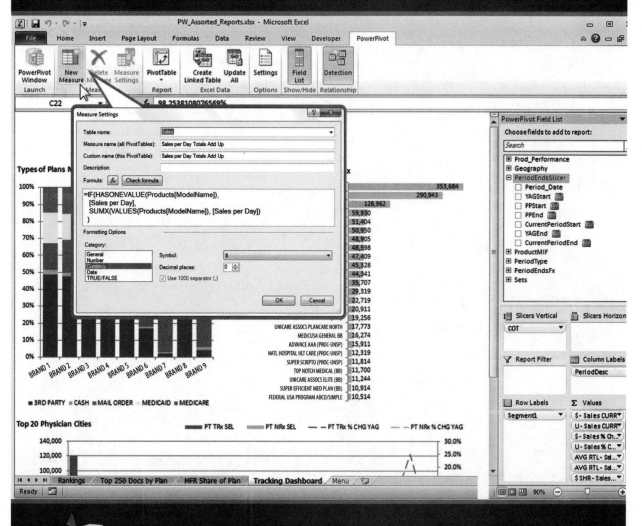